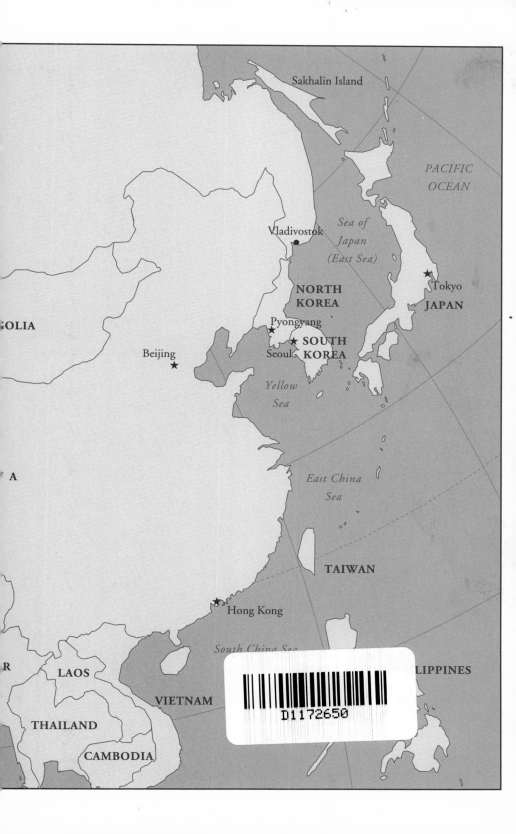

# SEPARATED AT BIRTH

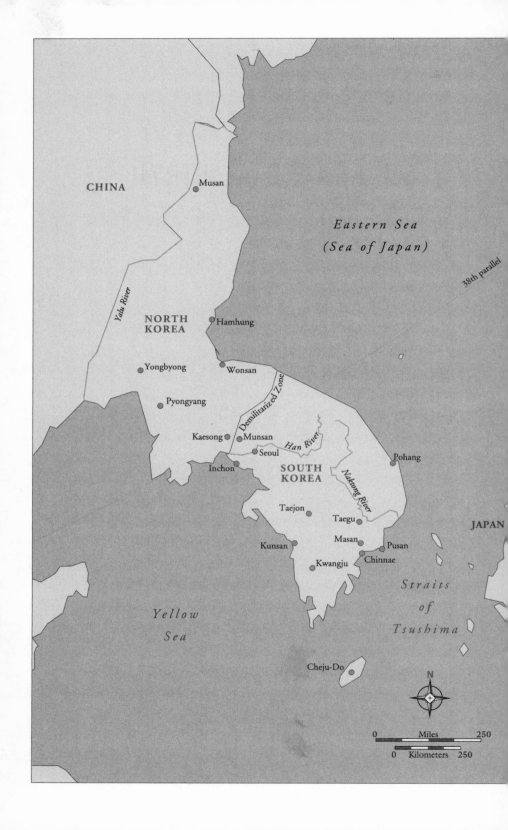

# SEPARATED AT BIRTH

## HOW NORTH KOREA BECAME THE EVIL TWIN

GORDON CUCULLU

THE LYONS PRESS
Guilford, Connecticut
An imprint of The Globe Pequot Press

The Lyons Press is an imprint of The Globe Pequot Press

10   9   8   7   6   5   4   3   2   1

Printed in the United States of America

Designed by Kirsten Livingston


ISBN 1-59228-591-0

Library of Congress Cataloging-in-Publication Data is available on file.

To those veterans, living and dead, who watered the

liberty tree in Korea with their sweat and their blood.

What an amazing thing you accomplished!

*Wish you were here to see it, Dad*

# Contents

# Acknowledgments

This book is a target of opportunity. Give full credit to my excellent literary agent, Joanne Wang, who called one day to ask if I could write about North Korea. "There just isn't anything out there from a perspective like yours," she said. After giving it a few days consideration—the idea of spending a lot of time thinking about an evil place like North Korea didn't appeal—I accepted the mission, but with my own unique twist: I would write about North Korea in terms of South Korea. It was important to me to show curious readers how their strange division came about and how it produced such radically different results. It is essential that we see a bigger picture to understand the situation fully and I wanted to paint one. Joanne liked the idea so much that she went out and sold it. So I was stuck. I actually had to write the thing. Five months later, I handed her a ponderous draft manuscript. She plunged in and did a superb job of preliminary editing. What a trooper!

After a long, seemingly fruitless search we found the right editor, Lisa Purcell. Lisa is perfect by background, temperament, and experience to take on a complicated challenge like this book and make it work. She diligently polished it into what you see today. Any smooth transitions and tight paragraphs you find are a result of her keen eye and quick pen. She works fast, is a consummate professional, and has a sense of humor. Lisa was well worth the wait. A great agent, a great editor, and a great publishing house—what more could an aspiring writer want? I hope you like the results.

Sometimes people introduce me as a "Korean expert," but that title scares me. Can you really be an expert on anything? A Special Forces sergeant once told me, "there are no *living* demolition experts." I suspect that rule applies universally. When I decline the approbation of expert it is not out of false modesty but from reality-based humility. Even though Korea is relatively small geographically, it is huge in breadth and scope. Thousands of years of history, complex philosophies, and ethnic bonding are all overlaid by invasion, stasis, and eventual metamorphosis into a bifurcated entity: half prosperous, free, and democratic, the other half gaunt, starving, ill, and terrorized by its own leaders. Who can grasp it all? The entirety is too much for any one person to understand fully, Korean or foreigner. The best I can claim is student status and even then not a terribly dedicated one, just a bit persistent. As a student, I learned from more teachers than I can possibly thank and name here. That list alone would consume the book.

A few of the teachers who come to mind are my language instructors in the States and in Korea. They tried to do more than just pound Korean grammar and vocabulary into my thick skull. Sometimes I got their real message and read between the lines. American mentors played a vital role in my development. Colonel Jim Hyinck steered me through his version of a graduate course in everything Asian. He taught me how to think analytically. Pals like Colonel Jim Young and a hardcore group of "old Korea hands" helped me over some rough spots and showed me different aspects of the country. Lieutenant Colonel Gordy Strickler, who died too young on the trail back from Everest, lived by the power of positive thinking. His example and friendship changed me forever. There is more than one Green Beret sergeant out there whose patience and persistence got a rookie officer through some extremely difficult times. They set tough standards and I tried to rise to them. Thanks to them and all of the fine soldiers and officers that I shared muddy boots and messy desks with over the years.

And what about all those wonderful Korean people who I know and admire? Koreans of all walks of life shared their knowledge, friendship, and love and I owe them a debt of gratitude that I can never repay. I hope that they see something here that they like, and that they are proud of a foreigner for learning from them. Many of the Korean Army friends I had—and even some officers who resented my presence—taught me a lot about their code of honor, friendship, and loyalty. They are tough and dedicated and I am grateful that they are our allies. From sharing frozen drop zones with their Special Forces (the famous Black Berets) to discussing complex tactical problems around a map at the Korean Army College, they were always there to help, prod, and nag. Whenever things got tough, we shared a laugh and a drink and persevered. Later, during the tumultuous days of coups and alarums, some of my former students at the Korean Military Academy risked their lives and careers helping me help their country. So did some of my classmates from the Army College. Those were difficult times and no one will know how much they did to help their country transition to democracy.

Closer to home, Ranyee Lee, who is very special to me, put up with more than any person ought to have had to bear over the past several years, but hung tough nonetheless. Without her continual support you would not be reading these words. I always had the support of my Mom, Louise, and my kids, son Gordy and his wife, Jill, and daughter Michele. They always kept the encouragement level high even at times when I was close to quitting. Thanks for their solid faith and prayers. Another who consistently helped was Gene Hanratty, who goes back with me even before Korea days and has been a special friend and confidant. We shared war, peace, and a lot of good times and difficult ones that have cemented our friendship. Jim Bell read the original manuscript line by line and made corrections that I never would have caught. It left cleaner thanks to Jim. There are many others who helped in ways small and large. You know who you are and I thank you sincerely.

Finally, I want to thank the uncounted soldiers—American, South Korea, British, French, Turkish, Greek, Filipino, Thai, South African, Ethiopian, and those from the rest of the sixteen-plus nations who fought for the freedom of a small country on the edge of Northeast Asia. Their sacrifices and efforts were lost in the cracks between the glory and popularity of World War II and the controversy and difficulty of the Vietnam War. But today a shining beacon of freedom lights an otherwise dark spot in the world thanks to those brave veterans. My pledge to you is this: the Korean War—forgotten no longer! Thanks, guys, for all that you and your successors have done.

I learned a lot from all these people but it would be inconsiderate of me if I tried to stick them with the check. If I got something right, consider them good teachers. But anything you read here, especially in the way of opinions, analysis, and options is my responsibility, not theirs.

*De oppresso liber!*

# Introduction

He stands five foot two in stocking feet. He adds two inches to his dumpy physique with elevated shoes. He then gains a couple of more inches by greasing his hair and goosing himself with an electric cattle prod—at least that's the net effect. He runs a gulag—a collection of concentration camps—that would make Mao Zedong or Josef Stalin proud. It is replete with forced labor camps, brutal medical experiments, and mass executions. His policies have resulted in slow starvation for his terrified subjects—perhaps two million or more have already died according to independent reports. But who can trust statistics emerging from a country that tells its people that the first man on the moon was a Soviet cosmonaut?

He has taken a country blessed with abundant natural resources and an educated populace with a dedicated work ethic and reduced it to the level of the most abysmal third-world pesthole. He has assassinated foreign statesmen, blown up civilian airlines loaded with innocent passengers, and sold weapons to terrorist groups around the world. He is diverting resources that his country cannot spare to accelerate a program whereby he can become a nuclear power capable of peddling weapons of mass destruction to terrorists in return for hard cash. He has surrounded himself with sycophants and toadies, lives in hedonistic luxury, and threatens his neighbors and the world with nuclear destruction. Call him anything other than "Dear Leader" and risk your life.

Who is this strange person? He is Kim Jong Il, aberrant ruler of the Democratic People's Republic of Korea—or as it's better known, North Korea.[1]

There were good and sufficient reasons for President George W. Bush to brand North Korea part of an "axis of evil" in his 2002 State of the Union address. And all of those reasons ultimately result from the crackpot, Stalinist personality cults of Kim Jong Il and his father, Kim Il Sung. The more we are able to crack the façade of North Korea, the more we learn of the dark, repugnant secrets that have been held close for decades. Peering through the cracks, we are able to glimpse an implacable hatred of America, South Korea, and other free nations. We wonder to what depths North Korean leaders would sink to advance their power. They deliberately misuse *The Diary of Anne Frank,* one of the most heartrending stories of World War II, that of the Dutch-Jewish child who hid from her Nazi oppressors until caught and executed. They claim that the Anne Frank story details what would happen to North Koreans if the American "Nazi warmongers" took control of their country. Kim Jong Il glibly equates the president of the

---

[1] Officially, North Korea is known as the Democratic People's Republic of Korea. South Korea is officially the Republic of Korea. For simplicity and clarity, the terms "North Korea" and "South Korea" are used consistently throughout.

United States and the entire nation with Hitler and Nazi Germany. And we have to wonder: How could this country—ethnically and geographically a twin of its brother to the south—have become such an awful place?

The phrase "separated at birth" is almost a cliché. It is used in everything from drama to comedy including *Twins,* the Schwarzenegger-DeVito film that juxtaposed a tall, gentle athlete with the short, streetwise con artist. Cliché or not, it makes sense to apply the phrase to Korea. After a millennium of homogeneity, the country was arbitrarily divided at the moment of birth—liberation and independence. Separated, these strange twins went opposite ways. North Korea morphed into a twisted, evil entity that oppresses its citizens. Contrast this to South Korea, which went through a bumpy development process but ultimately emerged as a role model for the developing world as a free-market democracy that enjoys economic prosperity and political freedom.

Today, as it has for several decades, North Korea, under the regime of dictator Kim Jong Il, poses a threat to South Korea and to the stability and peace of Northeast Asia. The regime postures and parades, threatens and bullies, and uses the specter of mass destruction as a lever to pry more economic aid from grudging neighbors, who comply in order to pacify its temper. When Bush groups North Korea with Iraq and Iran in an axis of evil, Americans hear him and wonder: Just what is going on over there that makes it such a threat? Part of what we try to accomplish in this book is to address this concern and to fill in some of the gaps in our knowledge so that we can better understand this enigmatic nation.

While Korea seems a remote, distant place for most Americans, it has always been real for me. As a child living in Occupation Japan, with a U.S. Air Force father who commuted back and forth to the Korean War, my exposure to Korea started early. In our Tokyo home, around a coffee table littered with Camel-filled ashtrays and glasses overflowing with good Scotch whiskey (usually Haig & Haig Pinch), Dad and his colleagues would construct mock-ups of the ongoing battles and discuss how to attack, defend, and win the war. Squinting through the cigarette smoke that made the coffee table seem even more of a battleground, they talked of tactics and strategy, of capturing objectives, of burning napalm and the atomic cannon, of stopping human wave assaults, and of Truman firing MacArthur.

Once Dad told a story, his voice filled with deep emotion. He had been awakened in the early morning hours in his tent at an air base near Osan by the sounds of distant bombing. "I went outside. In the brutal cold night as I looked north I could see the fires from Seoul burning into the night sky. Fire reflected off of the low clouds that covered the northern horizon. I watched for a while and went back to sleep. A couple of hours later I got up and went back outside. Seoul was still burning." He described a country utterly destitute, completely destroyed, and uprooted by a brutal invasion and war. "Korea will never recover," he said with quiet finality. "It is totally gone."

I lost him to cancer a month after I returned from Vietnam, my first war. He was just fifty-two and I was twenty-eight. Both now seem like terribly young ages. Later I lived and worked in South Korea, first as an army officer and years afterwards, for GE Aerospace. In all my travels around the country, I never forgot Dad's story. I always wished that I could escort him around so that he could see what the South Koreans had accomplished. On several occasions I've been privileged to address groups of veterans or civic associations about Korea. Particularly to the vets, I like to explain how much their sacrifice meant to so many people.

It's human nature that most of us leave a place retaining a snapshot in our minds of what it looked like when we were there. It is the same with these Korean War veterans. They still see the place as a grainy black-and-white newsreel or like *M*A*S*H*: war torn, beat-up, and reeling. I like to tell them that today fifty million people live in freedom and prosperity because of their sacrifice. It is an amazing achievement when you think of it: a modern, vibrant, free country with engaged, participatory government grown from terrible devastation. What a significant thing those veterans accomplished, indicative of their sacrifice and worthy of great pride. Unfortunately, most Korean vets have never been told what great things they did. That is one reason that they call their war the "Forgotten War."

When I was at the State Department, at the tail end of my military career, I was asked to go out to the Midwest, to the small rural town of Matoon in central Illinois, to dedicate a memorial to Korean War veterans. The task devolved to me because it was in an unglamorous location—neither a place nor an occasion that appealed to a lot of the State Department–types who favored more sophisticated venues. How wrong those people were who passed up the opportunity and how glad I am that they did. The experience turned into a quiet highlight of my life. I was met by a nice bunch of folks, about my parent's age, who brought me to the vet's club where we snacked on white-bread tuna salad finger sandwiches. The chow improved the next day, when a major general, who was National Guard adjutant for the state of Illinois, hosted us at the local country club. Their plan was for me—representing the U.S. government of all things—to join two other presenters in the dedication ceremonies. One rail-thin presenter was both a World War II and Korean War veteran and a former prisoner of war in Germany.

The plan for the ceremony was for us to stand on a flatbed trailer positioned in the local square. The trailer was parked beside the memorial under a bower of spreading oak trees. When I saw the monument I was at first stunned by its size and its design. It stood tall, carved from locally quarried granite into the shape of the Korean peninsula. Major cities were marked. It was a gorgeous piece of work. Then came the shocker. Upon the memorial was carved the name of every man from little Matoon and the surrounding countryside, population about five thousand, who lost his life in the war. Upon that memorial were fourteen names. Fourteen! All from this little town in Middle America.

The memorial committee had worked hard to find relatives of as many of the lost men as possible. The plan was for the relatives to sit in front of the memorial, each holding a red rose, while the three of us made our remarks. Then as each deceased soldier's name was called the relative would lay the red rose on the memorial. A volunteer would then give them a white rose as a keepsake.

That Sunday was steaming hot, as only an August day in the Plains can be. The spreading oaks provided a bit of shade but in a wool suit and tie better suited for an air-conditioned office I felt every degree of searing heat and each wringing-out percentage of humidity. I had prepared a presentation and gave it, I hope with sincerity, for I meant what I said. My message, repeated often since then, was that these men and their companions went far away to a strange, exotic land that was very different culturally than their own. They fought not to conquer that land but to free the inhabitants from brutal invaders. Soldiers who survived were often confused and deeply disturbed by their experiences. They remembered, as Dad had said at the time, a devastated land sparsely populated by a shocked, stunned people. My hope was to bring them up to date and paint for them a picture of modern South Korea.

These veterans of what they, with bitterness or irony, called the Forgotten War still wondered—and some do to this day—why had they sacrificed their innocence, their youth, and in the case of these fourteen young men, along with 36,000 other combat losses, their lives. These veterans were not the whiny, sniveling complainers of my generation. These men raised their hands, served their country, and returned to civilian lives without bleating about post-traumatic stress syndrome, Agent Orange, ruined lives, or a zillion other complaints. Nor did their compatriots burn flags, duck the war by staying longer in college, or flee to Canada. The veterans stood at attention around the memorial. Some saluted. Under those tall oak trees—an apt metaphor for their strength, fortitude, and patience—the veterans dressed as they would have for church services earlier that morning. (Pleasantly absent were the bizarre camouflage fatigues and painted faces that appear at Vietnam veterans' gatherings, usually on the wannabe crowd.)

I told these men how tens of millions of people lived in peace, relative freedom, and growing economic prosperity in a land that in 1953 almost no one thought had a future. I told them that the South Korean people had accomplished this success despite the fact that they still live under the shadow of a looming, threatening North Korea that continues to harass, bully, and cajole them. At that time, 1984, I was back some three years from Korea and had already lost half a score of newly minted Korean army second lieutenants who had been my students at the Korean Military Academy—their version of West Point—to land mines and combat in the so-called Demilitarized Zone.

That steamy day in Matoon, Illinois, I tried to paint a vision of a Seoul that had risen from its own ashes of war like the mythical phoenix to grow into modern high-rise office buildings and apartments for ten million inhabitants. Of a burgeoning economy that was transitioning into that of a developed country as we spoke. Of a per capita income high enough that families had sufficient discretionary income to buy luxuries. Of a well-fed, well-housed, educated, motivated citizenry rapidly on the move from oppressed and beaten to world leadership. Compared to those fourteen names carved deeply into the granite, and the sacrifice implicit there, my words sounded hollow and weak even to me.

After the presentations, the relatives placed their red roses and we all milled around a bit, meeting and greeting. A tall elegant woman, probably in her late seventies, with white hair nicely cut and set and wearing a light, floral print dress, came up to me. I noticed immediately that she carried a white rose. We exchanged a handshake.

"All these years," she said gently in a soft, firm voice. "All these years, I've waited for someone to tell me why my son died. To explain to me what he died for and what came of it all. Today you did that for me and I just wanted to tell you how grateful I am. Your words were lovely and now I know why we lost him and I feel better. He died for a worthy cause."

I could no more hide the tears that came that day than I can suppress them now at the memory. Many times I've said that on that hot summer day in Matoon, Illinois, I may have done the most important thing of my military career. And had that gracious woman not approached me I would never have known. My thanks and prayers go out to her and to her lost son. Surely they've earned God's blessings.

And it brought home for me what is really at stake when we talk of Korea. It is a mission greater than simple defense of South Korea, although that is vitally important, and we as allies stand shoulder to shoulder with them. For reasons that I do not understand, we and the Koreans—two disparate cultures—have found common cause in a way that transcends culture, geography, and petty differences. More than simple defense from aggression—as important a task as that is—our mission in Korea and other troubled places is a people-to-people effort to ensure that no one must live in intolerable conditions. We have accomplished that mission in South Korea.

But in North Korea, their brethren still endure the cruel yoke of tyranny. They count on us one day to liberate them from the oppression that seems endless: the death camps, the secret police, the bombastic propaganda, the starvation, the mindless hatred, and the utter frustration of enduring even one more day under a dictatorship.

It is for the special cause of human freedom that this book is written, with the fond hope and firm expectation that one day we may include the entire Korean people in freedom, the ultimate prize to which all human beings aspire.

# CHAPTER 1

---

# A Painful Division

My father, an Army Air Corps officer assigned to the China-Burma-India theater of operations, had been deployed before I was born. His unit, supplying the forces of China by air from bases in India and Burma, fully expected that they would soon relocate either into China proper or to the Philippines for what everyone expected to be the final big push to demolish the empire of Japan.

By summer of 1945, World War II was going well for the Allies but much work remained to be done. First Italy then Germany had surrendered unconditionally. Hitler was dead, the Third Reich was shattered, and the Nazi dream turned to ashes. Now the United States and its Allies could focus on defeating Japan in the Pacific. The battle for Okinawa was underway.

Characteristic of the island campaigns, each successive island battle grew more intense and brutal as the noose tightened around the main Japanese islands. Okinawa—the largest campaign of the Pacific War—was a frighteningly graphic preview of what the ultimate invasion of Japan itself would bring. Defenders allowed the invading force to land almost unopposed then began a series of suicidal fights that made the attacking army and marine units pay for every inch of ground in blood. The civilian population of approximately 200,000 Okinawans ultimately suffered 100,000 casualties. Japanese defenders, many with families who lived with them on Okinawa, convinced their wives and children to commit ritual suicide, often by plunging off a tall cliff on the southern end of the island into the coral rocks and choppy waves below. Today, the place is known to the Japanese as Kinji-no-to or Suicide Cliff to American visitors. Significantly, U.S. losses were higher than in any other campaign and at sea, the first of the dreaded *kamikaze* pilots appeared, wreaking havoc with its fleet.

What's the origin of the *kamikaze*? you might ask. Historically, Mongol invaders, using Korea as a bridge to their islands, seriously threatened Japan twice. In the thirteenth century, the Mongols, who were at the apogee of their vast empire, set sight on conquering Japan. With characteristic industry, they constructed and supplied a fleet to do just that. On two successive occasions outnumbered Japanese samurai warriors manned defensive positions on southern Honshu and Kyushu, prepared to fight to the death. On both occasions the most remarkable event happened. As the Mongol fleet sailed in deadly formation across the Straits of Tsushima, a violent typhoon came roaring out of the China Sea to devastate the fleet and drown thousands of Mongols. Survivors were slaughtered on the beaches and their severed heads impaled on poles to frighten others away from the sacred land of Nippon. The intervention of this remarkable wind was considered a divine act and so the story of the divine wind—the *kamikaze* in Japanese—became a symbol for triumph over invaders and the survival of Japan. Hence, the suicide pilots—many mere teenagers—were recruited in the last stages of the war to enact the role of saviors of the nation. They were trained to earn the title of *kamikaze* by crashing their aircraft into American warships.

The significance of the suicide attacks was not lost on Americans. Reports were being intercepted from Japan of a civilian population prepared and mobilized to attack the invading Americans. According to Stephen Ambrose, "they were ready to fight to the last Japanese." Children were encouraged by government authorities to stab American soldiers in the stomach, abdomen, and groin—the softer areas—with sharp objects such as bamboo stakes, chopsticks, knives, glass, even pencils. Authorities noted that the young attackers would be killed but that they would also kill or cripple an American "for the glory of the Emperor." Based on these reports and similar combat experiences American planners estimated that at least two more years of war was necessary for victory, and that only invasion of the main islands would bring Japan to the surrender table. The Battle of Okinawa had been so brutal and destructive that, as a preview of what was to come on the home islands, casualty figures were continually revised upward. Ambrose notes that casualties "could have been higher than the 800,000 estimate." For the Japanese civilians, losses were projected to be in the millions. It would be a bloodbath.[2]

Fighting units were even then boarding transport ships in the European theater of operations destined for the Pacific theater in preparation for the invasion. The industrial machine of the United States was cranking out aircraft, tanks, and weapons at an unparalleled rate. The entire focus of the American military was on defeating Japan. And even the top-level planners thought exclusively in terms of a conventional military campaign since the

---

2  Stephen E. Ambrose, *To America* (New York: Simon & Schuster, 2002), 115.

highly classified Manhattan Project—development of the atomic bomb—was still very uncertain.

With the death of multi-term president Franklin D. Roosevelt in the spring of 1945, unknown Vice President Harry S. Truman stepped up into the role of commander in chief. Internationally, the new president was an unknown factor. An obscure senator from Missouri, Truman was there simply because FDR had needed a running mate in 1944. He had little contact with Roosevelt—at the latter's preference and direction—and was kept out of the circle of decision-makers and advisors on virtually every policy consideration, especially issues dealing with the war and its aftermath. This suited Truman to a T. He was by his own admission much happier with his friends up on Capitol Hill engaging in a regular afternoon game of poker accompanied by a tumbler of sour mash bourbon in the Senate chambers, than he would have been hanging around the White House. In truth, had he attempted to insinuate himself into FDR's inner circle, there is little doubt that he would have been snubbed at best and more likely haughtily ordered away. The self-anointed Northeastern elites who ran the country under Roosevelt had little truck with a man who they regarded as a mental pipsqueak cowboy from the Midwest.

Harry Truman was immediately challenged to prove his mettle at a world leaders' conference in Potsdam marking victory over Germany. There he met Winston Churchill and Josef Stalin for the first time. The two men were suspicious, cautious, and a bit uneasy about the new president. Truman, however, thought that he could "work with" Stalin. At Potsdam, he had decided to tell the Soviet leader about the near completion of the atomic bomb project. In a private meeting, he spoke of a "new super weapon." Stalin only commented placidly, "I know." Already Soviet espionage had penetrated what was considered the most secret project in the world.

Back in Washington, D.C., Truman faced what many regard as the decision of his life. The Manhattan Project was fast drawing to a close. A prototype had been tested at White Sands in the remote New Mexico desert. Nonetheless, many of the scientists and engineers at Los Alamos laboratory were uncertain. Several doubted that the device would function if dropped from an aircraft. Some were objecting to the president that the device was too destructive and ought not be used at all. Arguments were advanced that the Japanese should be warned—perhaps the atom bomb could be demonstrated to them, some said. Others disputed that prospect. We only have two useable bombs. If we demonstrate one and it fails, we will never convince the Japanese to surrender. If we demonstrate the bomb and it works, but still doesn't persuade Japan to surrender, then we have only a single bomb to use against hard targets. Some advised using the bomb on cities, others away from them. The cacophony of conflicting voices must have been deafening.

Truman, whose Oval Office desk was famously decorated with a sign reading THE BUCK STOPS HERE, had nowhere to turn but inward after all of his advisors had finished. In his notes, Truman makes the point that was most persuasive to him. How could he face the parents of a soldier lost in an invasion of Japan knowing that he had not used a weapon that was available that might have ended the war more quickly? The prospect of hundreds of thousands or more dead American soldiers was too overwhelming for him to face. With a backbone of steel, Truman authorized use of the atomic bomb on Japan. Target cities were to be warned by leaflet that an attack was coming but were not to be told the full extent of its power. In point of fact, no one alive then really could have made an accurate estimate of the power or the effect of these weapons. On August 6, 1945, the first atomic bomb, code named Little Boy, was dropped on the city of Hiroshima by the aircraft Enola Gay commanded by Paul Tibbets. Three days later a second bomb, code name Fat Man, was dropped on Nagasaki. Records from the time indicate that despite the atomic bombing there were still those in the emperor's cabinet who advised him to resist until the Americans bombed the country to death. The prospect of going up in flames in a glorious *seppuku,* or ritual suicide, appealed to many. Wiser heads prevailed, however, and Japan sued for surrender.

### An Abrupt Ending

Tokyo and other cities and industrial areas had been targeted by the huge B-29 bombers for weeks. These targets had undergone an unprecedented bombing campaign. Tons of magnesium incendiaries fell from the skies and sparked firestorms that literally sucked the air from people's lungs. In 1952, while living in Tokyo, I was occasionally farmed out to a Japanese family or two for a few days. One young woman, the eldest sister in the family with whom I was staying, walked me over to Edo Castle, the emperor's castle in the center of Tokyo. The ancient structure is surrounded by a wide, deep moat. During the firebombing, she told me casually, in the morning hours the moat would be choked with the bodies of people who had drowned during the night seeking escape from the terrible flames.

Truly, by 1945, between the firebombing, the atomic bombs, and the prospect of a brutal invasion, the war with Japan had reached an extreme state. Emperor Hirohito elected to surrender. When the documents were signed aboard the U.S. Battleship Missouri in Tokyo Bay, startled American Allied Military Government planners, the teams that were deployed to restore civil order in occupied areas, were faced with an unforeseen situation: the war had ended before they were fully prepared. Quickly, in the manner of competent military staffs, they reformulated plans and accelerated deployment operations. Then someone brought up Korea. What ought we do with Korea? Someone else noted ominously that he thought the Russians were headed that way.

The opportunistic Soviets had no such concerns. They had jumped into the war right after the atomic bombs went off. They were already racing across Manchuria headed south to Korea to try to grab off as much as they could in the way of prisoners, industrial capacity, territory, and loot. To their surprise they found the vaunted Japanese army in Manchuria in a far weaker state than anticipated. Much of its strength had been bled off over the years to reinforce army units fighting the Americans and the Chinese. The Soviets quickly eliminated any resistance, rounded up tens of thousands of Japanese POWs, and put them to work dismantling factories and installations and loading the material on railroad cars headed into Russia. After the last trains were loaded with stolen material, the Japanese POWs were loaded, too. They were off on a one-way trip to the Soviet gulag, into the darkness of the forced labor camps in Siberia from which few of them would ever return.

## Win the War but Lose the Peace?

In many aspects the United States was unprepared for the peace. Its focus for several years was on winning the war. FDR's policy, oft stated, was unconditional surrender. Many people thought of it like an American sporting event: they would have been content to win it, dust off their hands, and come home. In fact, American impatience got nasty in places as some overseas U.S. military units actually rioted, demanding immediate return and demobilization. It was a time of enormous decisions all carrying vast consequences.

Unfortunately, many small countries and regions found their desires—regardless of how worthy—ignored by overworked, overtaxed policymakers.

This was also a period of enthusiastic territorial partition. To many planners, the fastest, most practical, and expedient solution to any international problem seemed to be to cut the contested area into parts. It worked in Europe. In the Middle East, Palestine and Israel were cut up. New boundaries were drawn for many emerging nations. Similarly, when faced with a threat of Soviet occupation of the entire former Japanese possessions on the mainland of Asia, it was quite natural to suggest partition, even if some considered it only a temporary solution, a stopgap until something more permanent could be negotiated.

In no way did America have a Korea-based focus any more than it had a Taiwan-based, Greece-based, or Eastern Europe-based focus. Many Koreans, even those who are strongly pro-American, fault America for arbitrarily dividing Korea along the line of the thirty-eighth parallel into separate countries. From a Korea-based focus, which far too many revisionist historians and Korea-centric writers employ, the agreed division of the Korean peninsula seems brutally arbitrary and callous. Perhaps it was. But it is very difficult to fault people at the time for lacking a quality of foresight that we ourselves do not possess. Nevertheless, with Soviet armies racing to the south intending to grab every piece of land all the way down to Pusan, planners in Washington, including a lieutenant colonel named Dean Rusk who would later be Secretary of State himself, drew up a proposal for American forces to accept surrender of the Japanese army in the southern half of Korea, below the thirty-eighth parallel. The plan was that after demobilization of the Japanese military and institution of local civil government—similar to what was being done in Japan and Germany—a free election could be held re-uniting the country.

## Painful Division

Maybe that was pie-in-the-sky stuff considering the actions of the Soviets, but it was probably the best that could be done under the circumstances. It proved acutely disappointing to the Koreans who hoped to be restored to full independence after a brutal forty-year colonization by the Japanese. On the other hand, we have to wonder what else could have been done. Would it have been possible to restrict the Soviets to the area north of the Yalu River? Probably not, because their forces were too close to the Korean peninsula, and were moving too quickly to stop completely. And were we going to fight over Korea? Absolutely not. We weren't fighting over the Soviet occupation of Eastern European states, and those states were considered a higher priority. (There is a lot of irony here when one recalls that the war began in earnest in September 1939 over the invasion of Poland by Germany. In 1945 we overlooked a similar amalgamation of Poland along with Hungary, Czechoslovakia, the Baltic states, and the Balkans into the Soviet bloc without a peep.)

But in 1945, although it was a terrible misjudgment, Korea was considered a colonial backwater of little or no significance. Its problem was just one in a long line of postwar territorial disputes that needed resolution. It is perhaps the ultimate irony that two foreign policy decisions made at the time, neither considered a major decision—the agreement to divide Korea and the decision, however reluctant, to allow France to reoccupy its former colony of Indochina—contributed materially to two more major wars in the Pacific and caused untold human agony. But putting ourselves into the context of the time and place, it is truly difficult to imagine that it could have been done any other way. Finally, in defense of those harried planners who suggested and agreed to a split Korea, it can be said that their arrangement kept a significant part of the country free and allowed it to develop the institutions of a free-market democracy that it enjoys to this day. Had they taken the easy road and simply allowed the Soviets free reign down to Pusan, the world would have been very different. Although some diehard ethnocentric Koreans claim that they would prefer such a settlement—a united Korea under communism rather than a split Korea—it is interesting to note that they all live in South Korea or other free countries, and that most of them hold jobs in academia, the arts, or media or are students or professional agitators.

### The Postwar Plan

The initial plan of the major powers was ostensibly for the USSR to take the surrender of Japanese forces north of the thirty-eighth parallel while U.S. forces accomplished a similar mission south of it. Following the restoration of order it was decided that elections would be held countrywide to select a new government and leadership for a united Korea. There is ample evidence that the Soviets were interested in grabbing territory, not holding free and open elections. They had already begun to send people into areas in the South—especially into the cities—where they could begin to proselytize the population and try to form communist organizations and cells.

One of several faults of the arbitrary division at a make-believe border (the thirty-eighth parallel) was that it ignored economic realities. Most of the industry and wealth that remained after Japanese occupation was north of the parallel. South Korea was for the most part, resource poor and dependent on agriculture for a living. As a consequence, North Korea in those early days seemed to be the relative powerhouse.

## U.S. Naiveté

In contrast to the Soviets in the North, in 1945, the U.S. forces were woefully unprepared for the mission of occupying the southern half of Korea. Everyone had expected that the Pacific War would take at least two more years and include an invasion of the main Japanese islands.

No one in the field knew of the atomic bomb, of course, since the Manhattan Project was super secret. The plan was in place—a template of that used in Europe—for Allied Military Government units (AMG) to follow the invading armies and quickly establish civil control in areas that the army moved through. They would work down to the district level and be responsible for identifying, arresting, and removing suspected war criminals or those associated with the fascist regime; for restoring civil functions such as police, utilities, and communications; for distribution of food supplies; for implementation of medical facilities—the list was long and complicated. Each AMG team was slated to enter a specific area. They were trained in area studies for that location—geography, economy, personalities, language—and were ready to follow the invasion forces into Kyushu, the southernmost of Japan's four main islands.

An Army Reserve colonel who was a fellow student at the Foreign Area Officers Course at Fort Bragg, North Carolina, in 1976, told me a story of his experience with the AMG. In August 1945 he was a young officer AMG specialist on a team poised in Okinawa. His team was aimed at a district near Beppu, in Kyushu. After the atomic bombing and unanticipated surrender—including the afterthought of the division of Korea—his team

was abruptly ordered to Seoul. No AMG teams had been prepared for duty in Korea because no one had anticipated that
such a requirement would be needed until 1947, if then. All focus
was on winning the war and that meant fighting and winning
the land battle in Japan. Despite protests—"we don't speak the
language; we don't know anything about the place; we don't know
what to do when we get there"—the AMG team was sent immediately to Seoul.

## A Wrong-foot Start

As could be expected things went wrong from the outset. The
shock of liberation—after forty brutal years of Japanese
oppression—was unanticipated among the Korean people. Naturally, they expected immediate freedom, a renewal of Korean
government, and a fresh start. Instead, they found an American
AMG team that was even more confused than they were. Elements of the Japanese army had to be assembled, disarmed, and
screened. While that was being accomplished, the American
AMG team set about trying to restore civil functions. Fortunately, there was little or no damage to the urban infrastructure
from the war. In a human reaction, but one that was incredibly
shortsighted and insensitive, the AMG people had the existing
Japanese officials and administrators continue in place until
they could transition themselves. The AMG people were more
comfortable with the Japanese—after all, they spoke Japanese
and were trained in Japanese customs. The AMG people—being
practical Americans—were also interested in results. They figured
that the Japanese officials and administrators were experienced
in the everyday workings of civil affairs and could make a transition more efficient than if they replaced them with Koreans
who did not know the system. There was also a big unknown: How

would they know and identify capable Koreans who could handle these technical and skilled functions?

They opened an incredible can of seething worms. The Korean people, who were not disposed to tolerate the Japanese for one day—one minute!—longer than necessary, were angry, disappointed, and nonplussed by the American attitudes. There were daily demonstrations outside major office buildings occupied by the American forces, with Koreans rightfully insisting on being allowed to run their own affairs. Until this mess got sorted out, it caused extreme discomfort and friction between the Koreans and the Americans. What ought to have been a joyful occasion turned sour and it was an historic reminder to Koreans that Americans are not aware enough of the past to learn proper lessons from it.

Scholars who focus on Korean affairs, such as Gregory Henderson, former Foreign Service officer, have been extremely critical of American performance in Korea, including the division of the country, the initial occupation, and the eventual installation of government. Their criticism, while certainly valid, would have more credibility if the Korean operation had been the single one taking place at the time. Put the Korean liberation and occupation in context with requirements in Japan (after all we suddenly had to occupy all of Japan, not just island by island) and elsewhere in the region (the Philippines and Taiwan). As my colonel friend summarized it: "Sure, we screwed things up. We weren't prepared to work in Korea but in Japan. But we went there with good intentions and tried to do the best job we could under the circumstances. We probably stepped on some toes and I regret that we hurt some feelings, but we were part of the effort that kept at least half of Korea out of the hands of the Russians. That part I'm proud of."

## The Temporary Line Becomes Permanent

Not long after U.S. forces arrived and moved to Seoul they began to receive alarming reports from the field. Soviet military units, augmented by Koreans in Soviet-style units were observed conducting surveys and installing permanent markers along the line of the thirty-eighth parallel. South Korean militia or civil authorities who approached them were threatened and chased away. These reports were received with concern by American and South Korean leaders who began to be aware of a major shift in attitude by the Soviets.

It has long been the hypothesis of some revisionist or sympathetic historians, such as Bruce Cumings from Northwestern University, that the U.S. authorities in league with autocratically minded South Koreans conspired to thwart the proper reunification of the country and, in fact, stifled a free, open election because they thought it would be lost. In reaction to this hostile gesture, they say, the Soviet authorities were left with no choice but to consolidate their position and reluctantly set up their own government. Such talk is nonsense. It ignores the pre-planning and extensive preparation that was needed for the Soviets to have made such a swift, thorough takeover. But this "don't blame the innocent Soviets" line still gets credence in certain quarters. In the face of what was clearly going to be a rigged election in the North—one of the classic Soviet-sponsored "one man, one vote, one time" arrangements that coerce the electorate into picking their dictator—officials south of the thirty-eighth parallel refused to participate in a charade. They insisted that unless and until elections could be guaranteed to be free and open that delay was preferable to a backdoor Soviet land grab. In the face of intransigence from the Soviet-controlled half of Korea, officials in the South proceeded with their own electoral process, which, predictably, the Soviets condemned. Those who have been inclined to explain, exculpate, and forgive all Soviet transgressions deplore the action by the South as "detrimental to the process of establishing a unified Korea." It is true to a degree that as Gregory Henderson bemoans "there is no division for which the U.S. government bears so heavy a share of the responsibility" nor one in which "blunder and planning oversight . . . played so large a role."[3] Admittedly, the United States could have done things better. But given the exigencies of the era it is difficult to see how. The criticism makes sense only if one looks at a complex world situation through Korea-only blinders and only if one accepts the postulate that a unified Korea under Soviet control is preferable to a divided Korea living half free.

## Emergence of a New Japan

As the division in Korea began to solidify, a terrible civil war raged on the mainland of China between Chiang Kai-shek's Kuomintang forces and the Red Army under Mao Zedong. The fall of China to Mao's communist armies in 1949 sent shock waves reverberating through the region and all the way to Washington. The occupation of Japan had been proceeding apace with General of the Army Douglas MacArthur acting as proconsul in Tokyo, instituting democratic, free-market reform at a dizzying rate. MacArthur had taken on total reformation of feudalistic, fascistic, Imperial Japan as an all-consuming challenge. He brought such prodigious energy to the task that it was difficult to believe that he was well past the age when most professionals seek a quiet life of retirement and relaxation. But MacArthur had long grown used to making his own decisions about what was best for Northeast Asia, as he had when the Soviets had moved to partition Japan.

---

[3] Quoted in Don Oberdorfer, *The Two Koreas* (New York: Perseus, 1997), 7.

In September 1945, a Soviet military transport had landed in Japan and a high-ranking Soviet general disembarked. A car drove him to Supreme Headquarters Allied Forces-Far East where he met General Douglas MacArthur. The Soviet general was excited about the bright future he planned for himself in Japan. He explained to MacArthur that he was there to give notice that Soviet forces had moved into Sakhalin Island and the Kuril Islands. Soon, he said, his units would occupy Hokkaido, the northernmost of the Japanese main islands. The Soviets intended to move quickly from there to occupy northern Honshu, the main island, on which Tokyo and most major Japanese cities were located. He was here to meet with MacArthur in order to secure an agreement to a simple division of Tokyo that, unlike the messy four-party arrangement in Berlin, could be split evenly between the United States and the USSR. After all, the Soviet said expansively, since the Pacific was largely a Soviet and American show it was unnecessary to accommodate the British and French.

General MacArthur dispassionately glanced at his wristwatch and noted that it ought to take approximately twenty minutes for the Soviet general to get back to the airport. Longer than that, said the Supreme Commander, and he would have the Russian arrested and clapped into prison. As far as any moves by the USSR into Hokkaido, he MacArthur, would resist those incursions with the utmost power in his hands and bring that power to bear on any Soviet forces that dared approach the main islands. Such Soviet action would, he concluded, be treated as an act of war and aggression and answered appropriately. Apparently, the General did not consider it necessary to address division of Tokyo.

The history of Asia would be markedly different had such a terrible thing occurred. Of all that General MacArthur accomplished during his proconsulship of Japan this almost unrecognized act of defying Soviet aggression may have been one of the most influential and long lasting. In a bold act that continues to this day to be second-guessed, MacArthur insisted that Emperor Hirohito remain as titular ruler of Japan. The General envisioned a British-style monarchy arrangement whereby the office and person of the emperor would serve as a symbol of the nation and afford a line of continuity to the past so highly revered by the Japanese.

The core document of the sweeping reforms that the General put in place was a new Constitution. In its famous Article IX, the country renounced war as an instrument of government policy. This was a radical declaration. As a consequence, Japan maintains what are known somewhat euphemistically as Self Defense Forces that in any other country would be an army, navy, and air force. Over time, these forces have become increasingly modernized although Japan and the United States always flit along the thin line that maintains the illusion, if not the reality, of a non-militarized Japan.[4]

## Edging Closer to War

The prospect of a rearmed Japan was a long way off in the summer of 1950 when a series of events triggered renewed war in Asia. By then both North and South Korea had openly declared themselves as independent nations, although neither recognized the existence of the other and each claimed that the other rightfully belonged to

---

[4] Over succeeding years as demands on U.S. forces grew, especially in a post-Vietnam War world in which many American leaders were only too eager to withdraw from Asian responsibility and downsize the military, a series of quiet agreements transferred responsibility for security within a one-thousand-mile radius of the islands to Japan. That the radius includes Korea is explained by noting that ocean distances only are the references.

it. Hence, South Korea had a ministry for reunification and had shadow provincial governments in place for the lost provinces north of the thirty-eighth parallel. North Korea had the same. Official diplomatic recognition of either South or North Korea was generally governed by the Cold War camp to which the recognizing foreign power belonged. Competition for recognition by neutral or nonaligned states was fierce. The recognition game evolved into a numerical contest between the two Koreas, with either side using each fresh diplomatic triumph as an affirmation of its legitimacy. This somewhat silly, but deadly intense competition continued for many years until roughly the Seoul Olympic Games of 1988 when then president of South Korea Roh Tae-woo's northern policy opened lines to the communist world.

The idea of perpetual division was a concept that simply did not register as an acceptable state of affairs with Koreans on either side of the thirty-eighth parallel. Certainly there were those in South Korea who dreamed about the possibility of eventual reunification. There may even have been those in the South who speculated about their ability to reunify the peninsula forcibly. But most rejected the idea of the use of force and hoped for the promised, UN-monitored elections. But the prospect of a communist-controlled, rigged election was a legitimate concern. It had happened in other places around the world, and that frightened South Koreans.

The American presence in Korea was limited and shrinking. There was an embassy, of course, and a small group of officers and noncommissioned officers who comprised the Korea Military Advisory Assistance Group but they were highly restricted in any material assistance they could render. With the pathetic amount of supplies and equipment available to their Korean counterparts it was impossible for troops to even fire their weapons regularly.

Several of the American advisors fretted that the light weapons that were the best the South Koreans possessed would be insufficient to halt the North Koreans should the latter decide to attack. They reported increased activity in Soviet-advised North Korean units along the thirty-eighth parallel and anxiously waited for the attack that they feared might come with no warning.

CHAPTER 2

# The Cult of Kim

Like many enigmatic leaders Kim Il Sung appeared out of the fog of World War II. No one in the West had ever heard of him. He came pre-packaged with a legend that had been created around him by the Soviet intelligence services, a cover background that promoted him as a heroic anti-Japanese guerrilla fighter. Kim was purported to be a valiant Korean nationalist who spent the war in the mountains fighting the hated Japanese and bearing high the standard of a new, liberated Korea. It was a good cover story on many levels. First of all, it was heroic, patriotic, and stirring. It was a Korean version in miniature of what Mao Zedong had accomplished in China. The story was important because it played well to all Koreans regardless of political or ideological leanings. Who could not like the image of a modern Korean hero enduring hardship and deprivation in the mountains while he fought to liberate his country? This mythic guerrilla fighter story also sounded much more inspiring contrasted to the dull lives of the academic expatriates such as Syngman Rhee who spent the years of Japanese occupation and war in exile in Hawaii. They hid from conflict and buried themselves in luxury and decadence, the communists would say, while the Great Leader Kim Il Sung endured terrible hardship. So the propaganda line was packaged and sold.

We now know better. Kim *was* involved with anti-Japanese activity at an early age. He *may* have spent some time with a guerrilla group in the mountains, but he was recruited early by the Soviet secret police for a more ambitious mission. The purpose in installing him in Korea was total Soviet control. His legend, carefully crafted by his KGB handlers, turned him into a freedom fighter living in the mountains, striking repeated blows for Korean independence against the repressive Japanese in order to bring the glories of the socialist paradise to peasants and workers loyal to the tenets of Marxism-Leninism. Nowadays, after the demise of the Soviet Union and many of its satellites with the concomitant revelation of the horrors contained in the perverted philosophy of communism, such words sound tendentious and vainglorious.

The shining image for Kim Il Sung contrived by his KGB managers had enough of a grain of truth contained in it to make it at least believable. There were, for example, groups of Koreans who resisted the Japanese and took to the hills and mountains to establish base camps. Kim Il Sung, however, likely spent most of the war in Moscow or at secret training grounds east of Moscow in a hidden, protected area. He was not a field guerrilla in the mold of Ho Chi Minh or Tito. As were many native expatriates who were being groomed to return, it was imperative that these future puppets had the necessary ideological training and background to know where their loyalties lay. When Kim Il Sung surfaced on the Korean peninsula immediately after the war, he wore a Soviet military uniform and spouted the code words of communist ideology like a ruptured Moscow sewer pipe.

Kim received his schooling in dictatorship at the feet of one of the greatest mass murderers of all times, Josef Stalin. Like Stalin, Kim saw the advantage of a state in which the central figure—indeed the only figure of public note—was the leader. He therefore set out to construct himself as the "Great Leader" in the mind of every North Korean citizen. Photos and drawings of Kim in heroic posture appeared everywhere. Busts, carvings, and statues sprouted like an ugly orchard. Posters were slapped on walls, murals painted, and tons of concrete for monuments were poured. Musically talented North Koreans wrote operas, plays, and songs, paeans to the Great Leader. No excess—however tasteless or expensive—was left untapped to honor Kim. The entire country began to look like a twisted theme park: Kim Il Sung Land. But this was only the beginning. It became a punishable offense to refer to him in any way other than as the Great Leader. Places where he was born, attended school, or eventually even appeared in public, became People's Museums honoring the Great Leader. Park benches that he reportedly sat on became saintly relics. The apogee of absurdity was set higher and higher until inside North Korea the ludicrous seemed normal.

His deliberate development of a cult of personality exceeded anything that Stalin might have attempted. He bypassed even the mummified Lenin and Mao in terms of self-adoration. Kim Il Sung seemed to reach back to another time and another culture until he became almost like an ancient Egyptian pharaoh—a god and a man simultaneously. Western observers would see the outward trappings of the Cult of Kim and laugh because it had assumed such ridiculous proportions. Sixty-meter-tall bronze statues and universally required lapel buttons with his face upon them were just a few of the bizarre manifestations of his cult.

But the reality of the Cult of Kim was not funny. The success or failure of personality cults is based on degree of control. From time to time in America you might see sports, entertainment, business, religious, or political figures attempt to glorify themselves. Occasionally they succeed, but not for long and not with everyone. In a free society we have choices and exercise them. But in the rigidity of a totalitarian state behavior that appears fatuous or might draw derision in an open society is taken with deadly seriousness. The presence of secret police, a network of informers, and extensive prison camps—the time-honored dictatorial methods of enforcing order—requires constant adherence to every edict, no matter how preposterous. Under the watchful eye of a system in which even the whisper of suspicion is enough to condemn one to death or deportation to a forced labor camp, every citizen must adhere to the norm as established by the most powerful person, in this case, Kim Il Sung, the Great Leader. As we shall see later, Kim Il Sung even managed to carry his personality cult well beyond the grave.

## Installing Soviet Infrastructure

As the war came abruptly to an end in August 1945, teams of Soviets and Soviet-trained Koreans moved quickly to establish order under their control at every level. Even in remote hamlets and villages, the presence of the new rulers was felt immediately. After almost three decades of constant turmoil ranging from civil war to internal purges, Stalin had learned how to use threat and intimidation as effective tools. He trained his people to follow a template of required actions that imposed an atmosphere of fear and uncertainty onto newly conquered peoples as rapidly as possible. After the preemptory declaration that these teams were representatives of the new ruler, Kim Il Sung, several actions took place quickly. All weapons were confiscated on the spot without exception. In places where fighting had been severe there were abundant stores of military weapons and equipment. These were taken immediately, along with hunting and defensive weapons. Rule number one was that an unarmed populace was easier to control. Simultaneously, each person was required to register with the new central authority. This provided the new rulers with a rather thorough census and it also gave them a compilation of the professions and skill of the residents. In North Korea as elsewhere in the world, those professions deemed to be potential "enemies of the people" were in for the first major purge. Anyone associated with Japanese authority was removed immediately. The next groups were composed typically of teachers, religious figures, civil authorities, and other educated individuals. This might include people as innocuous as librarians and minor civil servants. Purges and removals were carried to such an extreme that in some cases merely wearing glasses was considered a sign of literacy, therefore a mark of suspicion and distrust. These unfortunates were taken away to labor and "reeducation" camps from which few reappeared. It was the initial chill of mind control and repression that continues to exist in North Korea today in the form of a Soviet-like gulag, a system of concentration camps.

Trained communist leaders, teachers, and administrators replaced the purged citizens. The Soviets were prepared for a complete takeover. Obviously such plans are to an extent time dependent but the Soviets had done sufficient preparation and were able to exert the initial shock that stunned the local populace. That gave them the opportunity to impose additional controls until the web was woven so tightly that it was impossible for ordinary citizens to escape.

In those early postwar days Kim Il Sung did little without clearing it first with Josef Stalin. Certainly, he was careful that any foreign adventures were vetted through the Kremlin.

Additionally, he was cautiously developing a relationship with his neighbor Mao Zedong in China. To the outside world in 1945, the dangerous specter of a monolithic communist state on the march invoked feelings of challenge, despair, or resignation—depending on the viewer's moral courage. At the time, communist leaders came together in lockstep when facing outside powers. While the cracks of historic national competition between China and the Soviet Union were forming and widening even in the 1940s they were less significant—and considerably less hostile—than they would become in later years. Nonetheless, it was important that Kim Il Sung tread lightly in those days as he delicately built relationships with the Communist Party of China. He did not want to appear to be disloyal, unreliable, or ungrateful to Stalin and his Soviet sponsors.

While Kim was occupied consolidating his position in North Korea he never lost sight of his ultimate vision. From the outset, he prepared to use North Korea as a springboard to launch an attack against the South. His goal was simple: total unification of the peninsula under his leadership, by guile if possible, by force if necessary. With that goal in mind the institutional military development of North Korea was dramatically accelerated. Soviet equipment in the form of tanks, artillery, and aircraft were shipped to North Korea. Aggressive military training programs started immediately. The new North Korean army wore Soviet-style uniforms and learned Soviet attack doctrine: combined arms in a concentrated assault with heavy artillery support and armor forward, producing maximum shock power and action.

### Kim Builds North Korea

Meanwhile, the buildup in the North was proceeding apace. Soviet T-47 tanks were transferred to a rapidly growing North Korean

People's Army (in Korean, the In Min Gun), which was turning itself into the most effective local force in that corner of the world. Conforming to standard Soviet military doctrine, large blocks of artillery pieces were also brought to North Korea. The infantrymen were armed with PPSH submachine guns and SKS bolt-action rifles, all Soviet vintage. In addition, heavy mortars and machine guns were distributed down to the company and platoon level. Realistic training schedules were implemented and the People's Army ran several large live fire exercises.

Kim Il Sung carefully noted the lack of American commitment in South Korea and the desultory beginning of the new South Korean government. In his mind, the situation was still extremely fluid. He correctly estimated that the institutions of democracy had not been firmly implanted in the South nor had any sort of self-sufficient economy developed. South Korea was teetering on the edge of the abyss, waiting for a shove. Kim was assembling the necessary military force to do exactly that.

Kim Il Sung was a man of eccentricities. He refused to fly in an airplane, depending solely on ground transportation, usually railroads. The dictator of North Korea made a series of long train trips to Moscow for consultation. Once there, Kim could not have appreciated the fact that Stalin typically kept him waiting in an anteroom, cooling his heels for hours before he was admitted into the inner sanctum. This behavior was quintessential Stalin. He loved humiliating and terrorizing subordinates. It kept them in line and apparently satisfied some visceral desire to hurt that characterized him. Being a good and faithful minion, Kim Il Sung waited hat in hand for admittance. Since the Chinese communists were only then establishing their reign, Kim had not been able to develop the balancing act between the PRC and the USSR that he performed so adroitly later. In the years 1949–1950, North Korea was simply one in a long line of developing Soviet satellite states, and not the highest priority in the queue by any means. Kim exercised a degree of patience in those days that he would lack in later years. It must have chaffed but he nevertheless stayed calm and humbly pleaded his case.

Stalin was initially lukewarm about authorizing North Korean offensive action. His focus was elsewhere. He had enjoyed some immediate success in Eastern Europe in the years following World War II. True, he had been rebuffed in efforts to overrun Greece and Iran, had discovered a more independent player in Marshall Tito of Yugoslavia than he preferred, and had been thwarted in his attempts to run the Allies out of Berlin by the amazing triumph of the airlift. But Eastern Europe was solidly conquered, China had gone well, and communist insurgencies in Indochina, Malaya, the Philippines, Indonesia, Africa, and parts of Latin America were taking root. His overt intrusion had been rebuffed in Japan but its internal communist movement was growing.

Stalin had to be pleased that his greatest operation—to steal U.S. nuclear secrets—had succeeded beyond expectation. His agents in the United States had performed well. With acquisition of the atomic bomb, the Soviet Union sprang into immediate parity with America and did not fear having to bend to American will because of a disparate military capability. The success of this espionage program was a defining moment in the history of the world. Had the Soviets not possessed the terrible weapons much of what would become an "empire of evil" could have been avoided. The blood and misery of untold millions would eventually stain the hands of those Soviet spies. With atomic weapons, the United States and the Soviet Union began to face each other in a different manner. The very idea of a direct confrontation would fade until the doctrine of Mutually Assured Destruction made a third world war unthinkable. Instead, both sides began to fight the wars on the fringes, through surrogates, using unconventional warfare tactics, and the snatch-and-grab operations that would come to define the next several decades of Cold War action.

## Support for North Korea

While Stalin was not overly encouraging during Kim Il Sung's first visit, he did agree to increase military aid and advisors and to monitor the situation in Northeast Asia closely. Back in Pyongyang after the tedious trip along the Trans-Siberian Railway, Kim Il Sung set about actively to pump up military capability while tightening his control over the population. Secret police penetration of society increased. The focus on Kim Il Sung the person became pervasive. A subtle mental transformation began whereby Kim insisted that he be referred to as the "Great Leader." Rather than simply representing the state, Kim transformed himself into *being* the state. He was proving to be a fast learner in dictator class and a worthy pupil of his teacher Josef Stalin.

Kim Il Sung continued to press his intelligence operations into South Korea. He could only be encouraged by what he saw: an unenthusiastic, almost casual support by the United States and internal South Korean political lassitude marred by infighting. The future of South Korea was turned over to Syngman Rhee, the expatriate academic with an American wife, as president of the newly founded republic. On the military side, stagnation was the operative word.

Kim Il Sung saw nothing but weakness. He chafed under Stalin's restrictions, convinced that his People's Army could overrun the weak South Korean republic and reunite the peninsula by military might. There remained one unanswered question, however, one that Stalin himself had raised. What would the United

States do if North Korea attacked? Stalin had to be careful to pick fights he could be sure of winning. He wanted this one to be on his terms—quick, overwhelming, and, most important, successful. Stalin was still not comfortable authorizing an invasion. Soviet matériel, weapons systems, and advisors continued to flow into North Korea, but Kim Il Sung would have to wait a bit longer before being unleashed.

Looking with admiration—and probably no little envy—at the success enjoyed by Mao probably helped spur the North Koreans to action. Many of Kim's advisors must have watched as the United States equivocated over assistance to Chiang and the Nationalists and yet stood by and did nothing as its supposedly key wartime ally was humiliated and defeated. This lack of action had to be interpreted by the North Koreans as a nonverbal message. America's lack of involvement was a quiet signal that its interests in mainland Asia, including Korea were changing. For the North Koreans this was a positive sign. Kim Il Sung probably didn't require much more encouragement to do what he had wanted to do for a long, long time anyway: conquer all of Korea and install himself as dictator.

Armed with this new development and with his most recent intelligence reports, Kim Il Sung hooked his private car to a locomotive on the Trans-Siberian and headed west for Moscow and yet another meeting with Josef Stalin. At this meeting Stalin reviewed the regional geopolitical status with Kim and also with his own military leaders and intelligence agencies. Stalin arrived at the conclusion that the timing was indeed propitious for reunification of Korea by force. They collectively read the U.S. withdrawal of interest as a green light to their aggression. Even if interpretation of the AJO line statement—wherein U.S. Secretary of State Dean Acheson defined the limits of American interests in the Pacific at a line bordered by the Aleutians, Japan, and Okinawa—was not the single critical factor in Stalin's ultimate decision to attack, it played a part. But that was not the only reason that the Soviet Union wanted to move on Korea.

## A Stronger Strategic Position

Stalin recognized certain long-standing realities. The need for Soviet expansion south from Vladivostok and Petrapovlosk was historic. By restoring a Russian presence in southern Korea, albeit through a surrogate, the Soviet navy would in a stroke have direct access to the China Sea. More significantly, owning all of Korea would move the Soviets into a position to box Japan in on three sides. Stalin was convinced that when pressured America would pull back behind its two oceans, thereby abandoning Japan. Stalin wanted to be in the strategic position where he could move quickly to snap it up into his expanding empire. As a result of postwar territory grabbing, the Soviets already had forces on the northern Kuril Islands and Sakhalin Island (to the present day, still referred to as its "lost Northern Territories" by Japan). This occupation put Soviet armies within an amphibious landing of the main northern island of Hokkaido. Occupation of the Korean peninsula would bring the Russians within striking distance of Honshu and Kyushu. Having a major Soviet naval presence in the southeastern Korean Chinhae-Pusan ports would permit them to sever resupply sea-lanes from distant America. U.S. ships were vulnerable to interception and any other reinforcements the United States might dispatch from Okinawa to the south would be in target range. Securing Korea would be a hugely significant shift of power positioning in the region, potentially freezing America out of Northeast Asia. Much more was at stake than simply the fate of South Korea, as important as that was.

Occupation of Korea had even more appeal to Stalin when he looked at China. While he was happy to see a communist regime triumph there, Stalin held the classic Russian view that China was a rival under the best circumstances or an enemy at worst. A Soviet presence throughout Korea would knock China out of its historical role as protector of Korea. A Soviet fleet based at Pusan or Chinhae could furthermore sail just a few nautical miles west and effectively close access to the Yellow Sea, intimidate Shanghai, and threaten major Chinese ports and Hong Kong. What the limits of Stalin's sweeping vision were we may never know—he was not shy or conservative when it came to imperial expansion. But one thing is certain: when Kim Il Sung boarded his car in Moscow for the long train trip home, he raised a glass of expensive cognac in toast. His dream had been approved at long last. He had received the go-ahead from Stalin to invade South Korea and reunify the peninsula by force.

When in spring 1950 Josef Stalin finally approved Kim Il Sung's invasion plans, he reinforced his decision by a guarantee of massive Soviet assistance. Military supplies, equipment, and even air support in the form of squadrons of MiG fighter aircraft based in the Soviet Union and flown by Soviet pilots would back up Kim Il Sung's People's Army. With this approval and support, North Korea prepared to launch an attack. Yet, in these instances of naked aggression, the one who initiates the attack feels compelled to invent a subterfuge, an excuse for why it is necessary. A pretext of choice is to take out some unfortunate prisoners—political, military, or criminal is irrelevant—dress them in the opposing force's uniforms, kill them, and photograph the bodies well inside your own territory. The scene is complete when the instigating party acts aggrieved, "regrets" having to take necessary steps, and attacks to "defend" itself. By the time everything is sorted out the war is already underway.

Recriminations and investigations are of little value then. This tactic worked for Hitler, Stalin, Mussolini, and Japan on many occasions. Kim Il Sung adopted it with alacrity. In June 1950, North Korea announced that a group of "Imperialist puppet aggressors" had attacked their nation. Bodies were displayed, the requisite photos taken, and the atmosphere of tension rose sharply. The North Koreans floated their fabricated pretext for war for the next four decades, repeating endlessly the allegation that South Korean forces led by American imperialists had precipitated the war by attacking the North first. There was always a ready, gullible audience for this propaganda and it was reprinted as late as the early 1990s. When Soviet archives were finally opened then, they revealed extensive discussion and planning of the North Korean attack, debunking the North Korean claims. Yet, there are those who still believe the original specious charges. It comes as no surprise that there are academics—American and expatriate Koreans primarily— who continue to espouse and teach the lie that South Korea precipitated the Korean War. Ideology dies hard for some of them.

Still, in the South at the time, no one was prepared to face the harsh reality. The predominant feeling was that this incident would be just another in what was becoming a continual series of minor clashes along the thirty-eighth parallel. But Kim Il Sung had other plans. He attacked.

### The North Korean Offensive

At approximately 0330 on a sultry Sunday morning on June 25, 1950, North Korean artillery flashed and roared along the thirty-eighth parallel. Observers said that it looked like heat lightning, like the onset of a terrible storm. Shortly thereafter, North Korea army troops pushed southward, their advance led by Soviet-supplied tanks. The greater military strength of the North Koreans gave them an immense advantage. In some cases they rolled over the lightly armed South Korean defenders without pause. But not everywhere. Despite their lack of effective anti-tank weapons and other equipment deficiencies, many of the new South Korean units had more than a basic load of raw courage. General Paik Sung-yup tells of his First Division soldiers charging tanks with nothing more than explosive charges and hand grenades. Similar incidents of suicidal bravery were tragically common. Units fought to the death to defend their new country from the terrible, unprovoked aggression by the North Koreans. Only when they were physically unable to resist any longer did some units give ground. But the juggernaut was too large, the force of the attack too great to buy more than minimal time. Within days Seoul was being pelted by North Korean artillery fire.

As the military situation deteriorated, civilian refugees choked roads southward. Clad in the traditional loose, white cotton Korean garb, entire families pressed along the roads carrying children and possessions. North Korean infiltrators mixed with the refugees, covering their uniforms in white jackets, pretending to be civilians themselves until they were close enough to a South Korean unit to spring up in ambush. Tactics such as this one increased the overall confusion and spread panic. In Seoul a young South Korean engineer officer, who said that he had received orders to blow it up, destroyed the main vehicle bridge over the Han River. Other, more senior officers had him arrested and summarily shot as a traitor for destroying the bridge too early because there were friendly units still north of the Han. Decades later his widow successfully cleared his name in a lawsuit supported by witnesses to the action. It was one of several panic-induced incidents indicative of how quickly the command and control structure of South Korea was unraveling.

The North Korean People's Army continued to press south. Given the geography that defines the southern half of the Korean peninsula it did not take a strategic genius to guess North Korean objectives. The primary road network in the South runs from Seoul to Taejon and then on to Taegu and Pusan. Once the North Koreans captured the southern port city of Pusan, reinforcing the peninsula would be extremely difficult. In theory, South Korea as a political entity would then cease to exist. North Korea could call for a ceasefire for "humanitarian" reasons, receive support from the Soviet Union, and end up with effective control over all Korean territory. With this objective in mind the People's Army juggernaut rolled southward.

Following on the heels of the North Korean army were the special political sections made up of secret police. They carried lists of those people who would be purged. The lists were broad, comprehensive, and inclusive. The North Koreans were not one to take chances. Mere suspicion alone was sufficient grounds for summary execution or deportation. Mass graves were later uncovered on the outskirts of Seoul where schoolteachers, government employees, politicians, and others considered subversives were shot. Thousands of others, including the Italian general manager of the Chosun Hotel, the best in Seoul, were last seen under armed guard marching northward in dusty columns never to be heard of again.

The main North Korean drive was toward Pusan with the goal of trapping any South Korean units trying to escape to Japan. Some North Korean units were diverted toward the southwestern city of Kwangju and the south-central port of Masan in order to counter any attempts to strike their flank, but for the most part the push was unwaveringly to the southeast. The mission was clear: Capture Pusan!

## CHAPTER 3

# Fighting the Forgotten War

On that tense weekend in June 1950 when North Korean army units attacked south toward Seoul, my family lived in San Antonio, Texas. Dad was training troops in the brand-new U.S. Air Force, declared independent from the Army Air Corps since 1948. We lived in converted World War II barracks a few miles from Lackland Air Force Base. In those days we had one car—a Packard—that Mom would drive to the base to pick Dad up after work. I had become a mascot of the training company, going through the ceremony of saluting and reporting to the commanding officer daily. I learned how to throw a perfect salute before I knew how to ride a bike.

We got word of the attack on our radio news the night of June 25th. Dad pulled out an atlas to show me where Korea was. The Berlin Airlift had been only two years earlier and the tension between the USSR and the United States had grown. China had fallen to the communists just a year before. Dad was worried. "See," he said, "the Soviets couldn't get anywhere in Europe. Now they're trying in Asia. Korea sits right next to both China and Russia. They're the bastards who are behind this. Stalin wants Japan. That's why we've got to stop him. If only Truman has the balls to do something about it. He's got the best in Japan. He's got MacArthur. We'll see." Within six months Mom and I were living with my grandparents. Dad and the brand-new Air Force were off to war.

In Washington, Harry Truman and his advisors were also worried. They were still trying to grasp strategic realities in a world that changed and evolved constantly. In Tokyo, then Lieutenant Alexander Haig was duty officer. He received a hasty telephone call from Ambassador John J. Muccio in Seoul telling him that "this was the real thing." Haig immediately called his boss, General Edward M. Almond, who notified General MacArthur. Supreme Headquarters Allied Forces-Far East began to gear up for war. In Washington, President Truman learned of the Sunday predawn attack by North Korea when his State Department received a frantic cable dispatched by Ambassador Muccio. The time was early Saturday evening in Washington, D.C., and the city was well into a warm summer weekend with officials scattered about. Truman's first action was to assemble his national security advisors.

No one was 100 percent certain what the president would do. He had been a stalwart in sending military advisors and equipment to Greece and Iran to help friendly local governments defeat attempts by Soviet-sponsored communists to overthrow their governments. He had stood strong in Berlin when the Soviets imposed a blockade of all roads entering the divided city in an effort to force the western Allies out of their toehold in East Germany. Truman authorized the Berlin Airlift, an imaginative, dramatic counter to the blockade that set an example of resolute fortitude and determination for the world and helped keep the people of

West Berlin free. But the Korean situation was something different. This was a full-blown shooting war and the hastily assembled advisors wondered what the president would do.

With his cabinet surrounding him, Truman frowned in concentration as he listened to reports of the North Korean invasion. After he was satisfied that he had received sufficient information, the president ordered the Joint Chiefs of Staff to begin immediate preparation to defend South Korea. American military units were already in the region, primarily in Occupation Japan. And while that was good news, there was an element that made many of the people sitting at that table in the White House uneasy. A legend in Washington was the idiosyncratic nature of one of America's most illustrious commanders, General of the Army Douglas MacArthur. General MacArthur had long ago become accustomed to running his own show. There were concerns about how he would react to being bossed by people he considered junior to him. Truman brushed aside such concerns. He was commander in chief and expected full loyalty from his subordinates. Truman properly thought that he had serious tangible issues on the table and did not intend to be distracted by hypothetical problems.

The president made his decision. The United States would prepare to defend South Korea. He would bring the issue before the United Nations. Meanwhile, he authorized MacArthur, as Supreme Commander Allied Forces-Far East to prepare for combat. As successor to the late FDR, a staunch proponent of the United Nations, it seems logical that Truman would turn there when the clear opportunity for the organization to be useful presented itself. Harry S. Truman was a man of the people. He also had a stronger personality and a larger ego than his popular image portrays. He smarted under the lash of criticism as Roosevelt's successor. When he squeaked out a victory over Republican candidate Thomas

Dewey in 1948, Truman felt vindication for the first time in several years. Yet anyone who had watched Truman even in those years would have seen an emerging strength. He had made the difficult decision to use the atomic bomb, an option that would have haunted a lesser man. He had tackled extremely controversial domestic issues, such as racial integration of the armed forces, although as a calculating politician he had to recognize the potential risk. And he had followed up on those programs of Roosevelt's that he believed in—the United Nations was one example—while quietly abandoning others. But he had also demonstrated a quick, hot temper and a very thin skin regarding possible affronts to his family, himself, or the office of the president. And his distrust of military leaders, particularly high-ranking, patrician career generals, primed him for an eventual clash with anyone who might challenge him. All of these factors placed him on a collision course with Douglas MacArthur. The outcome of that moving train wreck would establish Korean policy for all these subsequent decades.

## The United Nations Goes to War

The United States in June 1950 placed before the Security Council a resolution on the issue of communist aggression in Korea. Timing was, to say the least, fortuitous to support a resolution of condemnation. At the time, neither North or South Korea nor the People's Republic of China were yet members of the United Nations. Three of the permanent members—the United States, the United Kingdom, and France—saw the North Korean attack as an expansion of Soviet aggression and voted immediately to oppose it. Nationalist China also supported the resolution. China had the added motivation of obtaining UN support for its interests on the mainland. If the United Nations opposed communism in Korea it follows with some persuasive logic that opposing the same ideology in the more populous and important nation of China had to be an even greater priority. This turned out to be a false hope, but the possibility made sense under the circumstances.

Fortunately for the continued existence of the United Nations, the resolution condemning North Korea and supporting assistance to the South passed for one key reason. The Soviet Union was at the time boycotting the United Nations for reasons unrelated to Korea. Even though it would have been outvoted, the Soviet Union could have imposed a veto on the resolution condemning the North Koreans and authorizing the members to raise a force and expel the North Koreans from South Korea. With the Soviet delegation pouting at home, the condemnatory resolution passed unanimously.

So for the first time in history the powder-blue flag of the United Nations marched off to war. But did it really? It was true that in time fully sixteen nations supported the UN effort in Korea with troops, medical supplies, or other tangible contributions. Some of the names on the roll call of nations sound a bit quaint today—South Africa (air force), Ethiopia (support troops), Denmark (hospital)—but others such as the United States and the United Kingdom have been consistent workhorses fighting for freedom and democracy around the world. France sent a battalion of foreign legion troops to Korea who fought bravely. Turkey dispatched a very effective infantry brigade. Countries in Asia such as the Philippines and Thailand supported as best they were able with token forces.

On the other hand, one of the primary countries actively supporting the North Korean aggressor in every conceivable way, including supplies, ammunition, a safe base area, and even combat air forces, was the USSR, a permanent UN Security Council member. But this fact was intentionally ignored because to face it might cause the United Nations to suffer institutionally. This thought process demonstrates a crucial weakness of the United Nations: the existence of the institution became more valuable in and of itself than support for the values listed in the Charter. From its very inception the organization had the cancer of cognitive dissonance metastasizing within it. If the primary reason to support an organization, be it state, church, or international, is merely to prolong the life of that institution, even if that means acting in contravention to the stated reason for the very existence of the organization, then the entire process is morally corrupt. Refusing to hold the Soviet Union responsible for aiding and abetting aggression—an aggression that was universally condemned by other Security Council members—simply because the act of forcing the Soviets to be publicly accountable for its actions might collapse the United Nations itself, began to erode irreparably the value of the organization. The ineptitude that has spread through the United Nations decades later as it has failed to deal with a horrific series of international crises illustrates and reinforces this point. Before it even got started on its first big mission the United Nations was already a dead man walking.

But there was already in the eyes of the policymakers apparently too much political and diplomatic capital spent on the United Nations to let it die an honest death. Instead, the charade was not only continued but was also reinforced by formulation in Korea of an entire semi-fictional UN command structure (that exists to this day!). I call it semi-fictional because the UN command has always been headed by an American general officer and staffed primarily by U.S. officers, non-commissioned officers, and enlisted men and women. It has been U.S. forces that have carried the weight of the entire support package to South Korea since the late 1950s, virtually alone. While support from such longtime allies as Britain, the

Philippines, and Thailand continues with the UN command, it is strictly symbolic at this stage, comprising perhaps a rotating platoon of British Gurkhas, or similar platoons from the Philippines or Thailand. There are 37,000 plus U.S. troops currently in South Korea committed to its defense. Notably absent are any other nation's military to make up a real UN force.

One of the key issues concerning the Korea War, one that is debated to this day with hot emotion, was the conflict between General MacArthur and President Truman. It resulted in the relief of General MacArthur—one of a handful of five-star generals in American military history—by a president that many considered a hero and others a buffoon. There is far more written on this topic than will ever be covered in this book.

The conflict between these two men directly influenced the way the Korean War was fought and the objectives of that war. The decisions of the winner shaped the way all of Korea looked after the war ended. Hence the controversy between these two tough men was not simply an internal American bureaucratic squabble or even a Constitutional test as some have interpreted it. It was responsible for the continued North Korea-South Korea split and for all of the issues that resulted from it. Had the decision gone the other way the hypotheticals are legion, for MacArthur was fixed on victory, not limited war. But it is important to note at the start that the continued existence of two Koreas—good, bad, and ugly— as they appeared after the armistice in 1953 was a direct result of President Harry Truman winning the fight.

Suffice it to say that there were two extremely strong personalities involved in the fight, particularly MacArthur's. The general had grown accustomed to being the person in charge. He was far better at informing than at consulting, and certainly did not think that he required guidance from anyone who he thought knew less about a subject than he did. From the general's perspective, a lot of people—military and civilian—fell into that category. The one thing MacArthur knew well was operating and leading military units. He therefore chafed under constraints and orders sent to him from the Joint Chiefs of Staff. MacArthur deemed the staff officers in Washington generally misinformed, confused, and contradictory. He would not be the first and certainly not the last field general to make that observation.

MacArthur in Korea was abruptly handed what many experts considered a lost war and told to win it. After all, the North Korean People's Army was literally fighting around the outskirts of Pusan when he was given the order to enter the war. Through brilliant generalship and the determination of the American and South Korean fighting men, MacArthur was able to turn certain defeat into stunning victory. He then proceeded to throw it all away when his ego got in the way of his experience and training.

When war broke out in Korea, General MacArthur had a large pool of military units stationed in Japan as part of the occupation. On paper, these units were combat-ready and available for deployment to Korea. The unfortunate reality was that life was soft and easy in Japan. Even the troops called it the "Occupation Country Club." Individual and unit training had degraded during the postwar period so that infantry units were ill prepared to face an enemy. Many of the junior officers and enlisted men had been too young for World War II and had never seen combat. Of all the raps against MacArthur during this period—and his critics are legion and vocal—no one has focused on one of the most grievous errors a commander can commit—that is allowing his troops to fall out of shape to the degree that they are not prepared to carry out their mission. Since most of MacArthur's critics are inexperienced themselves in things military the error itself and the magnitude of the omission probably escapes them. More than likely they think that the soft Occupation Country Club–lifestyle is the military norm, and that units undergo a kind of "spring training" prior to being deployed into combat. That theory works as long as your enemy gives plenty of advance notice of his intention to attack and you have a good bit of space to trade for time in order to prepare. Obviously the exigencies of modern warfare give neither warning nor time. MacArthur should have seen the necessity of enforcing strict training discipline. It was the commander's responsibility to make certain that he was informed of the readiness of his units for combat. Not only is a high state of readiness necessary for any military unit to accomplish a mission but it also promotes high morale. Troops do not enjoy a constant slack lifestyle where they think they are merely killing time. In this case poor training and lack of preparation killed many of them.

The first units to deploy to Korea in that typical steamy hot, humid July of 1950 were from the U.S. Twenty-fourth Infantry Division. They advanced north in an ad hoc unit known as Task Force Smith (U.S. Army custom names a special task force for its commander). The Americans were confident and unjustifiably cocky—a fatal combination. They told each other that the North Koreans would turn tail and flee when they saw that they were facing the U.S. Army. Things didn't work out that way at all. Task Force Smith gave a reasonably good account of itself and slowed the North Korean advance somewhat in the first clashes near Suwon and Osan, and then small villages south of Seoul. But the North Koreans were not intimidated by the mere presence of the Americans. They had come to the fight with everything they owned: tanks, infantry, and artillery. The weapons Task Force Smith soldiers carried were light infantry stuff—rifles, carbines, small caliber mortars, and bazookas—and were not intended to take on armored units. There had not been enough time to deploy any armor units into Korea from Japan so the Twenty-fourth Division troopers simply brought what they could carry on their backs to the fight. It was insufficient.

## The Pusan Perimeter

After overrunning Task Force Smith and scattering lead elements of the Twenty-fourth Division (including capturing the Division Commander, Major General William F. Dean) the North Korean army pushed down the peninsula, bent on seizing Pusan. MacArthur and his staff recognized that loss of Pusan with its excellent port and rail facilities would add considerably to the challenge of recapturing Korea. It had to be defended at all costs. In reaction MacArthur ordered units and equipment dispatched piecemeal through Pusan. They disembarked and were sent directly into battle in a frantic effort to defend a line that became known as the "Pusan Perimeter." In setting up the Pusan Perimeter as they were able to do, the allied effort was aided by a geographical twist of good fortune. The Naktong River, which formed a long axis of the Perimeter, drains the mountainous area of southeastern Korea and bends in an odd, bow-shaped arc that cuts first west then south, then a bit east. It follows ancient fissures in the relatively steep granite hills that lie along the river's eastern bank. It is what soldiers refer to as "good ground," a quirky bit of geography that allowed defenders to take up positions on the eastern bank high ground while forcing an attacker from the western side to cross a deep, swift flowing river under the defender's guns. These river defenses became the main line of resistance for the U.S. and South Korean forces. As much as anything else, the existence of the Naktong River and the ability of the U.S. and South Korean defenders to quickly establish positions along it was responsible for the ultimate continued existence of South Korea as a nation.

Even as the defenders were digging in along the Naktong, getting stronger, the North Korean army began to show signs of shattering and breaking against the staunch defenses. They may have come to regret the units that they diverted to seize Kwangju, Masan, and Pohang and took away from the primary drive to Pusan. It cost them precious momentum and gave the Americans and South Koreans time to regroup. While the North Koreans, nearing the farthest extension of their stretched-out supply lines, pounded futilely at the Pusan Perimeter, U.S. reinforcements continued to pour through Pusan. Soldiers had no time for orientation but were directed up into the line. In some instances, less than an hour would elapse between the time a GI stepped off the gangplank until he was changing clips in his M-1, firing into attacking North Koreans. Given this massive effort the Americans had enough forces in the country in short order to prepare a counterattack aimed at cracking the increasingly thin North Korean lines. In hindsight it is clear that the North Koreans gambled everything on strategic surprise and speed. If they had stayed focused and been able to achieve both, chances are good that their attack would have been successful, even if the United States decided to intervene. The North Koreans achieved strategic surprise but the unexpectedly rapid intervention of U.S. units from Japan, as unprepared as those troops may have been initially, was just enough to disrupt the enemy timetable and place doubt upon their sure success. By the time the full force of the United States and its UN allies was marshaled and brought to bear, allied victory was assured. Meanwhile, MacArthur's masterstroke—the amphibious landing at Inchon—was set to place a major nail in the North Korean coffin.

## The Terrible Tide of Inchon

Much of the public thinks that amphibious landings are the sole
province of the Marine Corps. But even a cursory historical examination reveals that the U.S. Army actually made a greater number
of landings—and larger ones—than did the Marines. The Battle of
Okinawa and D-Day in Normandy are but two examples. During
the Pacific War there was vigorous competition between the two
strategies personified by General MacArthur and Admiral Chester
W. Nimitz. The navy strategy was composed primarily of a navy-
marine island-hopping campaign up the central Pacific, attacking
and securing Japanese-held islands. In contrast, MacArthur's primary army-navy-marine campaign in the western Pacific focused
on bypassing strong points. Both strategies were effective, each in
its own manner. But there was more to it than that. In a war effort
that clearly designated Europe First, everyone else fought jeal-
ously for scraps from the table, including the two main players in
the Pacific. Part of the game was to get enough publicity to win political support in Washington. In this the Marine Corps has always
excelled. Battles such as Guadalcanal, Saipan, Tarawa, and Iwo
Jima assumed almost mythic portions in the public mind. Films
were made that reinforced this image, John Wayne's *Sands of Iwo
Jima* being one of the best known. The effectiveness of the marines
in storming heavily defended islands and overcoming fierce resistance has never been questioned, nor has the remarkable bravery
and courage they exhibited in going straight into the deadly
Japanese guns time and time again.

MacArthur's strategy in the western Pacific differed from
Nimitz's. He preferred the indirect approach. Perhaps the difference in strategy comes from his background as a muddy-booted infantryman who had lived and fought in the trenches as opposed to
the khaki-clad admirals who watched marines wade into blistering

fire through binoculars in the comfort of a distant battleship's bridge. That the western Pacific was a miserable, muddy, jungle-covered, leech-infested place, loaded with poisonous snakes and insects that carried a full menu of tropical diseases, made these campaigns appear far less glamorous than some of the South Pacific island ones. They were also far less deadly to the American soldiers who executed the missions. In any event the battles of the western Pacific are virtually unknown today to all but a few military history buffs. Few Americans know that there were many parachute assaults in the Pacific for example, or really understand the magnitude of the battles fought there.

For MacArthur preferred to bypass Japanese strong points rather than attack them head on. He called this a "wither on the vine" strategy intended to isolate Japanese redoubts and cut their supply lines rather than sacrifice thousands of American and Japanese lives to capture these strong points by frontal assault. In order to carry out this strategy MacArthur used a variety of tools including extensive amphibious operations, available air power, and paratroop assaults. For the most part the western Pacific campaigns were characterized by a series of well-coordinated strikes that kept the Japanese defenders confused and disrupted their defensive plans. It worked exceedingly well as the Allies made their way steadily up through New Guinea, the Solomons, and into the Philippines with casualties kept to a minimum.

So in 1950, when MacArthur looked at Korea he saw another opportunity to employ the surprise, indirect-approach strategy that had served him so well in the past. In an incredibly bold move, he put his finger on the map and announced that he was going to outflank the entire North Korean army by conducting an amphibious landing in force at Inchon harbor. MacArthur's staff was stunned. Inchon was a muddy port city west of Seoul, the South Korean capital, but it was home to one of the greatest tidal changes in the world, second only to Canada's Bay of Fundy. Military analysts—including some on MacArthur's staff—considered an amphibious assault at Inchon an impossible mission. A nasty bureaucratic brangle ensued between Washington and Tokyo over Inchon's selection, which over time, erupted into a full-blown fight between the president and the general. But, at first, MacArthur had to get past the Joint Chiefs. And field commanders are very far away from Washington, while the Pentagon is just across the Potomac River from the White House.

Reduced to essence, the initial controversy was this: MacArthur used the same reasoning when picking Inchon as he had when choosing similar battle sites in the past. In his mind, Inchon, which lay well behind the North Korean lines, was perfect for a classic indirect assault. It would be lightly defended and would open the door to recapture Seoul, laying just to its east, while simultaneously severing over-extended enemy supply lines. That it was considered an impossible place to stage an amphibious assault just made it more desirable to MacArthur. To him, it meant that he would have absolute strategic and tactical surprise—factors he always sought. Moreover, the very audacity of the location—others said it couldn't be done and he *would* accomplish it—certainly appealed to his ego as a Great Captain.

Military leaders in Washington—primarily within the Joint Chiefs of Staff—had already been well politicized. They were attuned to the Washington scene, to possible criticism from the press and the Congress. These Pentagon generals feared the downside results of a loss more than they desired the positive outcome of a win. It was an early manifestation of the risk-aversive nature of "command from long distance" that would eventually influence several decades of American military decisions and actions.

Seventy-two-year-old MacArthur had fought his previous wars, beginning with the Philippine Insurrection in 1902 up through 1945 when he accepted the Japanese surrender aboard the battleship Missouri, under a very different institutional system. He was now dealing with a complex bureaucratic restructuring of both the Department of Defense and the Joint Chiefs of Staff, institutions with which he had had no personal exposure. He would be likely to see their members as junior officers who had significantly less experience and understanding of things Asian than did he. After all, he was Supreme Commander Allied Forces-Far East and was in effect running the nation of Japan. MacArthur was described by many as the "American Emperor" in Japan as he reconstructed the nation according to what he thought was best for the Japanese people. That time has proven him successful in bringing free-market democracy to Japan is one of the most remarkable feats of modern history.

Adding to the overall friction between Washington and MacArthur's headquarters in Tokyo was the increasingly visible participation in the decision process of a president whom MacArthur didn't know personally. Unlike Franklin Roosevelt with whom he had a cordial relationship, MacArthur had never even met Truman. Furthermore, a few of Truman's comments that could have been viewed by a sensitive commander as disparaging filtered down. While Truman probably wanted to let the world know who was in charge, the comments rubbed field commanders the wrong way. And MacArthur for all his courage, endurance, and machissimo was as sensitive to criticism as Truman. And while Truman was connected to the American people and thoroughly familiar with the postwar cultural changes that were taking place, MacArthur had been operating with an extraordinary amount of freedom since the days prior to the Japanese attack on the

Philippines on December 8, 1941. He had lived abroad since the mid-1930s and the America of 1950 was far, far different than the America of 1930. He was in many ways unaware of the sweeping trends that had forever changed the prewar America he'd left.

The fight over Inchon—not the battle itself, but the bureaucratic tussle that preceded it—contributed to his undoing. It was what is known in military parlance as a "tactical victory but a strategic defeat." MacArthur and his staff considered Washington's attempt to micromanage the war as unwarranted long-distance second-guessing of their strategy. One of the characteristics of the Joint Chiefs of Staff system is that with increasingly improved communications the tendency is to oversee even the most minute operation detail. The temptation to call the shots from the Pentagon and White House has proven irresistible to chairborne warriors and their civilian counterparts.[5] No one on MacArthur's Tokyo staff disputed the contention that an amphibious landing at Inchon was risky. After all, they had already tried to persuade the General to pick another spot. They had used all of the logical reasons not to attack Inchon with their boss long before the supercilious Washington types weighed in. They had been overruled with vintage MacArthurian language and flourish. It was simply good staff work: they recommended options, the boss made his choice, and now they supported his decision as the professional officers they were and began working hard to implement it. They saw no need to drop everything and refight the decision with a staff in Washington. MacArthur himself simply would not

---

[5] This counterproductive tendency reached the ultimate lunacy in the Vietnam War days when President Lyndon Johnson personally picked targets that would be struck by American bombers on a daily basis. Fortunately, we seem to have moved beyond that extreme, but in 1950 the system was just beginning to crank up.

tolerate the idea of a group he considered much lesser qualified than he—and everyone in Washington fit into that classification—either contradicting his strategic vision or overruling him. In a final burst of anger, frustration, and pique MacArthur simply presented the Joint Chiefs with an ultimatum: approve the Inchon landing or get a new commander. He was secure—perhaps arrogant—in his confidence that they would fold.

MacArthur's threat to resign cowed the Joint Chiefs of Staff for the moment but left some bureaucratic abrasions that would continue to fester. Meanwhile, Truman and his staff in the White House were following the situation. The president was already grumbling at the independence and grandiosity of the Tokyo gang. He was beginning to personalize the dispute and treat the refusal of MacArthur and his staff to toe the Joint Chiefs of Staff's line as a direct challenge to Washington authority and by inference, to him as president.

MacArthur's stunning victory at Inchon against all odds, including the most unfavorable terrain imaginable for an amphibious assault, literally won the war (his logic that it was such an awful spot that he would achieve total surprise, proved correct). At least it won the war as it was then configured. Combined with a simultaneous successful Allied counterattack at Pusan that broke the spear point of the North Koreans, the Inchon landing laid a blocking force across enemy supply lines and severed escape routes. No army could survive under such conditions.

Overnight, the fast moving but overextended North Korean People's Army fell apart. The North Koreans tried to withdraw but allied counterattacks breaking out of the Pusan Perimeter quickly turned a hasty retreat into a rout. The pursuit was on. Within days after the landing at Inchon marine units liberated Seoul. They were joined by the U.S. and allied forces advancing from Pusan. The combined counteroffensive turned north and crossed the thirty-eighth parallel with the stated objective of a total victory over the North Koreans. The country would be reunited as one.

## Expanding the War

While there were those in Washington who spoke openly of expanding the war, of driving across the northern Yalu River into China, and removing Mao and the communists, this was not the case in MacArthur's headquarters where he continued to plan to surround the remnants of the North Korean People's Army and force it to surrender or die, thereby ending the war. He even spoke openly in November 1950 of having troops "home for Christmas." Nor was anything like an expanded war on the mind of the Truman administration. But a drive into China and return of the Nationalists to the mainland—a chance for Chiang to attack from Taiwan while UN forces drove west across Manchuria—was something that the China lobby in the U.S. Senate supported. Some of the Nationalist leaders were suggesting publicly that it could happen, but renewing the Chinese civil war was not part of anyone's strategic plan. Nonetheless, the new People's Republic of China leadership was profoundly disturbed by the way they perceived the war in Korea was developing, especially as UN forces moved north. It is odd that an old Asia hand like MacArthur and his more experienced staff missed the signals. But tragically, they all did.

MacArthur had been an expatriate for so long in Japan that he had not picked up on the particular line of thinking that use of nuclear weapons was now no longer socially or politically acceptable. Like other professional military leaders he did not reflexively or culturally reject the possible use of *any* weapon—

including atomic weapons—in the U.S. inventory. Good generals consider all the weapons in their inventory to be at their disposal and then they select the proper system or more likely combination of systems to achieve the objective. In other words, there would be no particular desire to select a nuclear weapon in a conflict any more than there would be an automatic rejection of something like heavy bombing. Even a weapon such as poison gas, which was prohibited by international convention, was part of the battle plan—not for first-use purposes but as a deterrent. The other side would not use them knowing that we were prepared to retaliate in kind. In any conflict—particularly a prolonged war—the weapons used in a military situation would be selected from need. Obviously, you don't go after a fly with a cannon and you don't try to stop a tank with a fly swatter. The idea of limiting force used against the enemy is not consonant with the very concept of war: increasing the other person's pain to the point that he submits to your will. So later in the war, when MacArthur's staff began to float ideas about using the atomic cannon or nuclear weapons, the reaction in Washington was one of shock and horror. It was a typical head-bumper. How can those idiots consider using nukes? the Washington crowd would ask. They're in the inventory, so how could we not? was the indignant response from Japan.

But back in Korea the war was going better than could be hoped. With typical bravado, MacArthur launched his paratroopers north in an attempt to bag the retreating North Korean army. The 187th Parachute Infantry Regiment executed what may have been one of the smoothest airborne operations in history at Sukchon and Sunchon north of the North Korean capital city of Pyongyang. The paratroopers landed behind the lines of retreating North Korean army remnants. Meanwhile, the British brigade attacked north from Pyongyang trapping the North Koreans between them and the 187th Paratroopers. With the defeat of this pocket of North Koreans, most organized defense ceased. The UN units then all faced north and moved up to the China-Russia border on a wide front. Their objective was to eliminate any pockets of North Korean stragglers and complete liberation of the rest of the country. The order of march was roughly the U.S. Army on the left supported by some UN allies, South Korean forces in the center, and the U.S. Marine Corps and Army on the east, along the coast of the Sea of Japan.

The seasons were changing faster than meteorologists predicted. Already the temperatures at night were dipping unpleasantly low. Soldiers awoke in the morning to discover frozen canteens. At this time UN forces had advanced north of the fortieth parallel. If you imagine armies traversing the northern Pocono Mountains in Pennsylvania in early winter, it approximates somewhat the conditions in weather and terrain found in North Korea. None of the Allied forces had been supplied with winter clothing or equipment, because everyone thought the war was drawing to a close. With North Korean resistance virtually melting away, leaders allowed defensive precautions to slip to a dangerously low level. Troops were sleeping in tents, if available, with space heaters and were snuggling down in their sleeping bags against the night chill. Many died struggling to get out of their sleeping bags when the Chinese attacked. GI survivors reported Chinese soldiers laughing and chattering as they moved from one helpless American soldier to the next, cutting their throats.[6]

---

[6] The Army ordered quick-release zipper systems on every sleeping bag it purchased since those awful, ugly winter days in Korea. Now a GI need only pull on a tab and then pop open the bag to defend himself.

## A Massive Chinese Ambush Turns the War

Reports had become more frequent of unknown units observed crossing the Yalu River into Korean territory. U.S. troops told of scattered firefights with fleeting enemy units who wore different uniforms than the North Koreans. Patrols would bump into these mysterious soldiers, exchange fire, and the strangers would disappear. Some of the new prisoners of war appeared to be Chinese, and not North Koreans. Again, we have to stop and place the right snapshot in time. In 1950, there were no such things as satellite imagery, sophisticated aircraft sensory devices, or precision signal intercept equipment. If an American pilot was in the air and happened to observe troops moving, he recorded it. Occasionally he was able to photograph them. If the enemy units moved at night it was difficult to see them unless moon conditions were favorable.

It was also possible—as it has been from time immemorial—to talk oneself into or out of a position as one wished. Chinese POWs were dismissed as stragglers from token units that had crossed the border. Troops crossing the Yalu were said to be North Koreans fleeing northward into China not Chinese units moving south into Korea. The reported massing of Chinese army units on the other side of the Yalu was considered to be just a reasonable Chinese precaution against a possible UN invasion, not a prelude to their invasion of Korea. There is also a tendency for lower units to report or not to report what they think the boss wants to hear. Word apparently had spread to certain levels that MacArthur was not interested in reports of large Chinese infiltration. By the time the reports reached MacArthur's level they had been sanitized to the point that they were sterile. There also existed a certain culture within MacArthur's staff of not bringing bad news to the Old Man. Part of this culture arose because of the amazingly accurate nature of his analytical abilities. The staff had said Inchon couldn't be done; he did it. They said it might be a long war; he won it in weeks. There was an aura of near-infallibility about him. Combined with the hubris of the moment it made the already serious strategic surprise of the Chinese intervention that much more effective.

The reality of the situation was that the communist Chinese leadership had determined that they could not permit a democratic, U.S.-controlled Korea to touch their borders. The possibility of using Korea as a jumping-off point for a future invasion may have seemed remote to American policymakers but was terrifyingly real to the Chinese. For them it was simply a repeat of historical patterns. They were determined to resist. For weeks, Chinese infantry units with troops numbering in the tens of thousands infiltrated across the Yalu River and disappeared into the mountains and ridges of northern Korea. They wore quilted uniforms against the cold and carried PPSH submachine guns, potato masher grenades, and Soviet-style mortars and artillery. In equipment, doctrine, and organization they most resembled World War II Soviet foot soldiers attacking Berlin. Many Chinese were veterans of the anti-Japanese war and their own civil war. They had been at this business of war for a long time. They knew how to use rough terrain to their advantage, were not bound by road and supply systems, and were clever with camouflage. They were already in attack positions well before any of the advancing UN forces were even aware of their presence or strength of numbers. Even those units that suspected the presence of Chinese infantry in their area could not believe that such large numbers were about to attack them. Using techniques that they had perfected against the Japanese and the Nationalists, the Chinese launched a simultaneous surprise night attack on all fronts, striking in the front and rear areas, creating confusion, cutting communications, and killing commanders and headquarters support personnel, leaving tactical units to their own devices.

It was a brutal, effective attack. American forces in the west reeled under the weight of the ambush and began to fall back. Most units regrouped as best they could and literally fought their way southward through a gauntlet of Chinese ambushes. Some regrettably fell apart under the weight of the attack and ran in panic. In the center, the South Korean corps was shattered and also began to retreat. In the east, the marine and army units that were near the Chosun Reservoir bent under the Chinese onslaught, then began to fight their way back through surrounding Chinese to the coast and evacuation.

Although no soldier likes to retreat, the withdrawal from the Chosun Reservoir was an extraordinary military operation done with heroism and uncommon valor under the most brutal environmental conditions conceivable.[7] Winter set in with a force that had not been seen in Korea in decades. The winter of 1950–1951 is the one that sticks in most people's minds to this day when they picture Korea: everything frozen solid and covered with ice and snow, bearded troops huddled in blankets, breath steaming with fatigue, and shock glazing their eyes. It was not a pleasant scene. The shock of Chinese intervention and UN retreat was exacerbated by the earlier optimism. Suddenly it seemed as if defeat was snatched from the jaws of certain victory. Americans were faced with what MacArthur called "an entirely new war." As UN units poured south, many in acute disarray, the public image of an ignominious retreat to Pusan and the specter of being pushed into the sea loomed terribly large. Seoul fell for the second time in the war and the stream of refugees grew even greater as some who

---

7  When informed that his unit was surrounded by Chinese infantry, legendary Marine General Chesty Puller is reported to have said, "Good, we've got the bastards right where we want them. We can shoot in any direction we want now."

had returned north now fled for a second time. The civilian death toll to hostile fire and the elements was horrific.

It was at this time that MacArthur began discussing the use of nuclear weapons, favoring the employment of low-yield weapons along the Yalu River to destroy Chinese army assembly points and supply routes. The idea of laying a radioactive barrier along the Chinese side of the Yalu was brought up as a sort of "invisible fence" to inhibit continued infiltration of men and supplies. He wanted to use nuclear artillery rounds (called the "atomic cannon" in the press) against the human wave assaults the Chinese continued to throw at the UN defenders. When thousands of Chinese gathered close together in an assembly area prior to the attack, the argument went, a few atomic artillery rounds would seriously retard their capability to mount the attack. In civilian-speak, the atomic cannon would be the most efficient tool to kill the Chinese soldiers before they could come at our guys. As can be imagined, all of these ideas stirred controversy back home—especially since many of them surfaced in the press before the White House issued a policy on them. Or worse, some statements were attributed to people in the field *in spite* of contrary White House policy. Noses got bent way out of shape. Truman was faced with some difficult options. He had the distinction of being the only leader who had ever authorized the use of atomic weapons in combat. So it must have seemed clear to people fighting in Korea that given the proper set of circumstances he might be persuaded to use atomic weapons again.

So what had happened in the five years since 1945 that might have made President Truman so reluctant to use something from his nuclear weapons inventory in Korea? From a policy point of view, the Truman administration saw Korea as a limited war, with objectives that were considerably less than the traditional World

War II idea of unconditional victory over an opponent. Korea had turned into a war with self-imposed restrictions and limitations that seemed artificial and bizarre, especially to the fighting men. The whole "limited war" concept is one that many had difficulty understanding at the time, and some people have trouble with it to this day. The administration had even begun to engage in the terribly destructive practice of official euphemism, calling Korea not a war but a "police action." To those fighting the war or supporting the men and women who were fighting and dying there, this practice became especially repugnant. Rather than bring about acceptance of the situation, the police action comments gave the impression that Truman wanted to minimize or trivialize the war and, by extension, the soldiers fighting it. The entire limited war concept made Truman—previously hailed as a stalwart, brave president—seem weak and vacillating.

The United States was entering a period where caution was replacing boldness and where fear of the ultimate nuclear exchange trumped all other policy concerns. The situation in Korea deteriorated to the point that the Air Force was forbidden to attack the bridges across the Yalu River even with conventional bombs because we didn't want to offend the Chinese. These were the same Chinese who were fighting the UN forces in the bitter trench warfare that characterized the last two years of the war. U.S. pilots were forbidden to use hot pursuit to shoot down the Soviet MiG-15s that engaged their F-80s and F-86s in dogfights over Korea and then escaped to a sanctuary in Russia. Concepts of limited war, measured response, self-imposed restraint, undue fear of international opinion, deference to the UN, and enemy sanctuary areas were introduced during the Korean War. These concepts would haunt the military and the country for decades and persist to present day.

Meanwhile the fighting continued for possession of the barren, useless ridges and hills. Hundreds of men died fighting for possession of places such as Pork Chop Hill, the Iron Triangle, and the Punchbowl. And more battle streamers were logged in the annals of the U.S. military as troops fought valiantly, always outnumbered, to capture or defend terrain that had become little more than a bargaining chip at the armistice talks. To the west, north of Seoul, tents had been set up near a village known as Panmunjom that without the war would have continued to live in pleasant obscurity. Representatives of the warring forces met at the table to discuss armistice terms. On one side were representatives from the North Korean People's Army and the Chinese People's Volunteers. On the other were the UN forces and the South Koreans. Exchanges were heated and accusatory. Name-calling and unchecked anger were common. Tempers flared; representatives walked out in a huff. Negotiations proceeded at glacial speed while men died in the heat and in the cold, in the dry and in the rain on the hills and in the valleys of Korea, watering the thin soil with their blood.

It is amazing to the visitor to see how much of the original Panmunjom survives to this day. Tents have been replaced with buildings but the original battle lines remain; the bridges and roads into the area are paved rather than dirt but the locations are precisely as they were when the armistice was finally signed in July 1953, and a ceasefire put into effect. What was known as the "military demarcation line" was an imaginary line drawn between the warring factions. Two kilometers from the military demarcation line to the north and another two kilometers from the military demarcation line to the south two other lines were drawn that ran parallel to the military demarcation line. The entire area encompassed by these lines formed a Demilitarized Zone. The military demarcation line itself became a de facto international boundary separating North Korea from South Korea. The boundary exists today exactly as it was in July 1953 when the armistice agreement was accepted.

North Korean and South Korean combat units that opposed each other in 1953 sit opposite each other today, watching, waiting, preparing for the attack they hope never comes. Mines that were emplaced during the war continue to lie in wait, shifting and heaving in the rains and frosts, waiting for the careless foot to trip them. Many young soldiers are maimed or killed every year by these uncharted mines. In military doctrine, minefields are defined as temporary barriers. They are placed carefully with a distinct purpose: to stop tanks, to disperse an infantry attack, or a combination of missions. Minefields are carefully emplaced, usually by combat engineers, and a detailed, precise scale map of the minefield is made in duplicate, one copy kept on site and another at higher headquarters. Doctrine calls for removal of mines as soon as they are not needed. In the DMZ of Korea are untold numbers of mines, many of which were laid by the enemy forces or in haste by allies. Many fields are unmapped as a consequence. Laneways through the minefields have been opened through the years and patrols are instructed to stay on the cleared ground. But the mines shift in the weather and the point man in a patrol will occasionally trip a mine, usually killing or injuring himself and the patrol leader who is often a second lieutenant walking second or third in line. Several of the cadets who were my students at the Korean Military Academy were killed that way by unmarked mines that may have been placed by their fathers—or their fathers' enemies.

CHAPTER 4

# Getting to Know Korea

My family came home by troop transport from Japan in the fall of 1953. When the Korean War ended in an unsatisfactory armistice many of the veterans, including Dad, felt cheated and let down. After his relief and return to America, MacArthur had given his famous "no substitute for victory" speech. While it was derided as sentimental and outdated by the left, it rang true to the core with the veterans. Dying for a winning cause was unfortunate but necessary. One performed one's duty. Dying for a "limited war" with poorly understood objectives was uncomfortable. Dying while available weapons systems went unused and enemies had privileged sanctuaries was unacceptable. Like many career soldiers burnt out by too many wars in too short a period of time, Dad decided to leave the military.

As our ship, the USS Anderson, passed beneath the Golden Gate Bridge we were met by fireboats streaming the green Pacific into fountains of foam and an enthusiastic band on the wharf. We took a train to Los Angeles and the Sunset Limited back to New

Orleans. Dad hung up his uniform but not his opinions. He was not one to dwell on the past but neither did he shy away from issues. He thought that the Korean War was justified and ought to have been fought but was furious about what he considered a disgraceful lack of support from American political leadership that translated into apathy from the American people. This was the genesis of the Forgotten War syndrome that has troubled Korean War veterans ever since.

Somewhere in those years I must have decided that the military life was for me. Although I flirted with a string of career ideas, the concept of serving was bred in me from birth. With a father, three uncles, a cousin, a grandfather, and back and back all in the military the idea of serving myself seemed to be both a duty and a right. By the time I was in graduate school at the University of North Carolina the Vietnam War was burning hotly. As I sat in dark carrels worrying over pre-World War II German documents for a thesis, the sense of responsibility and a call of adventure were too tempting to resist. I gave up my three-year fellowship and enlisted in the army, destined, I was certain, for Vietnam. Korea never entered my mind.

People say that you never know which are the big forks in the road, those decisions that loom large later in life. Seemingly innocuous incidents happen and you never realize that you made a directional change until years later. That happened to me twice within my first year in the army. The first incident was one of those "you don't know you just did something important" ones. It took place on a hot, humid June day in Fort Dix, New Jersey. We had been in the Reception Station several days. Each day we got more and more adult leadership until after a week or so we were shuffling from place to place in a semblance of a military formation, had drawn boots and uniforms, and began the testing, medical inspection, inoculations, and haircut phase. One day we stood in line in the sun after having been up most of the night for a barracks cleaning detail. My head ached and the sweat inside my new fatigues put out an unpleasant combination of body odor and chemicals. A corporal amused himself by yelling at us and pretending he was a drill sergeant. A few minutes later we were ushered into an older wooden building (these were all "temporary" World War II construction. They built them solid in those days.) Inside was cool and quiet. The corporal stayed outside. For me just out of school, a classroom-type environment was within my comfort zone. We began to take a bank of tests designed to assist the army in placing us within a Military Occupational Specialty, or MOS, that would influence the type of job we would do and in some cases whether we were to live or die. Most of us expected to receive the 11B, or Light Weapons, Infantryman, designation that in 1967 could easily have read "Cannon Fodder, Vietnam." Indeed, I had enlisted for exactly that MOS, a fact that had some of my contemporaries in Reception shaking their heads at my stupidity.

Among the bank of tests designed to assess mechanical ability, leadership potential, and other critical skills was a language ability test. It was given in what seemed to me almost an Esperanto-type format: an invented language with its own vocabulary, grammar, and structure. By that time I'd had two years of Latin in high school, three years of German, and two of Russian in college, and on reflection I think most important, had learned some Japanese as a child. But on that day I just took the test and immediately forgot about it. Months later, on my way to Infantry Officer Candidate School at Fort Benning, Georgia, with a khaki uniform laden with the crossed rifles of a newly minted 11B, PFC stripes on my arm, and Expert Rifle and Machine Gun badge I opened my records and saw a score of 36 on the Language

Aptitude Test. Gee, I thought, accustomed to scores out of a 100, that was pretty poor. Guess I must have boloed the test. I dismissed the score as irrelevant to a future infantry officer and leader of men. Boy, was I was wrong.

The second big fork in the road was one that I knew when I saw it. It happened toward the end of the rigorous Officer Candidate School. We began the program with more than 220 candidates in our company and barely graduated 100. Toward the end of the program we eagerly looked for our assignment orders to be cut in Washington. Just a couple of weeks prior we had been issued a volunteer form. On the form were four choices. A candidate could check all or none: Airborne, Ranger, Special Forces (Green Berets), and Language Training. Having fled graduate school for the adventurous life of the army, I had no desire for further schooling, so I checked only the top three.

We had still not heard anything from assignment branch when I was tapped one morning to sweep the orderly room. While pushing microns of dust into a pile on the already spotless floor, I shamelessly eavesdropped on the first sergeant's phone conversation. Information, we had learned as privates, was the currency of the lower ranks. It took only a moment for me to piece from his side of the conversation that he was speaking with an assignment officer. "Okay," the first sergeant said, "you're saying that if Abernathy and Maxwell volunteer for Airborne and Special Forces that you'll grant their request for language training? Hold, please." The first sergeant looked up at the designated runner. "Find Maxwell and Abernathy and haul their asses down here. Move!" He spoke into the receiver, "On the way, Sir," and waited, drumming his fingers. In a flash I realized that this was the critical moment. As I stood there with a broom in my hand, someone in Washington was filling in blanks for the coveted Special Forces slots. With a surprising prescience, given my brief time in the army, I also deduced that the persuader for being assigned to SF seemed to be language training. A chill hit me: Had I eliminated my chances of selection by declining language school? The fork in the road loomed closer and closer. In those days it was unheard of for a candidate to initiate conversation with any of the cadre upon pain of long and arduous physical punishment. My fingers gripped the broomstick so hard I must have left imprints. Now or never, I figured. Besides, for the past months I'd been "pushing up Georgia" anyway, what were a few more? "First Sergeant?" I asked tentatively, "Is he asking for volunteers for Special Forces?" He must have had a good night because the crusty First Shirt didn't explode as usual, but simply nodded. "Would you ask if I volunteered for language could I go to Special Forces, too?" He nodded again. My heart jumped in my chest. This was it!

"By the way, Sir, I've got someone else here who would volunteer for language training if he could get Special Forces. Is that of interest? Yes, Sir. I spell, C-U-C-U-L-L-U, that's Charlie, Uniform, Charlie, Uniform . . ."

I shouted with glee, dropped the broom, and ran down the hall. I knew my roommate, Ron Crawford, among others, wanted to go to Special Forces, too. I yelled the news to him: "Quick, go to the orderly room. Tell the first sergeant you will take language school to get Special Forces. Go," I repeated into his disbelieving face. The word spread until a line formed outside the orderly room and the First Sergeant would say, "Sir, I have another volunteer . . ."

Most Officer Candidate companies sent two, sometimes three lieutenants to Special Forces. The Ninety-fifth Officer Candidate Company in spring of 1968 sent fourteen! Who dares, wins.

When orders came down a few weeks later, there was no doubt in my mind that it would be for Vietnamese language. After all, with the war building to a crescendo what else made sense? But, no logic in the army, they say. "Korean," I read on the orders. Korean language training. Where had that come from? I was to go to jump school right there at Fort Benning, head on up to Fort Bragg in North Carolina for Special Forces qualification training, and then on to the language school in Monterey, California, for Korean language training. How in the hell had that happened? When I mentioned my low aptitude score to one of my instructors at the Defense Language Institute he noted that the perfect score was 40 and that most soldiers scored 10 or lower. So my 36 taken in the fog of the reception center was high enough to stick me into a difficult language. The army rank-ordered languages in declining order of difficulty. Korean was at the top followed by such tough nuts as Arabic, Japanese, Russian, Chinese, and others. Spanish was at the bottom, which is not surprising, considering how many shared root words we have. So from one unknown crossroad and one known I was linked to Korea.

It was a marriage made by the army but it has lasted for thirty-five years and seems destined to endure until I die. Even when I tried to change courses a couple of times later in my career, I kept getting pushed back to Korea. After a time I came to accept the fact that there was a reason for all of this and just because I wasn't bright enough to figure out just what that reason was did not make it less valid. Some might call it divine intervention, others fate; some of my friends over the Pacific might call it my Tao. Whatever it is with me and Korea simply is. Now I just grin and accept the fact that we seem stuck with one another.

## Monterey by the Sea

There are probably places as scenically beautiful as Monterey, California, but none can surpass it. In the nineteenth century the primary threat to coastal cities came from the sea. American military planners selected the spots that gave them the greatest fields of fire—meaning higher elevations to extend range and fire down upon an enemy ship with unrestricted line of sight. In the twentieth century that translates into the most desirable-view real estate in the area. Thus the fortifications—the presidios—of San Francisco, Monterey, and Los Angeles were all some of the most coveted property in the area. Developers continue to salivate over the site of the Defense Language Institute overlooking the famous Cannery Row and Monterey on one side and Pacific Grove on the other. Just over the mountain lie Carmel, Big Sur, and eventually San Luis Obispo. Up the road a bit are Half Moon Bay, San Francisco, and the Redwood country.

In 1969 Cannery Row was more Steinbeck than yuppie. The abandoned piers and decaying warehouses and factories lent a rustic air to the place and provided opportune diving spots. I spent most afternoons after class in a wet suit in the bay. In class we learned more than simply the intricacies of the Korean language—as challenging as those were. Along with the hangul (the Korean alphabet) came the culture, traditions, and a bit of the history of Korea. Most of my instructors were long-time expats who had come to the United States with little more than the clothing they wore. They fled the grinding poverty of postwar Korea for better opportunity in America. What they brought with them was far more than the ability to teach the Korean language. While that was surely challenge enough, they took on an even greater task with me: they tried to teach me what the heart and soul of Korea itself is.

Where did these Koreans come from? Korean people like to brag about five thousand years of history, a figure that boggles American minds. Anthropologists speculate that the original settlers on the peninsula were nomadic tribes who had migrated there from the Lake Baikal region of Central Asia. In prehistoric times, these groups of hunters moved restlessly around the globe even crossing the Bering Strait into North and South America. It can be uncanny at times to travel in the New World and run into people who you would swear from physical characteristics alone are Korean, Chinese, or Japanese until you speak with them and learn that are they are locals.

When these ancient nomadic people arrived from Central Asia into present-day Korea they probably rode horses. "Look at traditional Korean clothing," my instructor Mr. Park said. "See the gathering of baggy trousers at the ankle. That indicates a horse culture." No longer. Horse culture faded away over the years through disuse. "Korean people are practical," Park said, "and un-like Mongols or American Plains Indians who had to cover vast distances of relatively flat, open terrain in order to make a living, the close, hilly confines of the Korean peninsula encouraged a more settled, stable culture. And so it became. But we still keep the reminders."

One of the defining points of Korea is the homogeneous ethnicity of its people. In this way Koreans are very similar to the Japanese and Han Chinese who also have a tradition of a very close ethnic homogeneity. This contrasts sharply with southern China and Southeast Asia, for example, which are crazy quilts of ethnicities, languages, and peoples who have come together to make a very mixed population grouping. Within Korea there is a sharp, well-defined sense of what being a Korean means. I was to see many examples of that trait.

But that is not the way it started. Korea as we know it underwent many transitions. One of the important steps was in a period about a thousand years ago when the peninsula was divided into the Three Kingdoms. Imagine a Korean peninsula in which the territory that roughly approximates present-day North Korea into Manchuria was one kingdom, called Korguyo. What is now South Korea would be divided roughly in half by a north-south line. These were the other two kingdoms: Paekjae in the west and Shilla in the east. International alliances and rivalries typically checkerboard themselves (for example, my direct neighbor and I may quarrel, so my natural alliance is with his direct neighbor). Therefore Paekjae, the kingdom in the west, leaned toward Japan. Its rival to the east, Shilla, tilted toward China. Eventually Shilla conquered the others and unified the peninsula by force. The legacy of this ancient conflict lingers to this day and colors much of the politics and provincial rivalry in contemporary South Korea. But from the time that Shilla triumphed to modern times, Korea has looked toward China for friendship, guidance, and leadership.

There were other reasons for a strong tilt towards China. For one thing, Japan in those days posed the more fearsome threat. It was a disorganized feudal island state. Possessing few natural resources of its own, it looked outward for wealth. It became a nation composed of aggressive seafarers who had little compunction about attacking Korean and coastal Chinese settlements where they indulged in a raider's usual trinity: rape, pillage, and plunder.

There is growing evidence that advanced civilization and culture moved from China through Korea and into Japan. As you might suspect this is not a theory that strikes a popular chord with some Japanese traditionalists. One of my language instructors, Justin Kim, was able to demonstrate how the commonly used Chinese characters of the time passed through Korea and were then modified in Japan to be the hiragana writing that is used in Japan along with the kanji or more traditional characters. It is important to note that trade, communications, and travel were common throughout the region.

By the late fourteenth century, a period began in Korea that saw it literally freeze in time, earning it the apt description of "Hermit Kingdom." Philosophically the Koreans became even more of a perfect Confucian state than had ever existed in China. And they remained that way under the leadership of the Yi (Lee) Dynasty from that time forward. Korea lasted as a unique, uninterrupted dynasty for nearly five hundred years until the bottom fell out from China at the end of the nineteenth century. It is an amazing historical record. Confucius taught Koreans the value of position and relationships. He stressed that humans are bound by duty and family and that education is a worthy goal in and of itself. Confucius taught that one looks to the past for solutions to present-day problems and that interpretation of laws and rules depends on the situation at the time. The Korean people grasped these teachings and embraced them with an awesome enthusiasm and commitment. For five centuries, the Master's teachings permeated Korean culture, reaching every corner.

Because of this extraordinarily long period of relative peace, stability, and harmony, many living Koreans idealize this time, if not in reality then certainly in myth. All cultures have their myths and Korea is no exception. The period of the Yi Dynasty provides a huge historical comfort zone for many Koreans. Today South Koreans—while they are extremely friendly and pleasant—still have a suspicion about foreigners that dates to those days of the past when anything foreign probably did not bring good news. They—like the ancient Chinese Middle Kingdom from whom they borrowed the concept—look on an independent, self-reliant, sealed-off nation as an essentially good state and a desirable outcome. New ideas, new cultural influences, and new trends tend to disturb even as they are grabbed and absorbed.

South Koreans wring their hands in frustration and sadness occasionally about the "cultural pollution" that enters their country, particularly from the United States and its ubiquitous entertainment, fast food, and consumer goods industries. They fear the alacrity with which their citizens gravitate toward these goods and ideas. Some look at North Korea, standing in isolation and apparent self-reliance, or so that myth goes, with a bit of envy and nostalgia as representing the ancient, desirable Hermit Kingdom tradition. Mr. Park, like many expatriates, tended to be even more nostalgic for these days of old than most. His dreams of peaceful ancient times became more understandable to me as he slowly, almost painfully, related his own bitter experiences.

Mr. Park told me one day, after class, privately, about being drafted into the Imperial Japanese Army during what they called the Great Pacific War. His eyes grew narrowed and misty and his voice, usually very soft, fell to a whisper. "Life for us was a horror story. Discipline for ordinary Japanese recruits was brutal. For Korean men it was worse." Physical punishment was one action that was delegated down to the lowest noncommissioned officer level. Even corporals were authorized—actually expected—to levy frequent, heavy doses of physical punishment. One of the favorite methods was beating the buttocks with a paddle, bat, or stick. The unfortunate recipient was made to assume a bent-over position, often baring his butt, and was made to stand quietly while being struck. Severe bruising was normal; bleeding and blood clots were common. In many cases, recruits and enlisted men suffered permanent damage (for the beatings continued in their regular units). And that was for native Japanese. "Imagine," Mr. Park said, "the reaction of Japanese NCOs to recruits who were not 'real' people but were *eta* from Okinawa, Taiwan, or worse yet, from Korea. These men were frequently beaten to death by NCOs and officers who were consumed by fits of rage exacerbated by alcohol, boredom, or psychosis."

Mr. Park, told me how embarrassed he was that even after almost twenty years at the Defense Language Institute he could not bring himself to return the daily greetings of the Japanese instructors. This presented a constant problem because the Japanese language department was on the second floor of a long building and the Korean language department was on the third floor. So several times daily my teacher had to pass through the Japanese language area. He inevitably came in contact with his Japanese colleagues. "In the entire time that I was forced by the Japanese to be a soldier in their army, I cannot remember a day—not a single day—in which I was not beaten by my Japanese sergeant or corporal, often to the point of fainting and unconsciousness. On more than one occasion my fellow soldiers had to carry me to the dispensary where, if the medical orderly was sober or in a good mood, he might give them some ointment to spread on my wounds. Otherwise he would throw all of us out and leave us to our own devices."

"Why were you beaten like that?" I asked, horrified. "What could you have done to merit that kind of retaliation?"

"I was a Korean," he said with a shrug. "And some of the worst NCOs were themselves Koreans who had been appointed by the Japanese. They seemed to have to prove that they were even harder on us than the Japanese were. I was posted with my unit in northern China, fighting against Mao Zedong and the Chinese Eighth Route Army. We owned only the meter square of ground on which we stood. Everything else belonged to the guerrillas. They didn't care if we were Korean or not. As far as they were concerned, we were the enemy. If captured they did not take prisoners. Everyone they captured was killed, often after extensive torture.

Our units were spread like a long chain across the landscape in a series of small outposts. Each was too far away to support the others directly but we would be called upon to assist in time of crisis.

"I remember one time we were told late in the afternoon to get our combat equipment and fall in. We were ordered to reinforce an outpost that was under attack by the Chinese. In the Japanese army when you moved out on one of these operations, it was at a shuffling trot. Not running exactly but faster than walking. We kept going hour after hour. Long after the sun sank we continued to jog along that dusty track. After what must have been six or eight hours, we were given permission to rest for a few minutes.

"That was the first opportunity we had to drink since we departed. We had only a single canteen per man. And no food. We continued to run all that night and all the next day. Men fell out, exhausted by the roadside. We could not assist them. We did not even turn around for we knew that they would be killed by the guerrillas as soon as we were out of sight. Sometime in the evening of the second day, we arrived at our objective. It had been overrun by the Chinese guerrillas and all of our soldiers had been killed. Most of the bodies were horribly mutilated. We were ordered immediately to gather the bodies for burning. Throughout the night we burned the bodies, collected the ashes, and placed them in containers.

"We turned the ashes in to our officers. The ashes would be labeled and sent by mail to the families of the dead. Or they would simply be tossed into the garbage pit. It depended on the mood of the senior officer. After all night working to gather wood, keep guard, and dispose of the bodies we were ordered back on the road and jogged back to our base camp. They treated me like this for eight years in their army until 1945 when Korea was liberated. I am ashamed but I still am not able to bring myself to speak to a Japanese person to this day."

For the first time, after repeated conversations with Mr. Park about his experiences, I began to fathom the depth of antipathy that exists between the Korean people and Japan. Americans are quick to forgive and quicker to forget. But the Koreans clearly had much to remember. Another of my instructors, a Mrs. Choi, often discussed some of the unique cultural and historical characteristics of Korea. One afternoon I stayed behind and asked her about Mr. Park's story. "Is it possible that his experience—horrific as it was—was something different and unique to him?" I asked.

She shook her head firmly. "Mr. Park suffered much. I know his story. But I also know of hundreds, perhaps thousands of people with stories as terrible or worse. When the Japanese stole from us they did not only steal our men for their armies, they stole more. They took from us the very soul of Korea, our women." For factory work that required smaller hands and more patience—including putting together sensitive military equipment—Korean women were first recruited and eventually impressed into the labor pool. The same bait that attracted the men initially lured these women: good-paying jobs, safe working conditions, and clean quarters. What waited for them in the huge, sprawling industrial areas of western Japan bore little resemblance to the recruiting posters. Slave labor conditions similar to that of the Korean men was the norm—except women had to endure the added stress of physical and sexual abuse by overseers. In other cases women were deported into the cold northern island regions to process tons of fish and other sea creatures that were brought in by fishermen, themselves enslaved by the Japanese. Conditions were common of semi-starvation and terrible physical danger with little or no medical backup or thought toward health and safety. To a lesser extent than the battlefield but with every bit as heartless a nature, the factory system of Japanese slave labor accounted for the deaths and wrecked lives of hundreds of thousands of Koreans.

## The Horror of the Comfort Women

One of the most brutal actions against Korea in that terrible colonial period was not spoken of openly by my language teachers. The enormity of the issue overwhelmed them. It was not until I was engaged in discussions with a scholar at a nearby institute that I learned of the ultimate horror. "Of all the crimes against humanity perpetrated by the Imperial Japanese Army and government" he said, "one of the most heartless and cruel was the policy by the Japanese government to kidnap young women from occupied countries and force them into prostitution to service Japanese troops." Among the many euphemisms for these women was the term "comfort women" that today seems especially repugnant. They were also referred to as the "body donating corps" in order to perpetuate the fiction that they were somehow patriotic volunteers whose sole purpose in life was to support the morale of the Japanese troops in the field. Of course, had that been the truth, there would have been no rationale for the abysmal way in which they were treated, again by official policy. They were kept in brothels close to troop units at a ratio of approximately one woman for every fifty soldiers assigned. They were available for the convenience of the troops who were instructed by their officers and noncoms to treat them as brutally and impersonally as possible and under no circumstances to form a friendly or loving relationship with them. Women were often beaten, sometimes to the point of permanent maiming or death, often on a whim by a soldier or a group of soldiers. Sexual and physical torture was reported and the women were denied basic needs such as cleanliness, medical treatment, and decent food or living conditions.

What made the practice even more heinous was that the Japanese intentionally sought young women, girls really, in the twelve-to-sixteen-year-old range to be comfort women. They targeted this age group because they knew in the strict, somewhat puritanical Korean society girls this age were more than likely to be virgins and therefore not infected with venereal disease. In the days before modern medical care and antibiotics disease was more feared in many instances than combat injuries, and venereal disease could produce debilitating, occasionally fatal results. Consequently, the goal of the Japanese teams sent out to kidnap women was to capture them as young and as sound as possible. Although women were sent to the mobile prostitution units from virtually every country and land conquered by Japan, the largest number by far came from Korea. An exact count is impossible to obtain but reasonable, realistic estimates based on the number of Japanese troops deployed and on records recently discovered in Japanese files dating from the period indicate that upwards of two hundred thousand Korean women may have been kidnapped and sent out to be comfort women. Even one would be too many, but this is a mind-numbing number.

## Pitifully Few Survivors

Most of the comfort women did not survive the war. Far too many died of abuse and disease contracted from the troops. Some committed suicide when the opportunity presented itself, knowing full well that they would not be welcome back in their homes. There was no return for these women in their society; this was truly the end of the road. In most cases the retreating Japanese army simply executed them before abandoning a position. They rid themselves of the evidence so to speak.

Predictably but sadly those few women survivors returned to a world that rejected them. They were a living, visible symbol to Korean men that they were incapable of performing a man's most basic, essential task in his society: keeping his women safe. That they could not do this caused Korean men to be angry at the Japanese but also, irrationally, at the women themselves. As a result, the entire issue of the comfort women was tacitly ignored for the most part by Korean people who did not wish the shame to be brought up and by the Japanese who were, and remain, in deep denial. It was not until the few surviving women passed age sixty that they could no longer keep their torment bottled up inside and created a huge, justifiable, and long overdue fuss. They went public, got the media attention they needed and forced the issue to be addressed at a bilateral level. It is still a sensitive issue between Korea and Japan and in the Philippines, Taiwan, Indonesia, and other countries as well from which women were stolen. Truly, these women were sacrificed into the insatiable maw of the Japanese war machine that consumed millions before it was killed itself. The tragedy that most died anonymously, alone, sick, and hurt is a wrenching memory and one that ought to be kept in mind, especially in Japanese minds, so that it will not happen again.

### Korea Given up by Treaty

These conversations spurred me on to learn more. Clearly there was a lot about Korea than I was learning simply from the language. I began to dig around on my own, including frequent conversations with my friend at the institute. A picture of Korea emerged that depicted a remarkable story virtually unknown in the United States but in which, ironically, we were a key player. At the turn of the nineteenth to twentieth century Northeast Asia was a tumultuous place. No one realized how strong Japan had become in the previous thirty years as it moved from samurai swords to modern weaponry until it attacked Russia and fought a brutal two-year war beginning in 1904. Ultimately the combatants sought a mediator and the United States volunteered. A peace treaty between Japan and Russia was negotiated by President Theodore Roosevelt at Portsmouth, New Hampshire, in 1905. It was a singular accomplishment in international diplomacy for which the young president was awarded the Nobel Peace Prize. It is a treaty and an event of which most Americans are ignorant. Conversely, every Korean schoolchild is taught about the Treaty of Portsmouth because it is considered the first of several cases of American meddling in Korean affairs that resulted in unfortunate things happening to Korea. In this instance Korea was awarded to Japan as a protectorate. In the language of the time this convention was used in order for an "advanced" country to supervise a "backward" one, ostensibly for the backward country's "own good." In practical terms it usually resulted in unwanted suzerainty by one country over another and was abused more than it was honored. The case of Korea would prove no exception.

Why would Teddy Roosevelt, with his reputation of being fair-minded, agree to this? Partially because of the reputation that Yi Dynasty rulers had made internationally for Korea. By their own choice the Yi rulers had erected an anti-foreign, closed atmosphere that repelled outsiders and gave the world the impression—correct or not—that Korea *was* a backward, ignorant country, little more than a province of China, incapable of governing itself or, for that matter, of handling its own affairs without causing harm. The Yi Dynasty had rejected several opportunities for reform. In order to keep the entrenched aristocracy in power the Yi rulers had refused to back away from its deep-seated, stubborn insistence on maintaining a pure Confucian government. These acts cemented the impression that the Yi Dynasty and its aristocrats were corrupt and inept. The international community looked at Korea the way a parent would look at a two-year-old playing with the cutlery. Right or wrong, no one took the time or effort to dig deeper. But some of the responsibility for the way Korea was handed off to "adult supervision" at the Treaty of Portsmouth must devolve on the inability of Yi Dynasty rulers to see beyond their limited horizons. Trying to lock up their country and keep foreign influence at bay forever only served to weaken their defenses and made the inevitable foreign intrusion that much more painful.

## Establishing Control and Annexation

Japanese authorities wasted no time in establishing a presence in Korea. At last Japan was positioned in such a way as to be able to move with alacrity to snatch off all or part of China, for that was their unstated but ultimate goal. Korea would be their base to build up Manchuria, which would be the jumping off point for the invasion and conquest of China. All would be economic and political vassals of the Japanese emperor. The wheels began to turn.

By 1910 the Imperial Japanese government, sensing neutrality, indifference, or acquiescence from the international community in its treatment of Korea moved to annex Korea formally to Japan. Few voices were raised in protest and those under Japanese control were swiftly silenced. Henceforth, Korea would be considered part of Japan. Interestingly, maps from that period depict the two areas painted in the same color. It is a method cartographers use to indicate with a glance territorial commonality. From 1910 onward, the world community considered it all one country.

In Japan the military exerted increasing control over the Japanese government. Military officers pledged fealty to the person of the emperor, now Hirohito. They brought their armed troops into the streets to intimidate government officials, and assassination of members of the Diet or moderate politicians became common occurrences. It was a combination of the most extreme traits of the old *bushido* philosophy—the way of the warrior—linked to modern technology. The product was a scheme called the Greater East Asia Co-Prosperity Sphere in which raw materials and labor would be supplied to Japan, where manufacturing would occur, and the products used or exported. Great quantities of resources would be needed to build the kind of industrial might and military machine necessary for the Japanese to excel. And by that definition that meant conquering all of Asia as well as any other power foolish enough to oppose them.

Japanese administrators, engineers, businessmen, educators, and specialists followed closely on the heels of the invading army and secret police. As part of the annexation process there was a conscious policy decision at the highest levels—Emperor Hirohito himself—that all vestiges of Korean culture were to be systematically eradicated. The Korean people were to be converted into second-class Japanese and used as the Japanese colonialists wished to further the glory of the imperial cause. Oh, and the Koreans were to be appreciative of the leadership and guidance brought to them by the Japanese and were to keep their ungrateful mouths shut if they didn't like it. Any aspirations the Korean people might have had toward self-rule were ignored or, if they surfaced, crushed.

The process of eradication of everything Korean began, as these things tend to do, on the surface levels and then penetrated more deeply. The theory was that you first erase those things over which you have easy access. These included visible markers such as road signs, place names, communications media, shop, and advertising signage, maps, and other outward symbols of things

Korean. An early edict forbad the use of the proud, ancient Korean language itself. It became a crime to speak, write, or otherwise use it. From the outset, the Japanese renamed the country, replacing its traditional name with "Chosen." People were then told to forget their own names, the Korean names that had been given to them and kept for centuries in family books passed from generation to generation. They were to discard them and substitute Japanese names. Generations of Koreans were to be raised without being able to use their own language publicly or to call themselves by their proper names. It was the ultimate insult, striking at the core of hundreds of years of venerated tradition. As author Richard Kim recounts in his fictionalized memoir of the period, *Lost Names: Scenes from a Korean Boyhood,* "lost names" became a fitting metaphor for the brutal, mindless Japanese colonial period.

I am frequently asked why Koreans dislike the Japanese. But the wonder is not that animosity exists between the two peoples; the wonder is that they are able to somehow overcome it and work together. Yet, the specter of the past can continue to haunt the present and future. In today's world these old acrimonious feelings and attitudes are buried, but not deeply. They reside just below the surface and are simply one more element that must be factored into any ongoing analysis.

At the beginning of the twentieth century Korea had been wrenched from the false comfort of an ancient Yi Dynasty, where they lived in a fragile Confucian world of the past, into the status of a subjugated people under a brutal occupier. Because of the intensity and comprehensive nature of the Japanese occupation, it was virtually impossible for Koreans inside the country to put together an effective resistance. The two postwar leaders who emerged in North and South Korea respectively, Kim Il Sung and Syngman Rhee, were both expatriates for decades, one living with the Soviets, the other with Americans. Each was faced with the challenge of putting together a country and government from a people who had been repressed, abused, tortured, isolated, and brutalized by a tyrannical regime. And yet from these dismal conditions, well within living memory, one became an international role model while the other became an international basket case.

Interestingly enough, most of my instructors in language school openly acknowledged their Christian faith. Many had in fact been sponsored to come to the United States by churches or congregations. Christianity originally entered Korea in the mid- to late-nineteenth century and like foreigners themselves, was considered an unwelcome intrusion. Despite persecution and repression, including during the Japanese colonial period, Christianity in Korea persevered, until it became the fastest-growing Christian community in the world. I could see evidence for myself as can visitors to Seoul who are often impressed by the number of crosses they see at night glowing neon red from the tops of many, many buildings. As did those visitors, I too first presumed that these were dispensaries or possibly first-aid stations or even physician's offices. Wrong. They are churches and chapels. Perhaps with the promise of salvation, an afterlife, and a belief in something larger than the individual or the state, Christianity offers a ray of hope for people that typically have had none.

CHAPTER 5

# North Korea after the War

From the beginning of his rule, it was clear where Kim Il Sung's priorities lay. He was not particularly concerned with the economy or building agricultural or industrial infrastructure, but focused exclusively on raw military strength to attack and defeat South Korea. Despite rather transparent protests of defensive measures against a South Korean invasion, the entire North Korean People's Army was configured and postured for an attack, not a defense. The North Korean military absorbed all things Soviet. Its uniforms were the high-collared, broad-shouldered, belted tunics that would have been completely at home in Moscow's Red Square. Doctrinally the Soviet strategy made as much sense on the Korean terrain as it did in Europe. The presence of South Korea's capital city, Seoul, only thirty-five miles from the Demilitarized Zone, was a significant geopolitical advantage to the North. Soviet quick-strike doctrine made capture of Seoul the perfect objective for the massive combined arms strategy of artillery-armor-infantry. It also meant that defenders—

including the American units that sat across the probable invasion route—would not be able to trade space for time in event of
a North Korean attack. One of the best defenses, if the circumstances permit, is for a defender to fall back slowly over a long distance, allowing the attacker to expend resources and making him
pay for every foot of ground captured. Then, when the attacker is
extended to the breaking point, the defender counterattacks and
rolls over him. This tactic worked for the Soviet army when Hitler
attacked them. With Seoul almost within hailing distance of North
Korea, however, this tactic would be infeasible. The U.S. and South
Korean defenders were therefore put into a hold-or-die scenario,
which is the most difficult in battle. Both sides were fully aware of
their respective advantages and disadvantages.

North Korea rapidly modernized its forces with the accumu-
lation of massive amounts of material assistance from the Soviets.
Meanwhile, the South Korean military also built up but at a
slower pace. As Kim Il Sung constructed and reinforced his absolutist dictatorship, he did so with the complicity of the army. The
North Korean People's Army was Kim's primary tool in solidifying
his hold on the people. In return they had all of the support that
he could provide them. The army had priority on all goods: equipment, food, fuel, medical support—virtually anything that it
needed. In return it pledged unswerving loyalty to the state and
more important to the person of Kim Il Sung, the Great Leader.
Meanwhile, Kim had plans to expand his role even further.

Before the ink had dried on the armistice agreement, in July
1953 both sides were probing each other with infiltrators, patrols,
and hostile acts. It was North Korea, however, that began to extend military actions far beyond the acceptable limits. Kim Jong
Il, son and anointed successor to Kim Il Sung, was raised in this
atmosphere of tyranny and hate. One of Kim Jong Il's duties when

he was being groomed to succeed his father was to oversee, plan, and execute terrorist operations. In those days Kim Jong Il was even more of the enigmatic figure than he is currently. He would stay out of the spotlight and avoid international press. Few photos of him existed, at least that were shown outside of the closed walls of Kim's palaces. He was referred to obliquely in North Korean government releases, usually by a vague title such as the "party center." This was well before his official anointing as the "Dear Leader." In those days he was still making his bones as an intelligence organization boss and international terrorist. He was rather successful at his job.

## Assassination Sights on President Park

Sometime in the late 1960s Kim Jong Il was involved in supervising North Korean terrorist operations. It was apparent that the South Korean president, Park Chung-hee, had already been selected as a high-priority target for assassination. While many observers, primarily from academia and the left, have long criticized President Park for human rights abuses, authoritarianism, and other unacceptable behavior, it is wise to recall that Park originally was very much the man of the people. After he came to power in the 1961 coup, he made a habit of public appearances, often unscheduled and spontaneous. Frequently Park would simply direct his driver to pull over and wait for him while he got out and mixed with the happy crowds. To a South Korean populace more accustomed to older, aloof, distant leaders it was a joyful sign. The casual mixing brought him in touch with ordinary citizens and was a source of inspiration to him and to them. But it also exposed him to attack by unscrupulous North Korean agents who were quick to take advantage of any opportunity.

## The Blue House Raid

The most infamous of the many assassination attempts on President Park by North Korean agents took place in 1968. A team of twenty specially selected and trained North Korean commandos infiltrated at night through the American sector of the DMZ. Their presence went undetected at first. They then stumbled upon a party of South Korean woodcutters and, in an odd act considering the import of their mission, wasted precious mission time lecturing them on the glories of North Korea and communism. The North Korean infiltrators left the woodcutters with a stern injunction for them not to tell anyone of their presence.[8] The commandos then raced southward, keeping to high ground when possible and remaining hidden. That night then U.S. Army Lieutenant Steve Ciardelli was duty officer in the Second Infantry Division tactical operations center (TOC). He received reports from the woodcutters but initially discounted their veracity. "We simply didn't think that many people could get through our lines undetected," he relates. "So we figured that the woodcutters were drunk and ignored the first reports." Ciardelli was a fairly new lieutenant, too junior and inexperienced in normal times to be pulling the job as division level duty officer, a task typically assigned to a seasoned field grade officer. He had not been around long enough to have confidence in his own judgment. When others in the TOC were dismissive of the initial reports Ciardelli was reluctant to call a senior officer fearing that if the

---

[8] One of the things that consistently upset plans for North Korean infiltrators or terrorists was their own propaganda. Once they saw what South Korea was really like, the flimsy North Korean propaganda house of cards toppled. They had been told that the South Koreans were brutally oppressed, destitute, starving and would welcome them as liberators. When the North Koreans discovered the truth, many felt cut loose from their moral base, which drove some of them to defect, commit suicide, or simply surrender.

incident turned out to be a false alarm—as most others present in the TOC assured him that it would—he did not want to be on the receiving end of an ass-chewing for unnecessarily waking up an officer and bothering him.

As additional reports began to reach the TOC the initial skepticism turned to slow, embarrassed realization that a major North Korean operation was underway. Late enough after the fact to draw criticism, the Americans reported the infiltration and alerted higher command. While angry retorts and recriminations flew through the air South Korean and American units tried to locate the North Korean infiltrators. There was something about the intensity, focus, and speed of the North Koreans that counterinfiltration units found unsettling. Usually infiltrators conducted clandestine sabotage or espionage missions against military targets. But this unit was moving steadily and unswervingly in the direction of Seoul. Only one target in the city could merit such near-suicidal behavior: President Park Chung-hee himself. The superb physical conditioning of the North Korean commandos disconcerted counterinfiltration forces. The infiltrators literally ran away from pursuers. Combat-ready units were thrown into position along the route to block the infiltrators only to discover that they had already passed. The blocking forces then set up in a position where it would not be humanly possible, they thought, for anyone to have passed that way, only to discover that they were again too late. Frustration fed panic as the entire available military, police, and paramilitary leadership began to question themselves: Will we be able to stop these guys?

The infiltrators ran rapidly southward directly toward Seoul. They tried to avoid contact with locals but as population density increased they were forced to pass through farm areas then villages then into the suburbs of Seoul. No longer able to use forest and hills for cover they were easier to spot and came under sporadic fire. Whenever they were spotted South Korean citizens alerted authorities who then tightened the noose. A running firefight erupted. Gunfire spilled into populated areas. One after another of the infiltrators fell as a few engaged their relentless pursuers to give covering fire while the main body escaped. More and more police and military units were alerted. Soon thousands of troops were looking for the infiltrators. And then another chilling question was raised: What if this is just a feint and the real team is covertly approaching the Blue House from *another* direction?

Inside Seoul, the Blue House, official residence of the president of Korea, sits behind the ancient Yi Palace of Kyongbok, tucked into an area with tall granite hills surrounding it on several sides. Fences, guards, and sensory devices protect it but security personnel began to fear penetration by the determined band of North Koreans. Presidential security forces, already in near panic, insisted that President Park leave. He was too much the old soldier. He adamantly refused to flee before assassins and stayed put, closely monitoring the situation.

As reports from the field were collected and processed, the number of infiltrators was estimated at twenty. The count of killed infiltrators grew—none surrendered and a few wounded took their own lives to avoid capture. Slowly, some feared too slowly, the cordon closed on the few remaining enemies. By now they had reached Seoul proper. Reduced to a handful, the North Korean infiltrators fought a bitter, no-quarter gun battle through the streets of Seoul. They knew the city from maps and briefings, and by this time no one doubted that their objective was indeed the Blue House. President Park still refused to evacuate despite repeated pleas from his advisors. The ring of South Korean security tightened around the Blue House. In desperation, the commandos hijacked a civilian bus, murdered the innocents on board, and roared toward the Blue House in a fusillade of gunfire. Less than a thousand yards from their objective, the last commando died in a hail of bullets reminiscent to Americans of the demise of criminals John Dillinger and Bonnie and Clyde.

### Assassination in the National Theater

Undeterred by failure, Kim Jong Il recruited Mun Se-kwan in Osaka, Japan, and trained the twenty-two-year old Mun in assassination techniques. The opportunity to employ Agent Mun came on Liberation Day, August 15, 1974, a Korean national holiday celebrating the end of World War II and freedom from Japanese oppression. President Park Chung-hee spoke at the National Theater, an old-fashioned building nestled into the side of Namsan Mountain in Seoul. It was the standard kind of speech a Korean leader could be expected to give on an occasion like this. Security was there—bodyguards present in the theater and guards outside—also normal for a presidential appearance.

As Park delivered his speech that stifling summer day, Mun exited a chauffeur-driven auto rented at a luxury hotel and entered the National Theater. He carried a concealed .38 caliber pistol—later proved stolen from a Japanese police station—which he had smuggled into South Korea in a radio. Mun was not stopped by security guards, a fact that shows that the security net around Park at the time was still not the hypersensitive barrier it would later become. As he entered, Mun pulled out the pistol and began firing as he ran toward the head of the theater and the podium.

Near President Park on the podium was his wife, Yook Young-soo (Korean women retain their family names after marriage), an extremely popular figure with the Korean people. She wore a bright orange traditional Korean costume and sat with hands folded in her lap, listening. As Mun neared the stage firing wildly, the first lady slumped forward, shot in the head. Mun was apprehended and carried from the theater. He would be interrogated, tried, and executed. After Mun was removed President Park resumed his speech, only departing the theater after he had completed it. This behavior, seemingly unconcerned or emotionless toward his injured spouse, shocked veteran reporter Don Oberdorfer, although as an old Korea hand he should have known why Park behaved as he did. Within the strict dictates of Confucian culture, it would be incomprehensible for him to leave incomplete a serious responsibility to his public. As one of Park's advisors later told Oberdorfer, "the president is a man of responsibility, who has got to finish what he has set out." When his responsibility to his people was complete, Park immediately rushed to the hospital to be with his mortally wounded wife.[9]

Meanwhile North Korea kept steady pressure on the South through many unconventional means. Patrols in the DMZ were often aggressive to the point of firefights and ambushes as South Korean and American army patrols would be engaged. While military patrolling in the DMZ was permissible under terms of the 1953 armistice agreement, it was forbidden to enter into the opposite side of the military demarcation line from one's own side. In other words, North Korean military patrols were prohibited from venturing south of the military demarcation line and vice versa for South Korean patrols. The North Koreans in those days were nevertheless coming down across the military demarcation line with disturbing regularity, probing American and South Korean defensive positions, setting up booby traps, and laying mines.

---

[9]  *The Two Koreas* (New York: Basic Books, 2002), 48.

Firefights between clashing patrols within the DMZ were becoming almost routine. Units that were dug into defensive positions outside of the DMZ had North Korean patrols bump into their positions and engage them. Examination of uniforms and documents found on a few of the enemy bodies indicated that they were attempting to work their way past UN units and into South Korea. It was clear that one of the tactics the North Koreans employed was to make contact intentionally, and then use the normal confusion associated with a firefight to cover the infiltration of agents or other soldiers southward. It was an effective strategy.

North Korea engaged in constant probes of the South Korean defenses by land and by sea. Special Marine commando units were formed. These troops—highly trained in espionage, sabotage, and hand-to-hand combat—would use a tool called a "skunk boat" by the American navy and their South Korean counterparts. Usually the North Koreans would try one of two general strategies to get past the South Korean defenders. Either they would disguise themselves as fishing boats or other innocent merchant craft or they would try to make up with stealth and speed what they gave up in suspicion.

Missions varied and the method of infiltration was often dictated by the task at hand. Sometimes the skunk boats simply wanted to sneak ashore, land an agent or party of agents, and sneak out again without detection. This was especially productive on long-range espionage missions when South Korean bases, support facilities, or operations were the target. Or the skunk boat might land a sleeper or penetration agent who would try to blend in with the South Korean populace. These agents were dispatched to many kinds of missions, including setting up spy networks; infiltration of labor, student, or political opposition organizations; or simple observation and reporting. Because of the large number of displaced refugees who originated in North Korea it was possible with cleverly forged documentation for these agents to blend into the population, find employment, and lead outwardly normal lives.

No one knows how many of these agents may still be active in South Korea. Some could have discovered what life is like in South Korea compared to the repressive state they left behind in North Korea. They could have tried to sever ties with their past and assimilate into the larger society. Some could have gone to the authorities in South Korea, explained who they were and what their backgrounds were. At first glance this might seem risky but defectors are usually received well in South Korea. It might be more dangerous to try to hide. Finally, we can be certain that some are waiting patiently, working anonymously and quietly, for the word of activation from North Korea. That word might be to transmit information or to commit assassination or sabotage. No one knows who they are or how many are out there. The very presence of North Korean agents—even a strong likelihood of their activity—encourages an attitude of suspicion within South Korea that plays into Kim Jong Il's hands.

### "Tunnelin' Little Bastards"

North Korea, devoted to frantic engineering efforts for military gain, began tunneling beneath the DMZ, probably in the late 1960s. For years troops on the South Korean side of the DMZ regularly heard muted explosions and odd sounds. The occasional aerial photo might disclose the existence of large amounts of excavated rock in places. A follow-up photo would show it cleared away. But in 1973, Korean troops noticed steam rising from a field behind their defensive positions. On investigation they discovered what looked like a collapsed section of earth. When they poked into the opening they were received with gunfire. What became known as North Korean Infiltration Tunnel Number One had been discovered. Over the next several years, three additional tunnels were intercepted and cleared. As many as twenty others have been identified by seismic detective work. These latter have not yet been intercepted by South Korean forces.

In order to picture one of these tunnels properly clear your head of scenes of Wild West mineshafts or claustrophobically narrow laneways such as those in *The Great Escape* film. Imagine instead standing in a roomy basement—about 250 to 300 feet beneath the ground—in the middle of a solid granite room with a flat floor and a rounded archway ceiling. The tunnel is easily wide enough for several people to stand abreast and for a small truck towing an artillery piece to transit. South Korean and U.S. analysts estimated that several hundred men an hour could have passed through the tunnel, emerging battle-ready on the southern end. They also estimate that the tunnels ran for at least five kilometers—the North Koreans did not permit the investigating teams to measure the portion on their side of the DMZ, so the northern portion is a guess. Even if they came up a few score meters on the north side of the DMZ, ran under it for another four kilometers, and then almost a kilometer behind the South Korean lines, you have a long, long tunnel.

In those days I tended to be sophomorically cynical and a bit of a wiseass, so I challenged one of the Tunnel Neutralization Team engineer officers. "If you know there are twenty or more of these damn things," I asked, "why haven't you busted them open yet?" It was common knowledge at the time that the teams were conducting extensive drilling, sending down drill pipes to intersect with the North Korean tunnel. They then would flood the tunnel with water and dig what was called an "intercept tunnel" down to meet the enemy tunnel. This intercept tunnel was usually not very long because the North Koreans had learned from earlier efforts and stopped short of the surface. Their plan apparently was to complete the tunnels just before an attack. So why, I wondered, haven't you opened all the rest?

"Stand on your desk with a spool of thread," the Tunnel Neutralization Team officer said patiently. "Have a friend hold a needle an inch or so above the floor. Now, thread the needle. That's easier than sinking a drill hole to hit a three-to-five-meter-wide tunnel more than 250 feet beneath the surface. Remember, Gordon, these are some tunnelin' little bastards." I decided to stop harassing the TNT guys.

It is quite an experience to visit one of these North Korean tunnels. I've been in three of the four cracked open so far. The opening for the intercept tunnel is frighteningly far back from the edge of the DMZ. It gives you pause to wonder what the military effect of these guys pouring from these tunnels with machine guns blazing would be. Not a comforting thought. The intercept tunnel is usually angled down at a fairly steep grade. Visitors are advised to wear sensible shoes, boots preferably. The cave or mine effect—high humidity, constant cool temperatures—hits almost immediately. You know right away when you hit the North Korean tunnel. It is wider and higher than the intercept tunnel and more finished. In other words, the intercept tunnel is a matter of haste and expediency. The North Korean tunnel was constructed for the purpose of allowing smooth passage of moving troops and equipment. It is usually flatter, wider, and has a much gentler upward grade than the intercept tunnel. The South Korean end of the North Korean infiltration tunnels was designed to reach only so close to the surface. The North Koreans did not want to reveal the location of the tunnel the way they accidentally did in tunnel number one. Just prior to initiating hostilities the remaining distance would be cleared by engineering specialists. The infantry and light armor would then follow in an all-out attack. It all makes sense when the guide—himself an engineer officer—explains it to you.

Inside the tunnel the officer points out how the drilling and blast marks made by the North Koreans run north to south—for like all solid stone tunnels this one was constructed by the "drill, blast, and muck" method. You can clearly see the difference, especially if contrasted to the intercept tunnel. This is important because with typical North Korean deceit and bombast, the North Korean representatives to the Armistice Commission at Panmunjom first denied the existence of the tunnels when confronted with evidence of their discovery, and then tried to blame the South Korean and U.S. military for constructing them. It was all a propaganda effort, the North Koreans maintained, by the imperialist aggressors and their running dogs to make them look bad in the eyes of the world. So for nonexperts, being able to see how the shaft could only have been drilled from one direction—north to south—is an important point in understanding the key elements of the situation, and avoiding falling into North Korea's propaganda trap. One day these tunnels will be anachronistic reminders of a tense past. But today they remain hidden threats, lurking deep beneath hundreds of feet of Korean granite.

## Diplomatic Battles

In his single-minded quest to reunite the peninsula by force under his dictatorship, Kim Il Sung used every tactic imaginable to undermine the South. On the diplomatic front both governments engaged in a frantic "recognition battle" in which they attempted to establish legitimacy by having the greater number of

foreign governments acknowledge them as the true government
of Korea. Occasionally they would hit a tie, when a neutralist nation would recognize both, but on balance it reflected the Cold
War. Communist-leaning states recognized North Korea; democ-
racies recognized South Korea.

From time to time this would flip. At one point Australia had
a Labor government for six months and established an embassy in
Pyongyang. The experience of living in a totalitarian state trau-
matized many of the relaxed Australians. One of their diplomats,
Adrian Buzo, left the Australian foreign ministry afterwards and
moved to Seoul. While there he was a frequent invited speaker at
events organized by groups such as the Royal Asiatic Society, a
multi-national cultural organization. Even months after his post-
ing in North Korea, Buzo spoke with emotion about the intensity
of living in Pyongyang. There was, he affirmed, never a moment
when a foreigner, even a diplomat, was not under the most direct
scrutiny. In many cases the Kim Il Sung regime did not even
bother to disguise or soften the surveillance. He and his colleagues
were openly shadowed by North Korean agents, had rooms in the
embassy and in their apartments routinely and clumsily searched,
and were bugged by electronic eavesdropping equipment. He was
clearly rattled by such behavior and acknowledged that the stress
caused by the constant, cumulative scrutiny often reached unbearable levels. One can only imagine the effect on ordinary citizens for whom this life was their only option.

Buzo was struck by the totality of the cult of Kim Il Sung and
the pervasiveness of his communist philosophy. "There is nothing
pure Korean left up there," he said. "The communists have wiped
it all away." While one might make the case that five thousand
years of culture and history are tough to erase by any regime regardless of how totalitarian it may be, the fact that a keen, edu-

cated observer such as Buzo came away with that impression is significant. Certainly, on the surface traditional Korean society had been transformed by Kim's Stalinist-like personality cult. Only removal of the monster himself will one day show how deep the poison penetrated. It is unlikely, however, that Korean culture will be dramatically altered by relatively new ideologies such as communism or capitalism. These ideologies are still but a thin recent overlay on its solid ancient foundation.

## Training

Agent training inside North Korea is accomplished with the thorough approach that Koreans typically bring to any project. Fully in keeping with the Confucian method, agents are trained to anticipate certain things happening and are drilled repetitively on the processes and actions that they can expect to encounter in dealings with South Korea, Japan, China, or other countries that they may try to penetrate. The pair of agents who blew up a KAL flight crossing the Andaman Ocean in 1987 had been schooled on international travel and were well briefed on Eastern Europe and Middle Eastern countries. They were able to blend with the normal hodgepodge of international travelers without undue suspicion until the very end.

## Sleepers and Fishermen

For some agents, especially those whose mission called for them to remain in place for lengthy periods—perhaps for years—it made no sense for them to physically come and go. Not only would such a method be extraordinarily risky but few people would have an appropriate civilian cover that permitted them to be here then gone. One professional group, however, that does exactly that are commercial fishermen. Sailing in everything from leaky, small wooden boats to oceangoing metal ships, the fishermen of Korea have been renowned for years for the quantity and quality of their product as they ply the waters of the Yellow Sea and the Eastern Sea (Sea of Japan). Fishermen follow the currents and the vagaries of the ocean seeking their quarry. They are gone for long periods of time, away from oversight or control. As a consequence fishermen have been viewed with suspicion by the counterespionage services of both North Korea and South Korea. Systems have been put in place to monitor the fishermen and control their movements but such controls are difficult to enforce—in fact many of the defectors or refugees from North Korea are fishermen. One way of enforcing a type of control is by holding families, friends, and even entire villages hostage to their return. North Korea does this regularly. One must accept the fact that in fleeing for refuge in South Korea, fishermen from North Korea are risking more than their own lives. But few other professions or occupations give an agent the kind of freedom of movement that a fisherman enjoys.

## Positioned for an Offensive Operation

Over the years the North Koreans brought up all of their attack units and stationed them literally at the northern edge of the Demilitarized Zone. With a huge forced-labor supply, the North Koreans then dug artillery positions, fuel and ammo storage, even aircraft shelters right into live granite mountains. This further disguised any movement or improvements because it was all out of sight from American overhead cameras, and we have precious few human intelligence sources in North Korea. The North Koreans, having reduced attack warning time from weeks to days and now to hours placed the U.S. and South Korean commanders in a very tense position. In order to be combat ready, units had to be kept at a higher level of preparedness than might be necessary with a more conventional setup. But in Korea the advantage went to the North. The South was pledged not to strike first, and the location of the battle line was perfectly well defined. The issues have not gone away and still preoccupy American and South Korean military planners.

# CHAPTER 6

# South Korea after the War

After the Korean War the United States worked closely with each branch of the South Korean military to help them with modern equipment and training. In effect, America assumed the familiar Confucian role of elder brother to South Korea's younger brother. It was a role the Koreans fully understood and appreciated, perhaps more than the Americans realized. Relationships developed between officers that grew to genuine brotherhoods that spanned the years. I have sat with Korean officers in their seventies who spoke fondly of their American advisors from this period. Many still kept in touch and knew each other's families. Almost all of the assistance was funneled through a unit that went through several organizational modifications and name changes: the Joint U.S. Military Advisory and Assistance Group-Korea. During the time of the Cold War, developing countries around the world that were threatened by communist forces either directly or through insurgencies usually had an American military presence. At the time—living right under the North Korean guns—South

Korea had one of the largest assistance units, with more than 2,500 officers and men assigned. Its headquarters was in Seoul, near the headquarters of the UN commander and the Eighth Army commander (two hats for the same U.S. four-star general) at the Dragon Mountain, or Yongsan Compound.

In order to expedite and make assistance programs easier, Korean organizations and their equipment inventory were typically modeled after those of the U.S. Army. This came with many advantages for both sides. Use of standard weapons and support equipment augmented what the military likes to call "rationalization, standardization, and interoperability." Despite the convoluted terminology, it really is a significant simplification of a complex process. What it means in plain language is that if we all use the same equipment we can borrow from each other's supply bases in emergencies. And troops will know how to maintain, use, and fight with the equipment. It means our radios and theirs talk to each other. Ammunition for one fits in weapons that the others use, and so on. General Dwight D. Eisenhower proved in Europe that logistics win modern wars. Anything that can be done to expedite and simplify an incredibly complex logistics system contributes directly to war-fighting capabilities. These sorts of benefits are critical, as I was soon to learn firsthand when I came to Korea in a somewhat unconventional way—by parachute.

### Standing in the Door

The final command a parachutist hears before jumping is "stand in the door!" The jumpmaster then positions the lead parachutist in the open door, where ninety-mile-per-hour winds whip his clothing and gear as the aircraft bounces and turns in the thick, relatively low-altitude air. Since most Special Forces jumps are at night, the jumper looks out into darkness from the eerie interior of the aircraft in which red blackout lights are the only illumination permitted. They say the red light preserves a paratrooper's night vision.

In the fall of 1970 my Special Forces Detachment A was participating in Foal Eagle, an annual unconventional warfare exercise held with the Korean Black Berets. We were crammed into a C-130, four-engine turboprop aircraft headed for a drop zone in the sticks of North Kyongsang province. Our DZ was to be rice paddies north of the village of Sangju. Prior to takeoff we had sat on the tarmac at Osan Air Base, all dressed up with combat equipment and the extra weight of a main and a reserve parachute, hours ahead of schedule, as the army is so fond of having you do. We were jumping with a Captain Kim and a Sergeant Kwan, both Korean Special Forces. They were officer and noncommissioned officer, respectively, in charge of the national martial arts demonstration team that performed Korean taekwondo for VIP visitors. Captain Kim told me he had given demonstrations to President Lyndon Johnson in Seoul and to the Shah of Iran in Teheran.

I was one of the two jumpmasters on our aircraft. My team sergeant, MSG Richard Herald was the other. Sergeant Kwan approached the two of us, so weighted down he could hardly move. As well as his airborne equipment, he carried his gear—the team gear that we had distributed throughout the stick—and Captain Kim's gear (which his boss had dumped on him). Kwan was a great taekwondo master but was scared to death of jumping. The Koreans did not often jump at night and the pending night operation exacerbated his fear. He'd already had several pulls off his canteen, which was filled with milk-colored *makkoli,* a rice-based alcohol drink favored by Koreans. Between his broken English and my broken Korean I determined that he was worried that all the cumbersome equipment he carried would make him too physically weak in the aircraft to jump out of it. "Would we be kind enough to push him out?" he asked. He might lose face if the rest of us thought that he was refusing to jump. How could we decline? So as we approached the DZ I looked up at the lead man in the stick, Sergeant Kwan, and gave the order: "Stand in the door!"

Holding on to Kwan's equipment so that he would not exit early I knelt in the door and leaned far out to see the DZ. We were flying over Sangju village, which glowed briefly beneath us. Beyond I could easily see the inverted "L" made by a series of high-beam flashlights that marked our preferred exit point. Keeping the markings in sight I rose and gave a thumbs-up sign to Sergeant Herald who replied in kind from the other door. In a flash, the red lights in the aircraft switched to green as the pilot crossed the L. In one motion Herald grabbed one side of Kwan and I the other and we heaved him into the black maw. In seconds the door was filled as the rest of the A team followed him one after another. With a last glance across to Herald to confirm all out okay, he and I stepped into our respective exit doors and out into the cold, black night. Welcome to Korea!

It was the darkest night jump I ever made. The skies blazed stars but no moon. Every light was extinguished on the DZ. We later learned that the officer who set up the lights did not see us exit the aircraft and thought we hadn't jumped; it was that black. My first indication of ground coming up was when my rucksack, dangling on a line fifteen feet beneath me, hit the muddy paddy. Before I could cuss I landed hard and rolled. Had I gone just a few feet beyond I would have landed in a newly fertilized, flooded section.

As part of our exercise we walked from our DZ into Sangju, and then on to Kimchon and Taegu, sometimes bumming rides on police trucks. South Korea was largely dark at night then except for a few key areas that had electricity. Oil-lamp lighting and charcoal burning for cooking or heating was the norm. At no time did we encounter a village with potable water or anything other than latrine-type waste disposal facilities. Human waste was tossed into the rice fields or a vegetable patch near the house. Hillsides were largely denuded of trees, although we saw a few freshly planted pines in some areas, evidence of a government reforestation program. People were tough, cheerful, and hard working, greeting us everywhere with smiles and the occasional murmur of "Green Beret," from those who had seen the John Wayne film. When we arrived at Taegu, South Korea's third-largest city, we hit our first paved road. Poverty, dirt, and disease were my first impressions of Korea.

We were acutely aware of the danger from North Korean infiltrators and agents. Some of the Special Forces who were based in Korea had been involved in a harsh firefight with 120 North Korean infiltrators the year prior. It had been a long-running gun battle with a number of South Korean army casualties, but ultimately, all of the North Koreans were either killed or captured. Although we were told that it had come a long way from the war, South Korea to my eye looked like it still had far to go. When we boarded the C-130 at Osan for our flight back to Okinawa we were dirty and unshaven from lack of water and beginning to shiver in our woolen olive-green uniforms because the cool fall days of October had changed to the Siberian winds of November. As we roared off the runway and turned southeast for home I remembered Dad's words about Korea being so devastated by war that it would never recover. Seventeen years after he made that prediction it seemed that he was pretty close to the mark.

From a logistics perspective alone, from 1968 to 1972, the U.S. position in South Korea was virtually untenable in the face of a concerted North Korean attack. Ammunition was rusting in depots, supply books were poorly maintained, if at all, and the fuel pipeline—the artery carrying vital fuel for aircraft and combat vehicles—was in such terrible shape that it leaked, had places where fuel was regularly stolen, and was ready to collapse. A supply officer who served in those days told me that he'd found books that had been "cooked" for so long through so many generations of crooked supply sergeants and officers that very little on the ground matched what was in the official property inventory. In some ammunition depots case after case of ammunition for weapons systems that were no longer in either the U.S. or South Korean army inventory sat rusting. Rations were spoiled, medical supplies had in many cases simply disappeared—he suspected on the black market—and other items were in equal disarray. "If the North Koreans had attacked," he said emphatically, "we did not have the supplies to put up a sustained fight."

In that critical period thousands of tons of supplies were earmarked for the war in Vietnam. Other vital spots around the world—primarily Germany, where troops sat facing a huge Soviet army, and South Korea, where the guns of the North Koreans were in our faces—were left stripped of supplies and indefensible. We were waiting for the bad guys to attack but could do little more than give them the finger if they had. We were lucky.

### Shifting Troop Units

Until 1971 the U.S. Army maintained two full combat divisions in Korea, the Second Infantry Division and the Seventh Infantry Division. But as the Vietnam War continued to escalate, the U.S. military impatiently elbowed Vietnamese units off the battlefield, preferring to fight the war with American troops. In order to fill the increasing demand for units in Vietnam, the army was forced to pull troops from Europe and Korea. In 1971 the Seventh

Infantry Division was disbanded and its soldiers transferred to other units. The division's equipment—everything from trucks and heavy vehicles to weapons, communications gear, and supplies— was given to the South Koreans to make up for the removal of American manpower. The American ground force presence in South Korea was now limited to one division, the Second Infantry.

The decision to remove the Seventh Infantry had been made solely in Washington, without any consultation with its South Korean allies. This move, to understate it, rattled South Korean government leaders, especially President Park Chung-hee. Here was yet another example of Americans acting unilaterally without considering fully the seriousness of the situation that still threatened the South. In South Korean culture that kind of thing was not something allies or friends did to each other if they valued continuation of a trusting relationship. Understandably, their confidence was deeply eroded. In private meetings, South Korean leaders spoke in low tones, questioning the American commitment to their defense. For each one of the leaders, the Korean War was too fresh a memory to brush aside. And the presence of the North Korean military forces was far too threatening to dismiss. Their confidence in American resolution and commitment was further damaged by the United States' precipitous withdrawal from Vietnam in April 1975, following the tumultuous days of the terrible North Vietnamese spring offensive.

The net effect of withdrawing a division from South Korea was unsettling to the Koreans and to the American planners who worried about defending it. There has always been a permanency associated with the presence of ground troops that is reassuring to the place being defended by those ground troops. No other branch of the military—neither the Air Force nor the Navy—can give equally reassuring comfort as can the Army. The reason is simple:

if war starts and ground forces are involved, as they would be in Germany or South Korea in event of an attack, then the United States suffers immediate casualties and has no choice but to enter the fray. It is the classic "trip-wire effect" that produced a realistic deterrent to aggression for decades.

On the other hand, given their mobility, aircraft and ships can be here one day and gone the next, without a trace or without notification. Nor are air and sea assets capable of filling the trip-wire role as the army ones can, since they are normally positioned some distance from the immediate battlefield. It is critical to understand that when U.S. ground forces are withdrawn from South Korea or even the eventuality discussed hypothetically, it sends serious shock waves through the Seoul government.

The idea of removal of ground forces can also send the wrong signal to the enemy, in the way the announcement of the old Aleutian-Japan-Okinawa line sent the wrong message to North Korea and the Soviet Union in 1950. Wars are costly in terms of loss of human life and property damage. It is far less traumatic and expensive to maintain forces and prevent a war than it is to send them back to fight it once it has started. Unfortunately, by 1968 and the years following, the military situation on the peninsula was increasingly precarious. Replacement of positions was third priority to needs behind Vietnam and Germany. The preparedness level of the troops was thus extremely poor—most were recent enlistees or draftees with no more training than basic and occupational specialty training. Many had less than six months in the military and were woefully unprepared for combat.

As logistical requirements multiplied in Vietnam, forces in Korea suffered from basic shortfalls such as lack of quantity, type, and quality of ammunition. What was there was old, poorly maintained, and in some cases not the proper ammo for the weapons.

Replacement parts and maintenance capabilities suffered equally and the means of resupply in time of war of such essentials as fuel products, food, clothing, and other basics was woefully inadequate. The original plans for defending Seoul had also been overtaken by events. For example, no one anticipated its sharp population increase. Most plans simply wished away the horrific refugee and casualty problems that would be part and parcel of renewed war.

## A Secret Threat

Even when I was a kid in Japan we would occasionally see a full-body tattooed individual—usually in the public bathhouses that were more common in Occupation days than they are now. Dad would point out that many of these individuals were members of the Japanese gangster community, the *yakuza* class. When I returned to Japan in the 1960s and 1970s I learned more about this strange, fascinating community. Concomitantly, primarily through military intelligence links, I was finding out that a great deal of the political organizations, although located in Japan, were made up of ethnic Koreans who supported North Korea. Chosensoren was one of the largest. Japanese political and gangster elements were linking with the Kim Il Sung regime to form a coalition that was threatening peace and security in South Korea.

The main weak point in the South Korean defenses against clandestine agents was this North Korean linkage to Japan. When Imperial Japan imported—through persuasion or coercion—tens of thousands of Koreans as virtual slave laborers in their wartime industrial plant in the 1930s and 1940s they probably had no intention of creating a permanent minority. Now, fifty years and more after the fact, that is precisely what they ended up with. Today more than two million Korean nationals live in western Japan. This is the area in Honshu—Japan's main island—about two hundred miles southwest of the metropolitan Tokyo area that includes the big industrial cities of Osaka, Nagoya, and Kobe. During the war it was Japan's industrial heartland and considerable manufacturing is still done there. Cities and physical plants have long been reconstructed out of war rubble and the ports are humming. But the Korean population continues to grow, and neither Japan nor South Korea is quite prepared to handle it, although each for different reasons.

One of the cultural idiosyncrasies that define Japan, as well as some of the other Northeast Asia countries, is a strong xenophobia and a belief in racial or ethnic homogeneity. Japanese are unique, they believe, and the racial purity of Japan must be preserved. As a result, certain laws and ideas governing immigration and citizenship have been put in place that reflect these beliefs—and discourage naturalization. So what does a country do with millions of Koreans, who for successive generations have been born and raised in Japan? Most of these people speak Japanese as a first language, have never traveled outside of Japan, and consider themselves Japanese, with one small exception: they are not citizens.

Japanese authorities require them to register as resident aliens, which means they must have a passport from a country other than Japan because Japan will issue passports only to citizens. So what passport do they carry? Many of the original Koreans were brought to Japan from the northern provinces, which in the colonial days had the largest, most literate, most industrialized population. It was a natural place to recruit laborers. (The southern provinces of Korea furnished fishermen and farmers, many of whom were forcibly relocated to the Kuril Islands and Sakhalin Island where their descendents remain today.) When the time came to choose between North Korea and South Korea, many people therefore picked the North for family reasons. Over the years, a strong support base grew of Koreans living in a relatively more prosperous economy than either of the Koreas, and who were loyal to the North.

With exclusionary pressure from the Japanese that kept much of the resident Korean population from pursuing higher paying professional or middle-class jobs, many of them drifted into the underworld. A class of Koreans evolved—Korean yakuza—made up of criminals and other denizens of the social fringes who lived on income derived from the ubiquitous *pachinko* parlors that dominate the cityscape. Walk through Japan at night, especially the nightclub districts of Osaka and Nagoya, and the constant jingle of the pachinko machines plays a strange background music. Pachinko is a unique Japanese gambling game. Imagine if you will a pinball machine that sits vertically rather than horizontally. Players purchase small steel balls that are launched by depressing and releasing a handle and are pulled down by gravity across the face of the pachinko machine. Balls may fall into certain holes and score points. Points are automatically awarded to the player in the form of more balls (similar to coins from a slot machine). For the unlucky player, the ball falls into the return hole and gives nothing back (also similar to slot machines). When fortunate players have bunches of steel balls returned by the machine as a result of falling into especially desirable holes, attendants collect these balls and place them into plastic containers. Balls may be replayed by inserting them into the machine or the balls may be redeemed for prizes at the checkout counter. Since gambling for money is illegal in Japan, pachinko parlors do not pay cash redemptions but only award prizes. Fortunately for the players, adjacent to every pachinko parlor is a small store that purchases the prizes the players win at the parlor for cash. Each prize has a fixed value. The overstuffed teddy bear may be worth ¥10,000, for example. Since the pachinko parlors own the stores that buy back the prizes, the prizes may then be recycled for a new set of winners. In keeping with Japanese custom, form is satisfied: there is no gambling. Yet lucky winners are able to walk away with purses and wallets stuffed with crisp yen notes.

Since machines can be programmed to give so much and to take so much, pachinko parlors rake in huge returns for management, much as casino slot machines do. And in the parlors there is the same dark side of life one associates with casinos and gambling. Here too the Korean yakuza do not disappoint. Prostitution, extortion, narcotics, loan-sharking, and other illegal operations are intrinsic to the gangster life in western Japan. The deeper you walk into these areas at night, the more you begin to feel like an intrusive *gaigin*—an unwanted foreigner. There is a vibrant neon gaiety to downtown Osaka that becomes jarringly garish as you penetrate the increasingly narrow streets and the smaller alleyways. Passersby no longer grin and the hard edges you would naturally associate with underworld activities anywhere begin to show. If you're lucky, you may be approached by a Japanese man— it will always be a man—in an expensive suit. He will suggest with the utmost formality and politeness that you would probably be happier somewhere else. Take my word for it, you will definitely *not* be happy if you ignore this warning—for that is what it is. Time to get your *gaigin* bones out of there. Entrance into the inner sanctum of the yakuza is by invitation only. Foreigners need not apply.

Korean yakuza activity might be considered a localized phenomenon, if these people were merely a minority criminal element in Japan. But huge amounts of hard currency are regularly transferred from Japan to North Korea. This is accomplished by regular seagoing ferry traffic that departs from northern Honshu for Wonsan port in North Korea. Japanese customs officials have been instructed by superiors to ignore the large duffle bags of cash that are routinely couriered to the North from there. Over the years it has become one of the single largest sources of hard currency for a desperate regime in North Korea. At the same time, the Korean community in western Japan, with its loyalty and support of the North, has become a serious issue for South Korean authorities. Along with gambling and other crime money, quantities of hard drugs, principally heroin and methamphetamine, are being smuggled regularly into Japan for distribution within Japan or to transit for export to markets like Australia and South Korea. The Japanese authorities have recognized that once this traffic shifted from the internal yakuza environment to the general public it became an issue that had to be addressed. Japanese authorities are rethinking their previous policy of ignoring Korean yakuza activities. They are beginning to crack down on illegal export of currency, drugs, and espionage operations within Japan much more vigorously than in the past.

## Spies, Agents, and Dissidents

In addition to whiskey, drugs, women, and pachinko, the dark environs of the Korean yakuza community in Japan have been breeding grounds for North Korean operations against South Korea, both direct and indirect. North Korean intelligence operatives have for years used western Japan as a recruiting and training ground for agents. The disaffection that many young people feel being virtually stateless persons inside Japan combines with naïve idealism to produce a perfect soil to grow potential agents. It is the same kind of garden of evil from which terrorist organizations over the world harvest their recruits. Unlike Islamic fundamentalist terrorists with their penchant for suicide and martyrdom, however, North Korean terrorists typically rely more on subterfuge and guile to carry out their acts. Many die trying to complete their missions, but suicide is considered a last resort, a tactic to avoid capture, rather than a means and an end in itself. There is a huge difference in accepting a mission in which the odds are strong against your survival as opposed to one in which you intend from the outset to kill yourself as an intrinsic part of the act. Even the most desperate North Korean agents or commandos who take a mission guaranteed to end with their deaths hold out a faint glimmer of hope that they just might succeed after all and return alive. Contrast that attitude to that of a Hezbollah terrorist who departs on a mission with an explosive vest strapped to his body. There is a marked difference not only in attitude, but also in the amount and type of training necessary for the individual to carry out the terror mission.

North Korean agents recruited from among the Korean minorities in Japan usually undergo extensive vetting in Japan in an attempt to weed out possible South Korean double agents. These are people loyal to South Korea who pretend a desire to be agents of the North. After thorough screening, potential agents are sent to North Korea, often with their own legitimate passports, although false identities are easy enough for the North Koreans to provide. Inside North Korea, the fledgling agents are trained in sabotage, espionage, and terrorism. They learn how to fabricate and maintain a cover story, which gives them a reason to be where they need to be and who they pretend to be in order to carry out a mission. They learn the sophisticated methodology of having cover stories within cover stories, sometimes admitting to a lesser crime to avoid disclosure. For example, an agent arrested as a suspected spy in South Korea might under extensive interrogation, pretend to break down and admit to a lesser offense such as perpetrating a swindle or theft of corporate secrets. The technique is used in order to persuade interrogators that they have in fact busted a crime and need proceed no further. North Korean agent Kim Hyun Hee demonstrated the technique when she was arrested for her part in the blowing up of Korean Air Lines Flight 858. Initially, Kim pretended to be Japanese. She then "broke" and admitted that she was from the People's Republic of China (irritating the Chinese government no end). This was her cover story within a cover story.

It was far too easy for some of these displaced Koreans in Japan to get a South Korean passport and travel frequently. Not all such travel involves espionage of course; most is legitimate travel. Other travelers were linked to commercial organizations such as the *chaebol,* a large conglomerate of many companies clustered around one parent company, because certain elements of the South Korean business community used contacts with the Japanese-Korean yakuza to further their own interests in Japan. When Daewoo Group was at its height it was common to see Korean yakuza using the sauna facilities in the Hilton Hotel where they universally stayed when traveling over from Osaka-Nagoya. The Hilton was at that time owned by Kim Woo-choong, founder and chairman of Daewoo. The yakuza were easily identifiable in the sauna because their bodies were completely covered with dense, intricate, colorful tattoos. The artwork stopped at the neckline and at the wrists so that the gangsters could wear Western-style business suits and not reveal their yakuza affiliation. Missing joints on fingers, a typical yakuza punishment—forcing the miscreant to remove one of his fingers in the presence of the boss—were more difficult to hide. South Korean counterintelligence therefore faced the challenge of sorting through shady underworld characters from Japan who might or might not be associated with either crime or espionage, or both. And even trickier, they had to pick out the more dangerous spies traveling under cover as legitimate businessmen from Japan. Since South Korea and Japan have tight economic and business ties, the flood of legitimate businessmen made it relatively easy for an agent to hide himself in the mass. It also encouraged the Korean Central Intelligence Agency to conduct counterespionage activities within Japan. Operators from the KCIA began to appear in western Japan, trying to penetrate the closed, secretive yakuza societies. It was, to say the least, a tough assignment. If discovered by the yakuza, they would simply disappear—after appropriate torture and death. If uncovered by Japanese police or Japan's own counterespionage force, they could be tried or deported to South Korea, further souring an always-tense relationship.

Making matter even more complex, many South Korean dissidents—especially those with what seemed to be rather extreme left-leaning ties, including affiliation with North Korea—began to use western Japan as a sanctuary, a safe haven from the ubiquitous KCIA and police in South Korea. Moreover, using the formula that "the enemy of my enemy is my friend," these dissidents found natural allies in the North Korean yakuza elements. The heavy-handed manner in which each government treated its citizens in those days did little to gain either Park Chung-hee's or Kim Il Sung's side world respect. Loyalties and support tended to be divided on Cold War lines with European and American leftists and human rights activists vocal in their criticism of South Korea but far too silent on deplorable North Korean behavior. Since South Korea was largely dependent on the goodwill of the United States, and North Korea didn't give a fig about it, one is tempted to think that the critics go for the most vulnerable target, regardless of the degree of infraction. By the mid-1970s though, South Korean intelligence operatives were running around Japan, Europe, and the

United States with a stunningly blind disregard for sensibilities in those places. The South Koreans kidnapped dissidents and brought them back to South Korea. They may even have assassinated a number of political opponents that they considered most dangerous to Park. One famous dissident, Kim Dae-jung, who later became head of the opposition political party and eventually president of South Korea, was kidnapped by South Korean operators from western Japan in the mid-1970s and spirited away in a South Korean freighter. Word flew around Seoul that Kim Dae-jung was to be killed on the voyage, his body weighted and dumped into the sea. Only strong intervention by the American ambassador Philip Habib and especially by his U.S. Central Intelligence Agency chief of station, Donald Gregg (himself later a U.S. ambassador to South Korea), prevented a heinous political murder and a history-changing event. Had Kim Dae-jung been murdered the outcry for justice would have been so strong that it might have forced a restructuring of the U.S.-South Korean relationship, perhaps even leading to a withdrawal of U.S. forces from Korea, which could have precipitated a renewed war. At best it would have meant that the evolution of real democracy in South Korea would have suffered a major, perhaps irreversible setback.

Clearly the relationship between South Korea and America was strained in this period. The entire globe was at that time dependent on the concept of mutually assured destruction to keep nuclear missiles from raining down on it. Because the division between the Soviet Union and the United States was so deep and so wide, in this Cold War atmosphere, with both sides fighting through surrogates on every continent in the world, an unpleasant phenomenon surfaced among third-world and developing nations. Many of them tried to take advantage of the U.S.-Soviet divide. North Korea played both the Soviets and the communist Chinese like a virtuoso in obtaining additional aid and diplomatic support. For a time South Korea too fell into this pattern. Inside the United States, a South Korean businessman and wheeler-dealer named Park Tong-sun established himself in Washington, D.C., and began lobbying for support for the South Korean government. In the early to mid-1970s support for the government generally translated itself into support for the continuing presence of President Park Chung-hee. They had to walk a thin line: maintaining an arbitrary, authoritarian government but still avoiding U.S. criticism by being staunchly anti-communist. This led many to use the often heard but perhaps originally apocryphal line "yes, he's a son-of-a-bitch, but he's our son-of-a-bitch." This line or something akin to it was used to describe Park Chung-hee as well as a wide range of tough leaders of all stripes and positions on the political spectrum (Chiang Kai-shek in Taiwan, Lee Kwan Yew in Singapore, Pinochet in Chile, Somosa in Nicaragua, Pahlavi in Iran, and Marcos in the Philippines, to name but a few). Often overlooked but well to remember is that the Soviet/PRC gang had their own collection of roughnecks, including Honecker in East Germany, Ceausescu in Romania, Ho Chi Minh in Vietnam, Pol Pot in Cambodia, Allende in Chile, Ortega in Nicaragua, and, not least, Castro in Cuba.

**The Isolated Leader**

There were many reasons for the increased isolation of President Park Chung-hee, for the withdrawal from the ease with which he first mingled with the public. The reason that seems to have upset him the most was the loss of his beloved wife in the assassination at the National Theater. After that he became a changed man, harder, more suspicious, less tolerant of dissent. His initial comfort turned to a growing suspicion that slowly but thoroughly permeated all aspects of his life. Undeniably, the series of physical attacks on him and his family from North Korean assassins sparked his isolation and suspicion. These constant assassination attempts validated the advice of security people to install even greater safeguards and to appear less often in public. This left the door open for the head of the security force—a tough man by the name of Cha Chi-chol—to gradually insinuate himself into the command structure. The security chief became a go-between from the president to the outside world. Everything that came to Park had to pass first through the filter of the security chief. As with many power-hungry bureaucrats, Cha gave reports that made him seem indispensable to the president and as a consequence expanded his own power base. As Park relied increasingly on security and KCIA directors, such as Lee Hu-rak and Kim Jae-kyu, who saw threats everywhere and also used their access to him to build their own power bases, the president began to trust only his own judgment. Over time, even that was influenced far too much by the counsel of a small coterie of sycophants.

As the distance between the president and the outside world widened, his suspicions increased, and political rivals were portrayed not as loyal opposition but as tools of the enemy. This spiraling suspicion fed upon itself and grew exponentially. Park's absolutist tendencies grew with it. Park Chung-hee was a military officer and the product of a hierarchical culture. The tradition of democracy and popular decision-making was new to Korea. Many observers frankly stated that Korea could never function as a democracy and that only a strong leader would be effective. In that environment, with the economy struggling to stay afloat, and ambitious to move South Korea to the level of a developed nation while under the gun of hostile neighbors (North Korea, China, and the Soviets), Park not surprisingly consolidated power in the one place he had confidence: himself.

## Criticism

Park has been roundly criticized by the U.S. media, American diplomats, internal opposition party members, and of course the ever-vocal South Korean student population. All these voices added to the usual vitriol pouring south from North Korea. Indisputably, many of Park's actions merit criticism. He was especially harsh in his suppression of the opposition, including labor; he misused internal agencies such as the KCIA; and perpetrated a variety of human rights abuses. But there is more than that to the story. Despite abuses—and there were plenty to be sure— such measures were always directed against individuals and never institutionalized. Even though opposition figures were occasionally imprisoned, and at the most extreme, kidnapped or executed—inexcusable actions to be sure—the level of persecution directed against the opposition and the degree of control Park achieved paled considerably compared to what his rival in North Korea was doing. South Korea, for example, never had a gulag system under which hundreds of thousands of its citizens were worked to death or summarily executed.

Under Park's leadership South Korea was able to bootstrap itself into a higher and higher economic status. Moreover, Park himself lived humbly, was never corrupt, and made no attempt either to institute a hereditary monarchy or develop a cult of personality. The human rights abuses in South Korea, while inexcusable, never reached the degree of inhumanity that became routine in North Korea. Nor has terror ever been official policy as it has in North Korea. Park Chung-hee warrants criticism, but it must be tempered somewhat by context. Any judgment on him needs to be complete, fair, and balanced. He was a transition figure for South Korea, and his vision developed economic and security institutions that were precursors—indeed prerequisites—for the democracy that ultimately blossomed. It is interesting to speculate on how much more quickly South Korean democracy might have developed and how much less authoritarian Park might have been had the terrorism threat from North Korea not been so aggressive. Yet Park Chung-hee, warts and all, must be considered one of the giant figures of the twentieth century in Asia.

## The Post-Vietnam Era Begins

South Korea became increasingly concerned, as did many of its Asian friends and allies, when the United States abandoned Vietnam in April 1975. This sent a violent shock wave jolting through all of Asia, especially South Korea. Worse in their minds, even than those agonizing scenes of teeming refugees, helicopters gyrating wildly on carrier flight decks, and North Vietnamese tanks in Saigon, was the fact that President Nixon had guaranteed the security of South Vietnam and had through that guarantee convinced them to sign the Paris Accords. Yet when it came time for the United States to honor its agreement, the American Congress voted measures that refused to allow the president to act. Years of dishonesty in government, the media, and on campuses had finally culminated in brutal political backlashes that affect America to this day. But for South Korea in 1975 the stimulation for self-reliance in defense matters grew stronger, along with the constant fear of a resurgent North Korea.

In 1975 many of its Asian friends worried that America was, as had long been feared, abandoning its interest in the western Pacific, or at best, heavily ratcheting down its involvement. The severe internal conflict associated with the Vietnam War and its aftermath in America—street demonstrations, riots, assassinations, conflict between Congress and the president, rancorous media, and a depressed, indifferent public seemingly jaded on drugs and

self-absorption—were cause for concern. Allies up and down East
Asia trembled privately.

This concern over American commitment extended to South
Korea. As a consequence, South Korean leadership initiated several policy measures. President Park fretted about military equipment. He had seen the American Congress refuse to support South
Vietnam in the face of an overt attack despite in-place, sworn defense treaties by the United States to defend it. He worried that
the same thing could happen to South Korea, so he therefore appealed to the United States for increasingly higher levels of material support. His rationalization was that if America insisted on
cutting back its actual force structure at least he could move into
some limited manufacturing and thereby modernize his own
South Korean forces. He was desperate to take immediate measures to counter the huge North Korean buildup that he faced.
Park, along with most of his senior advisors, was looking northward, and did not like what the intelligence community told him
was looming there. Word was out on the intelligence street: North
Korea is building up to a major provocation, possibly to justify an
invasion. South Korea faced its sworn enemy on one side, with a
shaky ally on the other. On the Korean peninsula, that summer of
1976, tension seemed to rise with the thermometer as the summer
days heated up.

# CHAPTER 7

# Times of Tension

In spring of 1976 I received a set of orders for Fort Bragg, North Carolina, to be followed by an advanced Korean language course in Monterey, California. Afterwards I was alerted for deployment to Korea for purposes of working in the American embassy in Seoul as part of my training program to be a Korea-Northeast Asia specialist. The assignment would involve travel to Japan, the People's Republic of China, Taiwan, Hong Kong, and the Philippines in order to get a full picture of what was happening militarily in the region. I was delighted, although the prospect of returning to Korea with a family did not appeal. Nevertheless, I was told that the place had changed and become much safer, cleaner, and family oriented. There was a possibility, I was told by the people in Seoul, of my attending the Korean Army Military College, a year-long program of instruction analogous to the mid-level managers training we in the American army refer to as "command-and-staff-level training."

When I heard the news I was ambivalent to say the least. "My Korean language isn't good enough to make it in that kind of environment," I protested. "We don't care too much about that," Colonel Roland Rogers, the defense attaché replied, "because your primary mission down there is going to be to make friends and build relationships that will carry for years. Do the best in your preparatory training and you can improve language on the job." That did not sound very encouraging but as a captain at the time I couldn't raise much fuss. I was a senior captain, however, and that would help later with my Korean classmates, most of whom were majors and lieutenant colonels. Our promotions system was frozen after Vietnam and I stayed a captain for twelve years. My kids thought "Captain" was my first name.

But as I went through training at the foreign area officers' course at Bragg—tied into the Special Warfare School in those days—we began to notice serious undercurrents of unrest coming out of Korea. "Tension is growing," my instructor, Lieutenant Colonel Jim Hyinck said. "We have been seeing increasing bilateral friction develop between South Korea and the U.S. presidential candidate Jimmy Carter is talking about withdrawing American troops from Korea and that may be sending the wrong signal to the North. Also, President Ford is seen as a weak, interim president after Nixon's resignation. Be alert, because something big may be happening over there." Within weeks his words proved prophetic.

### The Axe Murders

In the hot, humid summer of 1976 some of us thought that the next war had come. The potential trigger incident took place within the Joint Security Area (JSA) in Panmunjom. At that time the entire area of the JSA, approximately two square kilometers, was open to soldiers from both sides. It was common for North and South Korean, American, and Chinese soldiers who were authorized to be in the area—distinguished by military police brassards or armbands even though they were not actually MPs—to wander wherever they desired. By 1975 there had already been several ugly incidents inside the JSA including everything from name-calling to pushing and shoving to outright fistfights. Since the North Korean and South Korean JSA guards were trained in their respective martial arts specialties, and the U.S. guards were selected for size and strength, the hand-to-hand fights were bloody and brutal. Even though the war was officially twenty-three years in the past, hatred was still palpable. The anthracite stares of the North Korean guards had become a topic of many photos and stories.

In 1976 the American-South Korean side had been urging the North Koreans to implement changes in order to minimize contact between guard factions. The North Koreans rejected any modifications in the original agreement and fighting, shouting, and cursing incidents became more frequent and increasingly bitter. South Korean and U.S. guards were sternly cautioned to avoid physical conflict at all costs. Men were selected for the highly stressful job in part for their patience and unflappable temperaments. Yet many men whose duty station was in the JSA, feared that a major incident lurked just around the corner. A serious American force weakness was lack of continuity and institutional memory due to the policy of the one-year tour for most officers, NCOs, and enlisted men. The one-year tour meant that by the time soldiers learned their way around they were being rotated to a new duty assignment. A U.S. four-star general who later became chairman of the Joint Chiefs of Staff, Jack Vessey, said that "we have twenty-five years experience in Korea—one year at a time." As a result each new assignee ended up having to invent the wheel. It was a self-defeating policy that continues today. This is yet another reason area specialty officers like me and my colleagues became invaluable assets to the commander.

The most recent serious North Korean act of brutality and aggression had occurred only a few years prior, when a Major Henderson, visiting the JSA from Seoul, was attacked in what was clearly calculated provocation. Several North Korean guards, using their distinctive martial arts–style of hand-to-hand combat, pinned the major against an exterior building wall in Panmunjom and systematically beat him. News photographers who were touring the JSA that day caught the tail end of the attack on film. It is clear from the pictures that the assault was thoroughly planned and choreographed.

Major Henderson was alone, wandering apart from his group, when the attack took place. He was not in a prohibited location; he was simply trying to look through a window into the building where the Military Armistice Commission talks are regularly held. The building screened him from view of friendly guards. His attention was then diverted from nearby North Korean guards, who on a verbal signal rushed him and began to beat him viciously. Onlookers shouted an alarm. From the opposite side of the building, U.S. and South Korean guards sprinted to the spot. Just before they were able to get to him, the North Koreans knocked Henderson to the ground. As he lay helpless on his back, barely conscious, his attackers deliberately used the heels of their boots to stomp his throat. Their intentions—captured for all to see on the film—are unmistakable. They were trying to shatter his larynx, obviously intending to kill him. The major survived, but had to endure more than a decade of repeated surgeries to repair his badly damaged throat. Knowing that this was the kind of behavior of which the North Koreans were capable, it is surprising that by 1976, as tensions mounted, more was not done of a preventative nature. From hindsight, the signs were there for all to see. But then hindsight is so very clear.

## The Offending Tree

By August 1976 there were several issues that were under discussion in the Joint Security Area that dealt with a combination of administration and behavior. Fights and name-calling had become almost daily occurrences. Over the previous months, the North Koreans—in violation of agreements—had established several illegal roadblocks and checkpoints within the JSA. These were expressly forbidden by mutual agreement and were clearly part of a deliberate provocation and harassment policy by North Korea. The U.S.-South Korean side continued to object to these but the North Koreans refused to dismantle them. As was typical of their style, North Korean representatives then issued a counteraccusation of a fictitious violation by the U.S.-South Korean side. It was business as usual at Panmunjom: hostile, inflammatory, and angry.

Along with the checkpoints there were many other contentious issues that grew from requirements of observation and security. Most of these were minor points—tree maintenance, personnel levels—issues that could have been settled in minutes if the North Koreans had the inclination. But every little thing, every point however minute, was instantly raised by them to the level of acrimony, argument, accusation, and recrimination. An example was in the northwest corner of the JSA near what is called the "Bridge of No Return." This was the bridge that was filmed during Operation Big Switch and Operation Little Switch, as prisoners of war came south from North Korean custody and those captured by the U.S.-South Koreans went north. It is doubtful than any but the most fanatically committed few of the North Korean or Chinese soldiers who returned to custody of their own people survived. Like Stalin, neither Mao Zedong nor Kim Il Sung trusted anyone "contaminated" by contact with the West. Any who were accused of open collaboration with the Americans were shot out of hand. Others went into the rapidly growing gulag to be worked to death. Thus, crossing the bridge northward truly meant no return.

Because this bridge offered the North Koreans direct access into the Joint Security Area, an authorized U.S.-South Korean checkpoint was located near it. The checkpoint was under constant observation by a U.S.-South Korean guard post several hundred yards distant. It was necessary that the various friendly guard posts kept constant watch on each other because North Koreans had taken to attacking isolated guards verbally or physically. If a guard was threatened someone else could call for assistance and alert a response force.

But over the years since the war ended trees had been planted or allowed to grow naturally in the area. Many had spreading branches that blocked easy observation. As a result, the U.S.-South Korean side had begun that summer to clean out much of the brush and remove a few of the trees. One, a forty-foot tall Normandy popular blocked sight between a U.S.-South Korean observation post and a U.S.-South Korean checkpoint maintained in consonance with the armistice agreement near the Bridge of No Return. On August 6, 1976, a U.S.-South Korean detail had been dispatched to remove the tree. At the time, North Korean guards abused them and chased them away, although they had no legal authority to do so. Faced with the increasing frequency and intensity of the hostile acts by the North Korean guards the American authorities attempted to find a solution that would be acceptable.

On August 18th, a U.S.-South Korean work detail was dispatched, not to remove the tree but just to trim the lower branches, thereby permitting visual contact between the checkpoint and the guard post. In command of the detail was Captain Arthur Bonifas assisted by First Lieutenant Mark Barrett. I knew Barrett. He and I had served in the same unit prior to him going to Korea. I thought of him as a bright, cheerful, action-oriented officer with great future potential. Along with the two American officers were several South Korean guards, a few other American guards, and a contingent of South Korean laborers. The guards were armed with .45 caliber pistols but had been sternly cautioned against using them. There was great concern at the highest levels that the North Koreans were looking for any reason to provoke an incident and all measures were to be taken to prevent giving them one on a platter.

When work first began, the North Koreans came by to see what was happening. Initially they did not object but, in typical bossy fashion, shouted commands at the laborers telling them what to do and how to do it. As the sun rose higher and the day progressed the work droned on. The North Korean guards returned, this time under the leadership of an officer, Lieutenant Park, who immediately ordered the U.S.-South Korean detail to cease work. Captain Bonifas refused and ordered the detail to continue. Park then began to make threats, which Bonifas ignored— he had become accustomed to regular verbal berating from the North Koreans. Park issued orders to his people. Before too long, more than thirty North Korean guards had assembled, far outnumbering the tree-trimming detail. By this point, Park's threats were borderline hysterical.

From a distant checkpoint, U.S.-South Korean guards filmed events and monitored radio exchanges. Tension grew palpable. A number of the guards grew concerned that this might turn out to be more than the usual North Korean harassment. Radios crackled back to headquarters. The Quick Reaction Platoon was told to mount vehicles just outside the JSA and to stand by. Meanwhile, Bonifas, supervising his detail, was not taking the threat seriously enough. He turned his back to Park. Unseen by Bonifas but caught on camera, Park removed his watch, wrapped it in a handkerchief, and stuffed it in his uniform trousers. A second North Korean officer present began to roll up his sleeves. The other North Korean guards spread out, surrounding the work party. Before an American sergeant could warn Captain Bonifas, Lieutenant Park issued the command, *Chuk!* or Kill!

In a premeditated assault, Park kicked Bonifas in the groin, knocking him to the ground. Suddenly, North Korean guards grabbed tools from the nearby trucks or snatched them from the laborers. Systematically they began to beat the U.S.-South Korean soldiers, isolating Bonifas and Barrett. While Bonifas lay on the ground the North Koreans yanked off his helmet and began striking his head and face with crowbars, axes, and other tools. It was later ascertained that he died from traumatic blows from the blunt edge of an axe. Lieutenant Barrett was pursued by six North Koreans who followed him into a creek bed and bludgeoned him to death in the weeds and brush. A South Korean sergeant was beaten badly but survived. An American drove one of the trucks into the melee allowing friendly guards and workers to assist the fallen. The reaction force arrived to lend help but by that time, the damage was done. Two American officers lay dead and bleeding in the dirt. Within minutes, the North Koreans fled back across the Bridge of No Return.

Upon examination, there can be no doubt that the North Korean attack was unprovoked, calculated, and planned. The manner in which the North Koreans deployed and acted in unison demonstrated that this without question was a deliberate, intentional attack. And that it was designed not to harass but to kill. It was also clear that the American officers had been targeted for assassination. Some have criticized the U.S.-South Korean side for trimming the tree in the first place and ignoring the North Korean objections of August 6th. A few apologists, in the most convoluted logic imaginable, even carp at the United States for giving the North Koreans reasons to attack.

That is a load of nonsense. Take the tree: the U.S.-South Korean side would have been derelict to ignore a situation in which some guard troops were endangered by the inability of their comrades to see them if they were assaulted. It was well within U.S.-South Korean rights and authority as outlined by Joint Security Area agreements to undertake such routine maintenance. The North Koreans were not reacting to a tense situation but were intentionally creating one—obviously on orders from higher authority. It must be assumed that in the top-heavy, stovepipe decision chain that characterizes North Korean military that such orders could have come only from Kim Il Sung himself.

The Axe Murders of August 18, 1976, were infamous, dastardly, cowardly murders and the most brazen provocation. The incident could easily have been the launching platform for a renewed Korean War. All Kim Il Sung needed was sufficient reaction by the U.S.-South Korean side to justify launching his own attack.

So in August 1976, with rhetoric from the American presidential election campaign hitting its ninety-day fever pitch, it seemed to the U.S. commanders, especially in South Korea, that this was an excellent time for Kim Il Sung to incite a war. If Kim responded to a U.S.-South Korean punitive attack he might be able to sell enough people on the idea that he was the helpless victim and not the aggressor. It would not have taken much for many Americans—especially led by a biased media—to be willing

to believe that the United States was the culprit. As a consequence, General Richard Stilwell and his South Korean counterparts had little confidence of being backed up in a crisis. Their
mission therefore was to prevent an explosion. Their challenge
was to answer the Axe Murder provocation with sufficient resolve
and yet not give Kim a chance to up the ante to open war.

Under the remarkably able leadership of General Stilwell
and his chief of staff, the illustrious Major General Jack Singlaub,
the task was accomplished successfully.[10] It was decided to con-
front the North Koreans over the core issue—the removal of the
tree—and force them to back down, thereby losing face internationally. By having a major show of force—B-52s flew in formation
toward North Korea, for example—Kim Il Sung would either have
to launch an attack overtly or choose voluntarily to reduce the tension. When the moment of truth came, Kim Il Sung blinked. The
restraint of the U.S.-South Korean command in not launching a
retaliatory strike was admirable. In a firm but restrained display
of strength, forces were assembled and in Operation Paul Bunyan
the tree was chain-sawed to bits under the protective guns of a
poised, motivated guard force.

Meanwhile, just outside of the Demilitarized Zone, unit helicopters filled with troops with loaded weapons circled, ready to
pounce if the North Koreans went on the offensive. After several
tense hours the North Koreans backed down and eventually Kim Il
Sung issued what was as close as he can get to an apology. The terrible tension ratcheted down a bit but the issues of confrontational

---

[10] Richard Stilwell was hard-bitten and tough; however, he had a warm spot for veterans of the Forgotten War. Later in his life, Stilwell was instrumental in overseeing the
funding, siting, design, and construction of the stunning Korean War Memorial in the
Mall at Washington, D.C. For details on the Axe Murder incident, see Jack Singlaub's excellent memoir, *Hazardous Duty* (New York: Touchstone, 1992).

forces remained in place. Inside the Joint Security Area a division line was imposed that prohibited guards from wandering into the others' area but the bitterness remained on both sides.

Back at Fort Bragg one of my classmates, in the kind of gallows humor that characterizes military friendships, pointed solemnly at news photos from the incident posted on our bulletin board. "Don't cut down any trees while you're over there," he cautioned deadpan. I promised not to. By the time the election was over—Carter was victorious—I was on my way back to Korea. I landed in Seoul just about the same time as Carter's "withdraw-the-troops" announcement hit—along with the revelation of a huge, unknown expansion of North Korean military capabilities. Events were exploding on the scene.

When I returned to South Korea after a seven-year absence, I had a dated snapshot in my head of what the place would be like. My frozen-in-time-picture was not pleasant: I remembered that it was necessary to be constantly alert for the presence of the predatory "stealie boys" who would dart from hidden alleys and doorways to snatch sunglasses, watches, briefcases, purses, jewelry, pens, and other salable items from unsuspecting passersby. The telephone system in the late 1960s and early 1970s had been primitive at best. It was necessary to shout at the top of one's lungs just to be heard. Operators running manual switchboards controlled the phone calls. In order to keep the maximum number of lines open they would constantly troll through the working lines. If they heard silence operators would arbitrarily pull the plug so that another call could go through on that line. Even a brief pause to think of a response would lead to telephonic decapitation. (To this day older Koreans who were a product of the early primitive communications days typically scream into telephones with deafening volume, and fill every pregnant pause with a barrage of *"yoboseao,"* the Korean word for both "hello" on the phone and "excuse me.") My other memory was of dirt, particularly in the backcountry. Virtually every road had been dirt, rock, or gravel. To drive from Seoul to Pusan you actually had to ford streams in some places, cross over single-lane pontoon bridges, and plan on taking three days to make the roughly 250-mile journey. Basic sanitation was of the most primitive sort, with chamber pots common in homes and country inns, privies rather than flush toilets, and non-potable well water—if a place had running water at all. If not, it was hauled in in buckets.

So when I landed at Kimpo that hot, humid August day my mind was still in a time warp. I felt as if I was visiting friends who had small children when I last saw them and who had now grown into large teenagers. After arrival, we were housed in the Naeja Hotel, a U.S. forces hotel in the center of the city within a few blocks walking distance of the American embassy, the National Assembly, and other government buildings. On my way back to the hotel on the first afternoon after arrival, I saw a well-dressed young woman walking toward me. The sidewalks were of carved stone. She must have caught a high heel in one of the cracks because she fell forward sharply. From a few feet away I could see that she had ripped a stocking over her right knee and scraped it bloody. We were right in front of the South Korean Foreign Ministry building and the two uniformed army guards watched from their posts. Instinctively I moved to assist her. Because of my previous experience there, with the ubiquitous stealie boys lurking behind every nook and cranny, I feared placing my briefcase on the sidewalk to use two hands to assist her to her feet. Surely the briefcase would fly away and I could not risk losing the contents. So awkwardly, fumbling with one hand I tried to assist the mortified woman who had not only fallen but also done it in front of a stranger—worse yet a foreigner! She tried desperately to get to her feet, ignore the pain, and flee while I flapped around helplessly with one hand. When she recovered and I turned to continue to the hotel I glanced over to the gimlet-eyed guard. "You are very kind," he said in rather good English and saluted. I returned his salute and walked away thinking (with great originality), "Wow! Has this place changed!"

## Discovering the Hidden Threat

Helping to guide me through my first days back in Seoul was the army attaché, then Major Jim Young, a long-time Korea hand. He had just come from a key assignment in the army intelligence staff at the Pentagon and brought a disquieting report: the military balance on the peninsula was tilted sharply in favor of North Korea. This was shocking news indeed. Despite years of observing the North Korean order of battle, new analyses based on upgraded overhead photography techniques revealed that a vast part of their army had been hidden for years. What made the discovery of these previously undiscovered North Korean military capabilities even more frightening is that but for the work of this group of intelligence professionals it might have gone overlooked. Jim's excellent team back in Washington had included a brilliant civilian analyst, former officer, and West Point graduate, John Armstrong. Through remarkably astute analytical ability Young, Armstrong, and the U.S.-South Korean authorities were able to determine that Kim and the North Koreans had not only reduced the indications and warning time of a possible attack on the South but had also assembled a massive special commando force unnoticed. Aided by information from defectors and a great deal of overhead photographic analysis, the team—working around the clock at a feverish pace to get their analysis in a form that could be disseminated to the community—put together the clues that determined that a major portion of the North Korean force had been totally overlooked.

They determined that North Korean armor force was underestimated by 80 percent, that artillery was considerably higher than previously thought, and that a special corps of ranger-commandos had been formed. These were troops that would race through tunnels, infiltrate by aircraft and parachute, and exploit breaks in the defender's position. Their mission would be to disrupt rear-area command, control, and communications sites; to assassinate high-ranking political and military leaders; and to commit acts of sabotage and terror. When a corps of this size was backed by an active army of more than a million and a staggering two million plus reservists, it was enough to strike a chord of fear into any commander's heart. "Not only was the North Korean army significantly larger than . . . had been previously estimated," Young summarizes, "but also its equipment inventory and deployment pattern indicated conclusively that it was an offensive-oriented force capable of attacking the South with little or no warning."[11]

General Jack Vessey, the senior American commander at the time, listened to the briefing with pained intensity. Vessey knew that the situation in Korea had changed gravely with this new intelligence. He immediately flew back to Washington to brief the Joint Chiefs of Staff and the newly elected president, Jimmy Carter.

---

[11] Now retired, Colonel James Young gives an excellent summation of this critical time in Korea and the years following in his partially autobiographical account *Eye on Korea* (College Station: Texas A&M University Press, 2003), a must-read for all interested in the current tense situation.

## Withdrawal . . . or Not?

What exactly senior officers such as General Jack Vessey expected to find when they met the new president is not known. Possibly they thought that as a Naval Academy graduate and a former officer Jimmy Carter would understand the problems and challenges associated with waging war. If that was their hope, they were disappointed. Carter appeared to most military contacts to be almost pathological about his need to be in control—or at least his desire to be perceived that way. Most senior military people came away from meetings with the new president convinced that not only did he not heed advice, neither did he listen to it. Senior officers who were not his handpicked pets came away from meetings shaking their heads in frustration. The consensus of those officers was that his mind was made up, and he refused to change it.

Given that stubbornness—which can be admirable to a certain point—the ironic characteristic of Carter administration foreign policy was the constant flip-flop. "Now we will; now we won't" seemed to be its motto. The withdrawal of U.S. ground forces from South Korea became a classic example of the Carter administration flip-flop. It was an on-again off-again policy that eventually soured the bilateral relationship and accomplished only a titular, face-saving withdrawal for Jimmy Carter. A case could be made that the net effect of the policy was to set back the progress of South Korean democracy for another decade. The threatened withdrawal placed the South Koreans in jeopardy and forced them to look internally for their defense products. As a consequence, American manufacturers lost hundreds of millions of dollars in contracts while Korean manufacturers were pressured to enter fields in which they had little experience or competitive advantage and which diverted scarce resources from development of a more balanced economy.

## A Shaken Ally

When North Korean actions had cut normal warning of a possible attack to days, if not hours, the South Koreans were gravely concerned. Not only did they have to gear up to defend against sudden attack, they also had to deal with an ally who was talking openly of troop withdrawal. And the United States had a history of abandoning allies; it had done exactly that just two years earlier in Vietnam. So, the question had to be asked: Could the Americans be fully counted on in a crisis? The South Koreans were desperate. Reflecting this new sense of urgency, the Seoul government began to work furiously toward an independent option for defense. They accelerated rapidly after the public pronouncements of U.S. President Jimmy Carter in 1977.

Carter benefited from the feeding frenzy the national media had had with the Nixon administration, especially the Watergate scandals that forced one president out and led to the swearing-in as president of a man never elected to that office or even to the vice presidency. Nonetheless, Gerald Ford was an exceptionally decent man. He was experienced, bright, and transparently honest, a welcome change from the darkness of the previous administrations of Richard Nixon and Lyndon Johnson. The press, however, was giving no quarter. Their consensus was that it was time for a change, and Carter was the candidate of their choice.

The election of Jimmy Carter probably had more to do with a general American rejection of the Republicans than of knowledge of Jimmy Carter the man. To an American public wire-brushed by a Nixon-hating media over Watergate, Carter must have seemed a mild relief. He was likeable, had a broad, toothy grin, and promised not to lie to the American people. He asked them to call him "Jimmy." But on balance, he was a lightweight, relatively inexperienced Southern governor with little national exposure. Carter nevertheless settled into the White House, bringing with him some radical concepts of foreign policy.

## Human Rights Policy Produces Human Wrongs

The Carter administration's foreign policy was to be based on a country's or government's respect for essential human rights. On this Carter was unyielding: any regime that violated human rights must be called to task by the United States. A violator state would not be considered a friend. The definition of basic human rights was an expansive one for the president and grew over the years to include housing and education. On the surface the idea of enforcing human rights worldwide can be a compelling philosophy. But consistency is an absolute necessity in any country's foreign policy. It may be appropriate to base foreign policy on a single, clearly defined principle—in this case human rights—but only if that principle is universally and equally applied. It is a fatal policy error, for example, to uphold your high standards with one particular country then compromise those same standards with another. To do so renders the entire policy hypocritical, and diminishes the credibility of the nation expounding it. That was the hurdle that tripped Carter.

Carter lacked the courage, confidence, or ability to go after the gross human rights abusers: the Soviets, communist Chinese, North Koreans, Cubans, Eastern Europeans, and other major offenders. Instead, he decided to take on smaller nations that were in many ways U.S. client states. These were places that for one reason or another were important to U.S. interests but which may have been run by regimes that Carter didn't approve of because of their human rights records. In virtually every case he put unbearable pressure on friendly states, frequently destabilizing them, causing a power vacuum and bringing in a hostile, brutal regime over which he had no control or even rapport. In so doing, Carter's meddling, however well intentioned, resulted in a significantly more grievous situation for the residents, a destruction of key U.S. relationships, and a delay in instituting a free-market democracy.

South Korea became a prime example. Carter spoke out in a highly critical manner against Park Chung-hee. He demanded immediate reforms and announced that he was arbitrarily withdrawing the Second Infantry Division from South Korea, the last of the American ground troops and the major deterrent against North Korean invasion. South Korea was stable enough to withstand the Carter onslaught, although institutions such as its intelligence service were compared to the world's worst internal police forces and Park was portrayed as a gross human rights violator. Was Park tough? Did he commit abuses? Certainly he did. Some of his actions were indefensible. But rather than throw the baby out with the bathwater, destabilize a friendly country, and endanger millions of people, Carter could have used moral suasion, diplomacy, and economic incentives to bring an increasingly freer democracy to the country. This method works considerably better than just dumping people to the fate of a new abusive ruler. Backing Park Chung-hee into a corner and putting excess pressure on the country set the eventual development of democracy back a decade in South Korea.

American troop withdrawal was extremely traumatic for South Korea. President Park wrote an essay on the subject in which he debated the point that the troop withdrawal was, as President Carter had stated, for purely economic savings. The amount of alleged savings to U.S. taxpayer was one of the embellishments that the Carter people put on the policy to sell it. But Park countered with the simple but compelling logic that it was far cheaper by any measure to keep the troops as a deterrent than to have to send them back in to fight a war. Korea even offered some cost-saving measures by which it would supply certain support for the American forces stationed there in return for promises of continued presence. It was a program called Host Nation Support that Germany and Japan both used to help maintain U.S. forces on their soil. But Carter was increasingly intransigent, complaining to a staffer, reporter Don Oberdorfer notes, "this is the only campaign pledge that I haven't changed." That ought to have told him something. As the tension grew between South Korea and the Carter administration, Park and his cabinet began to assume the worse.[12]

Rather than garner support for Carter some of his precipitate actions, including the relief of General Jack Singlaub, made him appear amateurish. They further called national attention to the South Korean troop withdrawal policy, forced hearings and debate on Capitol Hill, and in time effectively killed it. Carter ultimately withdrew a symbolic battalion but left the remainder of the troops. Nevertheless, while the possibility of war was avoided in the near term, the damage to South Korea was done. The point was made, just as had been observed in Vietnam, that America was capable of making fickle, changeable policy decisions that could plunge their country into the direst circumstances imaginable. And that it could be done completely without warning. At one point in the late 1970s it was reliably estimated that if North Korea attacked, Seoul would fall in a day. To think that under such circumstances the South Koreans would be content relying on such an erratic ally as America was proving to be foolish.

General Bill Livesey who commanded American forces in Korea in the mid-1980s noted that he was still trying to undo the

---

12 *The Two Koreas*, 127.

damage that Carter had done with his misguided policies. "Carter made two big mistakes at the time," Livesey said. "The withdrawal plan and the terrible way that he tried to punish General Vessey afterwards." General Vessey, who had risen from the rank of private in World War II to four-star general over the years, was a lock to be named Chief of Staff of the Army, a position appointed by the president but nominated by the services. Carter gave Vessey a cursory interview then elevated a three-star general, Edward "Shy" Meyer, over the heads of all serving four stars, including Vessey, to the job. He then offered Vessey the position of vice chief, certain that Vessey would retire. But Vessey served in the position proudly and was President Ronald Reagan's first choice to be chairman of the Joint Chiefs of Staff after he defeated Carter in 1980. In many ways Jack Vessey was truly a soldier's soldier.

What was involved in continuing the American ground force presence in South Korea? More than just the deterrent factor, although those on the ground know how important that is. Having U.S. forces on site also meant a sharing of doctrine, tactics, intelligence, improved weapons, fire support, communications, military systems, and technological transfer. The tech transfer element was important because struggling Korean companies were trying to move out of first-tier manufacturing, such as fertilizers, petrochemicals, and textiles into higher-end industries such as electronics, communications, and semiconductors. Being able to make parts for systems purchased from the United States had helped the U.S. defense industry, offset some acquisition costs, and improved Korean capabilities. Often U.S. industry could buy common parts made in Korea and reduce the price for all, including a savings for U.S. taxpayers.

For years South Korean industrialists, known as the chaebol, had been encouraged, supported, and secretly protected in their business ventures by the government in order to stimulate the economy. When Park Chung-hee assumed power in his 1961 coup d'état he was frustrated and impatient at the lack of economic growth. In his opinion, North Korea was prospering. This was a view shared by most observers and based on the fiction of the *juche* movement in which North Korea feigned independence and prosperity while its two communist sponsors—the Soviet Union and China—poured billions of dollars worth of aid and assistance into it. Meanwhile, despite a fairly steady stream of U.S. foreign assistance, South Korea seemed to languish.

The negative, almost contemptuous approach that American diplomats and officials took in response to suggestions of possible South Korean development had been echoed in a large part by President Syngman Rhee and his advisors, who thought like Americans, in many respects due to decades of expatriate life in the States. Park rejected the view that South Korea must remain forever the poor twin, the agricultural appendage of North Korea doomed to mere subsistence existence.[13] It was Park's vision that the South Korean economy would reach a developed stage under his tutelage. As a consequence he brought the chaebol family leaders into the planning and execution process, and involved the government in the economy in ways that Americans might consider conflicts of interest. Park would, for example, encourage a Korean company to bid on construction projects in Indonesia or the

---

13 Some of the American attitudes were classic in their error. In the 1960s there were three bridges across the Han River, the river upon which Seoul has been sited since the thirteenth century. Two were for vehicle and foot traffic, one was a railroad bridge. The South Koreans asked for assistance in constructing another bridge. U.S. embassy aid officials rejected the request, sniffing contemptuously that "Seoul will never in the foreseeable future require an additional bridge." At present there are at least eighteen bridges across the Han River, clogged with traffic, and the public is demanding new ones.

Persian Gulf region, assuring them that the government secretly backed their play. In other words, the Korean companies could not fail. As a result, during this time the chaebol seemed to exemplify the most dramatic, successful entrepreneurs in the world. South Korean businessmen were reputed to be consummate risk takers who always won.

The reputation hugely assisted Korea as it solicited around the world for foreign investment and joint-venture projects. Park even aggressively pursued industries from which the rest of the world shrank, such as shipbuilding and steel. Without a steel mill, Park hypothesized, a country could not call itself developed. So against all advice he pushed the Pohang Iron and Steel Company into creation and production. South Korea, the poor rice-farming country, now had a functioning, profitable steel mill that competed with the best in the world. But Park had wanted to develop the commercial, civil side of South Korean's economy first. He hoped to delay his defense industry development while he focused on commercial, export-oriented production.

The South Korean industrial giants, the chaebol—Hyundai ("modern" in English), Samsung (three stars), Daewoo (big group), Kumsong (gold star), Ssangyong (twin dragons), Kumho (gold house)—and other big guns, operated along with their silent partner, the Park government, on a simple, effective business model: (1) bring in raw materials, of which South Korea had none; (2) process the materials into finished products using cheap Korean labor; (3) export the final products to foreign customers who paid in hard currency; (4) use the hard currency to reinvest in production facilities; (5) expand into other fields; and (6) build, build, build! It was a sound plan but completely dependent on support from two internal constituencies: labor and the middle class. Korean labor had to remain willing to take a back seat in the growth process and the emerging middle class had to acquiesce to staying relatively poor. The government tried to give this unpleasant status some honor by promoting "belt-tightening" and "sacrifice-for-the-future" campaigns, but over time the slogans began to wear thin.

Unions in South Korea were tied to specific companies, not general industries. In other words, there was no equivalent to the American United Auto Workers Union, but each company automobile manufacturing plant had a union. This was a way of keeping labor diffused and decentralized. The labor movement and unionization, which were considered by the Park government to be undesirable organizations and hotbeds of possible communist influence, tried to stand up for the workers but were beaten down, often with clubs and tear gas rather than words. All of these issues were on the table in the late 1970s when South Korea, under the leadership of Park, was faced with a crisis of extraordinary proportions: how to survive and continue to prosper if the United States pulled out not only ground troops but also economic support and defense products. Nothing could be considered too far-fetched to be a possible destabilizing threat.

## Building the Defense Industries

Park and the South Koreans—and their supporters in the United States of whom there were many—tried in vain to convince Jimmy Carter to ease pressure on South Korea. Were we sliding down the road to a renewed Korean War because of a misplaced, unequal emphasis on human rights? What about human rights in North Korea? Many people were chastising the Carter administration because of his apparent unwillingness to tackle the egregious human rights violators and instead target only friends and allies. In Seoul there was a genuine, palpable fear in the air that in spite of all the hard work, belt-tightening, and international prestige, South Korea was being abandoned to its North Korean enemies by a fatuous, naïve president.

By that time I had begun class work at the Korean Army College, located on the picturesque southern coast in a cozy port city called Chinhae. I was the senior of three American students at the college. Our class, designated as Class 23, was scheduled to be a yearlong middle managers course. We had 185 Korean majors and lieutenant colonels attending and one officer from Taiwan. For years the South Koreans had sent officer students to the comparable U.S. program at Fort Leavenworth, Kansas. This was the first time the United States was reciprocating. It was a big step to have American students there. Our presence gave them great face for it demonstrated that their army had achieved true first-world status to attract American officer students. As the senior officer it turned out that I represented not only our tiny contingent but also the entire U.S. government. Every day it seemed as if each and every Korean officer classmate and half of the instructors and staff would find time to ask me "Why is the U.S. president pulling troops out of Korea?" The line was always delivered with the intensity of an accusation and the poignancy of a grievance. At the time I was a mere captain. What could I say other than such decisions were far above my pay grade? But for those of us on the ground with our Korean counterparts it was difficult to maintain an officer's code of loyalty to the commander in chief. Yet, despite our real sympathies, most of us tried to be loyal.

Those months at the Korean Army College were among the most difficult and challenging in my military career. We had eight solid hours of instruction daily, usually on a five-and-a-half-day week. All instruction and all training materials were in Korean. While I had just taken an "advanced language course" at Monterey and the instructors did their best (one was himself a former Korean army lieutenant colonel) I was woefully unprepared for the experience. I'm not certain that one can be prepared without devoting at least two years to intense language taught in a similar format as used at the school. This is impractical for American army students to give up so much time for a specialty. As a result we're simply tossed into the pond and told to swim. Or to sink. Naturally, the Koreans would not let us fail. Our presence was too important a prestige point for them to allow that to happen, so we were coached, prodded, and tutored. My brain typically fried early in the day from the intense concentration required to focus on the language coming from the platform instructors at machine-gun cadence. I'd then try to stay engaged—without much success. When I discussed these issues with the commandant of students, a dignified, elderly colonel, he simply waved his hand in dismissal with the dictum, "You must become a Korean officer!"

There were some amusing aspects to the grueling experience. Early in the game the commandant would seek me out almost daily and ask, "What percentage of language are you understanding?" It is a tough question because with me it was binary: I either got it or didn't. More often that not, the latter. I could see, however, that the commandant was serious and his seriousness made my sponsor, Major Lee, very nervous. If I screwed up it was Major Lee who was going to get reamed. So I decided that since "zero," which at that time was the truth, was too low I would instead settle for a modest answer of "10 percent." As the weeks wore on I found that the commandant had a steel-trap recall for what my last reported percentage had been. I had to show improvement without putting myself in too high a bracket, so I'd have reports of 15, 20, and 25 percent. As long as the number was higher the commandant nodded sagely, gave an approving glance to Major Lee, and walked away. After several weeks of the game, I, suffering from chronic smart-ass, began to report "33.25 percent," "36.83 percent," and other ridiculous numbers. The commandant never batted an eye but continued to take every report at face value. Major Lee caught on to my silly game, though, and told me to quit. Fortunately, in the latter part of the course we began to study maneuvering of units with extensive use of maps. At that point, I finally began to make some sense out of what was happening and almost enjoyed class.

But from the whole experience, as painful as it was on a daily basis, came a tie to the Korean military that lasted for years and still exists. On return trips to Korea I frequently meet former classmates and other friends who came out of those days. Many of them were to play a key role in the months and years that followed graduation. My relationship with them allowed me to access information of a kind and quality that was unavailable to other American officers. Commanders such as Generals Vessey and Wickham were quick to realize the value of such assets and frequently found themselves relying on the foreign area specialists for information that could not be garnered elsewhere. After graduation and return to work in Seoul with the newly activated Combined Forces Command, whenever a Korean officer would introduce me to a colleague he would always include the remark, "This officer was the first to graduate from our Army College." It was an unfailing door opener and relationship builder. Something that was to become critical as the days of tension mounted in South Korea.

By this time, without question, the pressure on President Park had reached near breaking point. In Seoul, Park made some strategic decisions. South Korea, he ordered, must immediately begin to develop its own basic defense industry base because it could no longer count on the support of the United States. Carter's equivocation, he explained, had been a revelation to him that despite formal treaty ties, shared history, and blood loyalties, an American president had the power to influence affairs on the Korean peninsula so adversely as to court national disaster. As president he could no longer ignore this situation and continue to trust naïvely in American constancy. That was a danger into which he could not in good conscience place his country. Park ordered his military and the chaebol to proceed without delay to build up a defense industry capability.

They selected a new industrial area in Changwon near Masan in the south to be the site. Changwon was about as far away as possible from North Korean interdiction for safety and yet close enough to road, port, rail, and air facilities to be practical. Upwards of fourteen villages were removed for site preparation. In typical Korean fashion the displaced villagers received womb-to-tomb compensation. Modern public housing replaced village housing. Villagers were paid directly for their lost land and in addition were given new housing, medical and education benefits, and scholarships for their children in the technical and engineering academies that were under construction. Villagers also had priority of employment in the new facilities once they began operation.

Because of where I lived and the kinds of assignments I had, I was able to watch the development of this special industrial area from ground breaking through construction and ultimately to manufacturing. First the presidential team ordered the ground to be surveyed and divided. Each chaebol was assigned its piece. Along with the land, each company received a mission. Each chaebol would deal exclusively and noncompetitively with its particular specialty sector. That way not all of them would cluster to one sector, fighting one another, to the neglect of the other sectors. Samsung, for example, with its background in electronics and high tech would enter the communications, radar, and aerospace field. Daewoo, which made heavy construction equipment, would begin to build light-armored vehicles and anti-aircraft weapons. Hyundai would make artillery cannon and a Korean tank. Everyone had a piece of the action and they all scrambled to find the engineering and production skills necessary to accomplish this mission.

## Helpful American Friends

There was under-the-table activity that few Americans are aware of associated with the South Korean defense industry buildup. At Park's reluctant decision to enter the defense industry field, uniformed military technical types from the Second Ministry in the South Korean Ministry of National Defense structure decided to look to their American counterparts for help. The word was spread throughout the South Korean military: approach Americans you can trust for assistance. Their goal was to secure as much technical knowledge as possible on American weapons systems. These systems were already in the South Korean inventory and would be a reasonable starting point for them to use to build their industry. Not surprisingly given the circumstances, most American officers were furious with the perceived indifference that the Carter administration showed to the South Koreans. Even more irritating was the knowledge that it would fall to the American military, whose advice Carter ignored, to clean up any mess he created. If there was a new shooting war the military would have to bleed and die to win it, not Jimmy Carter. Many of these U.S. officers had been shoulder to shoulder with the South Koreans in wars in Korea and in Vietnam and were not happy to see their friends abandoned.

American military services have extensive, comprehensive files of what they refer to as "technical data packages," or TDPs, that contain significant amounts of engineering and scientific information about a particular military system. The TDPs are intended to be used to make repairs or in some cases to tool parts that may be difficult to obtain in time of crisis. Hundreds if not thousands of TDPs were transferred, without authorization, from the U.S. services to the Koreans. Most of these TDP transfers happened at the Joint U.S. Military Assistance Group Korea and many, many others took place in Washington between the service representatives in the Pentagon and other facilities and the South Korean logistics mission based in Arlington, Virginia. Possession of these TDPs assisted the South Korean engineers immeasurably in their Blue House–mandated mission of reverse-engineering the defense systems for ultimate South Korean manufacture. Frankly, as one not completely in the know but watching a lot of this take place, it is amazing how quickly the South Korean military and industry were able to build facilities, translate and dissect the TDPs, learn from the actual pieces that they disassembled and analyzed, and begin production. I first visited the Changwon area when ground was being prepared for initial construction. A canal was underway to connect the complex with the ocean; rail lines were being graded and laid; and beautiful, wide boulevards (capable, incidentally, of landing and taking off transport aircraft in emergency) were being built. Over the years I continued to visit, each time impressed with the quantity and quality of the physical plants and the amazing progress made on the manufacturing side. One has to wonder what could have been done in the civilian sector if this much energy and resources had not been diverted to the defense industry.

One of the first products to be built by Daewoo was a Vulcan Air Defense System, an air defense weapon that was comprised of a Gatling gun, platform, and acquisition radar. This had been manufactured by GE Aerospace in its Burlington, Vermont, facility.

When the South Koreans were ready to test Daewoo's version of the Vulcan system they notified President Park who sent a Blue House delegation to view the formal test. Naturally, this was classified top secret. The last thing the South Koreans wanted was word of their activities to be made public. The test turned tragic as the gun system exploded, sending out fragments like shrapnel that killed several observers. It is a testament to the tenacity and determination of the South Koreans that they cleaned up the mess and went on with their mission.

Years later when I was employed by GE Aerospace our people estimated that the South Koreans had reverse-engineered the Vulcan Air Defense System quite successfully and had made more than 2,500 systems. One must ponder certain facts: had the South Koreans not felt so pressured by the threat of American abandonment, they would have not felt compelled to plunge into defense industries. The Vulcan system alone, if manufactured in the United States as opposed to South Korea, would have brought more than 400 million dollars into U.S. coffers with hundreds of associated jobs. Instead, by misguided pressure and confused foreign policy, the United States lost the sale, the jobs, and control of the product. This review of Park Chung-hee's decision and the South Korean move into the defense industry area is not intended to be a justification of reverse engineering, patent infringement, avoidance of royalty payments or the unauthorized release of technical data packages. Rather it is simply a commentary of the law of unexpected consequences. Before you do something you need to make certain you understand what forces you're putting in motion. The Carter people, by being myopic over a single issue, not only did nothing to improve the human rights climate but also upset many other apple carts along the way.

# CHAPTER 8

---

# Times of Uncertainty

By fall of 1979 I had graduated from the Korean Army College and become the special warfare officer for the newly formed Combined Forces Command in Seoul. This organization included Korean and American officers at all levels in an integrated command system. It was a quickly thrown together command designed to preserve a modicum of U.S. authority over ground forces in the event of a pull-out of the Second Infantry Division. Although the division remains, the CFC continues to function. In those days we were watching North Korea closely and formulating special operations war plans that would be enacted in time of crisis. Some of the plans were tested in exercises such as Foal Eagle, a successor to the special warfare field operation that had brought me to Korea in 1970. One instructive example was the Kunsan Raid, which became a legend in special operations circles. At midnight a USAF Combat Talon C-130 landed in total blackout conditions at Kunsan Air Base—an American fighter base near the Yellow Sea. No one in the control tower, including the exercise evaluator who knew the plane was scheduled to land, so much as heard the silenced black-bird touch down. It taxied to the end of the runway with props feathered. At the F-16 parking ramp the tailgate dropped and a combined force of U.S. and South Korean special operators raced to the aircraft, placed simulated explosives on the fighters and jumped back into the C-130. The Air Force personnel in the control tower watched in stunned shock when it roared away into the night while the simulators popped merrily on their precious fighters. It was a harsh lesson in vulnerability—a mission such as that one was well within the capacity of the North Korean commandos to execute. It embarrassed the Air Force but we had a larger mission: we were working our people hard and sharpening their skills for a war that we all hoped would never happen.

Meanwhile, on the political front, the presidency of Park Chung-hee was in its eighteenth year. As is the story with most authoritarian leaders his was a case of things done well versus things done poorly. On the economic side, even with a few recent glitches, it was on balance a strong case of things done well. The immediate perception of any traveler to South Korea was always "Wow! Has this place changed!" The phrase could have been on the welcoming sign at Kimpo Airport. In those days you could be absent a year or even less and still be surprised at the dramatic differences in infrastructure improvements, new construction, available food, proliferation of entertainment outlets, standards of dress, and number of automobiles on the roads. Certain things—such as a broad selection of consumer goods—were still in short supply but that was intentional scarcity. Absence of a wide variety of consumer goods did not reflect a soft economy but was national policy designed to be part of the countrywide "belt-tightening" move. Since most luxury consumer goods were imported—and the government's broad definition of "luxury" in those days might include toasters and small appliances as well as perfume, designer clothing, and jewelry—it was considered preferable to limit importation by imposition of extraordinarily high taxes. An imported automobile, for example, might carry a 200 percent import duty. This of course limited severely the availability of goods to the hungry emerging middle class but gave the status-conscious wealthy a way of flaunting their money.

More significantly, by 1979 real hunger was just about absent from South Korea. Petty street crime was now rare and casual prostitution a thing of the past. It was unusual to see a beggar on the streets. Some of this was a result of Park Chung-hee's anti-crime campaign but most of it reflected improved economic conditions. With the proliferation of growing businesses and entrepreneurial opportunities everywhere in the country, the population moved up from that terrible, lingering postwar period of hunger and deprivation.

By 1979 South Korea had strengthened many of the infrastructure weaknesses that were so familiar in my memory. A highway connected Seoul to Pusan. Paved roads were extending to all major cities and many smaller ones. The New Village Movement, or Sae Maul Movement, a favorite project of President Park, had poured money and science into the rural countryside. Improved wells and clean water were the most dramatic and life-saving measures. Along with this came replacement of traditional thatched roofs with tin ones. While not as picturesque as straw, the tin roofs were far more durable. Thatch has to be periodically replaced; tin lasts for years. Further, tin deprived rodents of a convenient living area near humans. "As big as cats," my team sergeant used to say of the legendary Korean rats. On an earlier Special Forces deployment we stayed in a country inn one night. After the evening meal the woman who ran the inn threw all the

leftover food scraps up on the roof for the rats to eat. Her explanation that it kept them from coming into the house looking for
food didn't convince me. All night long it sounded like a herd racing from one end of the roof to the other. I was happy to ruck up
and get back out into the uninhabited areas where we could sleep
on rat-free ground.

One of the most amazing and, to me, completely unexpected
benefits of the New Village Movement was a restructuring of the
old rice fields. For untold generations these fields had been laid
out in patterns that followed ancient boundaries, streams, roads,
and the like. They meandered, dikes twisting and curving like
an octopus's arms. Park brought in agricultural specialists who
assisted in re-laying the old fields into squares or rectangles. I was
later told by visiting U.S. agricultural scientists that this act alone
provided South Korea with 33 percent more arable land. What a
phenomenal stroke! To be able to add a third to the growing surface in a land-poor country was an amazing feat. Additionally,
the government, through the New Village Movement, provided
rice farmers with a mechanical tool—sort of a large tiller that a
man would walk behind, for the fields were not suitable for large
tractors—as a replacement for the traditional ox. (The farmers
even called it the "mechanical ox.") This device used minimal
amounts of fuel and freed farmers from the demands of growing
extra crops to feed animals. Although many farmers kept their
animals, the mechanical ox allowed a single farmer to work his
newly squared-off fields alone. Soon South Korea became self-
reliant in rice production. With fewer hands needed to work the
rice fields, farm laborers were free to move to the factory and
urban areas where new education and employment opportunities
awaited. Much of the benefit of the reform in the countryside was
to increase the ratio of how many people a single farmer could feed

in such a way as to alter the basic demographics of the country. As farms increased their productivity, far greater numbers of citizens became urban-oriented rather than rural-oriented.

Achieving self-sustaining levels of rice production gave South Korea a real as well as a psychological sense of independence. At least we won't starve, they could say. Meanwhile, continued agricultural reform saw the introduction of plastic-tent farming under which vegetables and fruit could be grown and the season extended by weeks on either end. By this manner farmers were able to harvest larger vegetable and fruit crops, thereby extracting a higher cash flow from limited acreage. In one stroke they improved their own standards of living and provided a greater variety of inexpensive, nutritious food to the general population. Among all of South Korea's remarkable accomplishments, its agricultural success is one of the most vital but often overlooked and underappreciated. These reforms—under an admittedly authoritarian ruler—stand in stark contrast to the corruption, abuse, inefficiency, and mass starvation by the two Kims in the "workers and farmers paradise" of North Korea. Same land, same people, different methods, different motivation—far different results.

General economic conditions had improved in South Korea to the point that citizens no longer feared catastrophe. Many were beginning to chafe under the restrictive import duties and the limited availability of consumer goods. A brisk black market existed that drew principally from U.S. military sources such as the Post Exchange and commissary stores. While some of the goods were sold by GIs looking for a quick profit, the majority of black market goods—large pallets of goods—simply disappeared from ports and warehouses courtesy of the universal lubricant: bribe money. It was always a surprise in those days to see how limited the range of choices was for the South Korean consumer despite a relatively high living standard compared to a place such as the Philippines, where the country was less visibly wealthy but had virtually unlimited choices of goods.

From an industrial standpoint South Korea had weaned itself from the economic umbilical cord of the United States and was busy exploring and developing new foreign markets. Not yet ready to challenge the United States and Europe in finished manufactured goods, Korea began to fill a niche in offering inexpensive labor for piece products that would be exported to those regions. Beginning simply with products such as textiles, low-end garments, athletic footwear, basic consumer electronics, and OEM products to Japanese and U.S. industry, the country had built a solid foundation upon which to expand.

As life improved the people reached up the hierarchy of needs scale and began to look for satisfaction at the political level. Since 1974 and the murder of his wife, Park Chung-hee had become evermore concerned about assassination. He was increasingly withdrawn from interaction with the people, and most of his information filtered through his security chief, Cha Chi-chol and his Korea Central Intelligence Agency chief and friend, Kim Jae-kyu. This phenomenon of gradual withdrawal from the everyday realities of living is a common symptom of an authoritarian leader who has remained too long at the helm. And as well as withdrawing from the public, Park was also instituting ever-tighter controls. He had imposed his own Constitution in 1972, although under pressure from the Carter administration, he liberalized a few of its provisions. As a gesture, he released more than 180 political prisoners, including opposition leader Kim Young-sam. Almost immediately, Kim Young-sam and other dissidents began to rally opposition to Park. Naturally, Park's reaction to opposition was repression and he turned to his police and military forces. Students, labor, and opposition party members nonetheless began to organize and participate in street demonstrations that grew rapidly in size and intensity.

Park and his government were under increasing pressure from the U.S. government to reform, but by this time the only real leverage the United States had to exert was the threat of withdrawal of U.S. forces. Correctly recognizing that the United States had more to lose than to gain by withdrawal—by late 1979 Jimmy Carter himself may have been the only person who failed to recognize and acknowledge this fact—it made effective pressure difficult. Nonetheless, Park was not eager to alienate his American allies and tried to walk a tightrope between increased toughness at home and promises of reform to foreign visitors. Many people in South Korea—both officials and the general public—were chafing under Park's increasingly strict rule and hoped for a way to transition peacefully to another political leader. At the same time the specter of a hostile, abusive North Korea hovered constantly. Assassination attempts, infiltrations, and subversion were at a high level and the Axe Murders and other atrocities were still fresh in people's minds. Nonetheless, the rising voice of popular opinion both in inner sanctums and on the streets called out for reform.

On the evening of October 26, 1979, a Friday, there was a dinner party at the Blue House, held in one of the small buildings scattered around the grounds that doubled as private dining rooms. Present at dinner were President Park Chung-hee, his security chief, Cha Chi-chol, his KCIA director, Kim Jae-kyu, and Kim Kae-won, a member of the Blue House secretariat, a brain trust of presidential advisors. Also attending were two women, a well-known model and an actress, who were there more for decoration than for substance. Both Park and Cha had been very critical of KCIA director Kim in the preceding months and weeks. Park was especially critical because he was an old classmate and friend of Kim and clearly expected better reporting on the internal opposition activities. The clash between Cha and Kim was entirely predictable as each jockeyed for power by positioning himself close to the president. Each tried to alienate the other in Park's eyes, playing the old zero-sum game of "what makes you look bad makes me look good by default." It is a familiar game to anyone who works in an organization—public, private, or nonprofit. Despite custom both Park and Cha railed against Kim Jae-kyu during dinner. Their conversation was increasingly acrimonious and accusatory. Kim, beside himself with anger, made a disparaging remark about Cha. Apparently Kim Jae-kyu was reaching a breaking point that no one perceived.

We will never know if he was mentally unstable, cracked under stress, or had some yet unformed grandiose scheme floating in his head. But Kim Jae-kyu excused himself, went to his nearby office, and returned with a pistol. On the way back to dinner Kim instructed his bodyguards to kill the presidential security guards—five were in an anteroom in the building—if they heard shots fired at the dinner. Minutes after returning, he pulled the pistol, shot Cha first, and then Park. Kim then had to get a new pistol since his had jammed. He used the second to finish the two men off. In the anteroom, his guards cut down the unsuspecting presidential guards before they could react.[14] Thus began a convoluted, murky series of events that followed the Park Chung-hee era.

---

[14] Neither of the women was harmed and they lived to testify to what happened that night. Nor was Kim Kae-won hurt, although he was later convicted of being complicit in the assassination.

## Aftermath of Assassination

By early Saturday morning on October 27, 1979, Park's death was still fairly close held. That day I was at Yongsan Army Base for their weekly 10K race. When I got there, my first thought was that today was my day because so few runners had shown up. A good friend then arrived with his wife, who was Korean, looking for me. She was weeping and said that reports from the Korean Broadcasting System radio station alluded to something tragic— an "accident" it was being reported—happening to the president. "Let's go find Gordon," she told her husband, David. "He'll know what is going on." Since I didn't know (I rarely listened to the news before a run—it was too distracting), I ran back home and called a friend, Jim Potratz, who was on the chief of station's staff at the embassy. Ominously, his wife said that Jim was at the office. Unusual for a Saturday morning. I dialed the number from memory and asked for him. "I was waiting for you to call," he said. "I can't talk about specifics. You know who I'm talking about, right? We are not sure what happened but he's dead. I've gotta go. We'll talk later. Take precautions."

The receiver was as dead as the president of South Korea. For those of us living there it was difficult to remember a South Korea that didn't include Park Chung-hee. What would happen now? We in the military were acutely aware of the security issues and the loathsome presence of a rapacious North Korea that would be itching for an excuse to attack. All they needed were some civil disturbances to give them the pretense to enter South Korea to "restore public order." If that happened we would be at war again. I told my family to pack: one hand-carry bag each and have passports ready to go in case of non-combatant evacuation. "Don't get a bag out for me," I said. "I'll be staying." So it went for the next several weeks. Three getaway bags, one each, packed and ready by the door, passports handy, and sufficient cash to carry them over for a few weeks. Fortunately, they were never used.

The weeks immediately following the assassination were dramatic, fraught with a gamut of emotional ups and downs—hope for the new government that seemed reform minded, concern that the army might stage another coup d'état, and real fear that the North Koreans might jump off. American forces went to a higher defense readiness status immediately upon learning of the death of the president, which was standard procedure in any emergency. We had seen it after the Axe Murders incident and in other times of tension. In North Korea Kim Il Sung made speeches welcoming the death of Park and calling for "liberation of the southern brethren," and espousing the glories of the "paradise on earth" that was North Korea. When nothing happened immediately, we relaxed a bit—but only a bit. The price of freedom is eternal vigilance. None of us were taking the North Koreans for granted.

## Capturing the Assassin

Every tale of political assassination seems to have its twists and turns. The assassination of Park Chung-hee is no exception. At the same time as the president's dinner party, the South Korean Army chief of staff, a four-star general by the name of Chung Seung-hwa, was also dining that night, but alone in yet another small meeting house on the Blue House grounds. The assassin, Kim Jae-kyu, reportedly had made arrangements to meet General Chung but never did so, either before or after he pulled the trigger on President Park. Upon hearing the firing, General Chung went to investigate but was blocked by KCIA guards from entering the other safe house. He was told that "number one"—a KCIA guard lifted a thumb straight up, the Korean sign for one—was dead. Fearing for his life and worried about possible internal turmoil,

Chung later said, he departed the Blue House grounds and went directly to army headquarters. His senior aide-de-camp, Colonel Hwang Won-tak, was addressing the retirement dinner of a sergeant major downtown and was not aware of events that had taken place at the Blue House.

The next day, KCIA assassin Kim Jae-kyu and his guards came calling on the minister of National Defense and his staff. The offices were in a relatively modern building adjacent to but not connected to the American Yongsan Compound. Kim had called ahead demanding a meeting, claiming that immediate action must be taken to prevent internal chaos and to thwart a possible North Korean attack. By now suspicion was already mounting against Kim. The generals and civilian leaders at the ministry worried that Kim might try to use his KCIA gunmen to kill or capture them or to force them to participate in a coup. When he arrived about mid-morning Kim was disheveled and appeared to be in a state of excitement. The generals had two goals: to keep Kim calm so that he didn't precipitate any irreversible action and, from a purely practical standpoint, to separate him from his deadly KCIA bodyguards. From the start the generals listened to his disconnected ramblings, nodded agreement, and assured him that he had their support. But, they noted, before they could act they must have approval from their senior officer. Kim therefore must meet with the chairman of the Joint Chiefs of Staff and personally explain his ideas. Kim Jae-kyu agreed but insisted that his bodyguards accompany him. The generals said that the chairman could not permit them in his office for security reasons but that they could stay outside in the anteroom where they could watch over Kim. Reluctantly he agreed.

As they walked Kim Jae-kyu through a circuitous route to the chairman's office there was time for specially trained security personnel to station themselves in rooms adjacent to the ante-room. Kim was then escorted into the chairman's office. When the door closed firmly behind him a silent signal loosed security personnel and military policemen with drawn weapons into the anteroom through several doors. The stunned KCIA guards, taken by surprise, were arrested quietly and confined. On signal to the chairman that the operation was successful, an aide pointed a weapon at Kim Jae-kyu and arrested him. The pistol with which he killed Park Chung-hee and Cha Chi-chol was taken from him at that time. With Kim Jae-kyu in irons the immediate fear of a KCIA-initiated coup was allayed. There was, however, still the problem of succession.

Under the Yushin Constitution that Park had imposed on the country the next step was for the vice-president Choi Kyu-ha to succeed. He was sworn in and assumed the mantle of president. Choi was a virtual unknown in South Korea, intentionally selected by Park for his anonymity, much as FDR had picked Harry Truman for the same reason. Surprisingly, in a more aggressive mode than most had anticipated, Choi decided that he would be president in behavior as well as in title. He picked a very democratic, reform-minded cabinet and appointed the first woman ever to a South Korean ministry, selecting the president of Ewha University to be his education minister. From early November until mid-December it appeared as if South Korea might be at the most desirable transition point, moving from an authoritarian regime to a full democracy. Unfortunately other, more ominous forces were at work plotting against this eventuality.

Many of us who were in Seoul in those days in late 1979 had great hopes for a new dawn in South Korean government. We watched with pleasant surprise as successor Choi Kyu-ha transformed himself into something more than a figurehead. There were many positive signs in those days that the transition to democracy might have paradoxically been accelerated by an act of violence—the assassination. Yet, other rumblings were afoot. Those of us who were trained Korean area specialists—Colonels Jim Young, Thomas "Reb" Sims, Bill McKinney, me, and a very few others—were watching the dynamics between two distinct and rival groups within the highest ranks of the South Korean army. The rivalry involved the most senior officers—who were commissioned prior to the Korean Military Academy graduating to a full four-year program—and those who were the first to graduate from the four-year program. To American officers, to whom region of origin and form of commission are less relevant than performance, the controversy seemed petty. But to the Korean officers these things had deep cultural value, and the clash was very real. Complicating an already confused situation was the existence of a core group of officers known colloquially as the "Taegu Seven Stars" who had been handpicked, some said by Park Chung-hee himself, to be the future leaders of the country. All of these officers were from the same four-year Academy class and all were from the same province as Park. Informal leader of the group was a young general officer named Chun Doo-hwan, who was thought to be unusually bright and extremely ambitious.

Chun had been associated with Park for years. He had assisted in the 1961 coup, and commanded the Capital Security Command forces in 1968 that intercepted the North Korean assassins during the Blue House raid. Chun was then appointed in spring of 1979 to head the Defense Security Command, a kind of intelligence watchdog unit that monitored the South Korean army. (The American military has nothing similar.) But the presence of DSC officers at all levels—but outside of the chain of command—who are charged with observing and informing on unit commanders, meant that the commander of the DSC had extraordinary power to spy on every South Korean military leader, even the most senior. Chun's appointment also reflected the degree of trust and confidence that President Park Chung-hee had in him. It was, to understate the obvious, a position that lent itself to abuse. Chun Doo-hwan was ambitious, of that there was never a doubt. He also displayed a Confucian loyalty toward his mentor, Park Chung-hee, even though the president was dead. It was a combination of desire for advancement, justice, and possibly revenge that drove Chun deeper and deeper into the murky political arena that proved so tempting to many South Korean officers in those unsettled times.

In North Korea, following the assassination of Park, Kim Il Sung called a Party meeting, denounced Park as a "traitor" and leader of "one half of our territory under the occupation of the U.S. imperialists and reactionaries, landlords, and capitalists." Kim went on to extol the virtues of the North Korean "socialist paradise" wherein its citizens enjoyed "a happy life to the full, without any worries about food, clothing, medical treatment, and education." (In some ways Kim was correct: if you are concerned about merely surviving possible arrest, imprisonment, torture, starvation, and death, then the more esoteric desires like education and retirement programs fade in importance.)

Meanwhile, we in South Korea continued to watch actions by North Korea closely. That they would seize on any pretext to intervene in South Korea was foremost on everyone's mind. Given the tenor of the times it was not out of line to wonder—as had the late President Park—about the constancy of the American government should a crisis erupt. The normal tension associated with watching your front was heightened by worrying about your back at the same time. Still, for the moment, North Korea seemed to be content to fulminate and wait. That suited us just fine. Nevertheless, the three packed bags stayed near the back door, ready for instant use.

## A Cold December Night

The popular rap on Korea is that the winters are extremely cold. Part of the cold winter myth arises from the frigid winter of the 1950–1951 war years. That may have been a century-plus record for cold, snow, and bitter weather. With photos of frozen Marines and GIs on the retreat from the Yalu burned into our collective memories, the idea of brutal cold may be permanently associated with Korea. Nonetheless, the winter of 1979–1980 started out exceptionally cold, too. About midway through the month of December a Siberian cold front drifted down and hovered over the region. The air was clear enough to pick the stars from the skies and felt thick enough to drink. A blanket of snow and frost crackled under boots when you walked about.

One odd phenomenon about nights such as those is the way sound behaves. Sometimes sounds that seem close by are really distant; it is difficult to tell. In the early predawn hours of December 12, 1979, I woke to a string of crackling, popping sounds. "What is it?" my wife asked. "Sounds like M-16s firing!" I replied, coming instantly awake. We had a small government-supplied house on the Yongsan Compound, located less than a good hand-grenade's throw from the quarters of the four-star commander in chief, General John Wickham. My first thought was that those North Korean ranger-commando units that we were so concerned about had infiltrated—possibly by parachute—into the compound and were trying to assassinate the Old Man. The shooting sounded like it could have been that close. By then it was possible to pick up the distinctive chatter of M-60 machine guns. What I did not hear was even more indicative: I did not hear the high-pitched *crack* of the AK-47 Kalashnikov, weapon of choice for the North Koreans. While trying to sort things out we moved the kids into a central hallway and put them on the floor. Should the house be fired upon the wooden walls would not stop a bullet, but most soldiers fire high in the night. Keeping the kids low would keep them out of the line of fire. So we hoped.

In minutes it was clear that the shooting was not coming from the neighborhood but from a few hundred meters away at a building just outside the Yongsan Compound. It was the South Korean Ministry of National Defense Headquarters, the equivalent to the U.S. Pentagon, although considerably smaller. The firing continued but seemed to diminish in volume. That was a good sign. I heard no hand grenades, mortars, or rocket-propelled grenade fire to indicate that the firefight was designed to restrict excess damage. And somehow the absence of the explosions associated with Viet Cong or North Vietnamese army attacks was oddly reassuring.

I picked up the phone to call friends who might have a clue to what was happening. Most lines were busy or simply didn't function properly. The antiquated switchboards were jammed. When I finally got through to a friend in the command bunker on the other side of the road from the quarters area, he cautioned me to stay in place. "We are not sure what's going on," he said, frustration and urgency in his voice. "Stay where you are so we know where to find you if we need you. Oh," he added, anticipating my next question, "It ain't the North Koreans." Then I knew. We were watching a coup d'état.

As soon as he was able, General John Wickham made his way to the command bunker. The Old Man was a physically small man, but a wire-tough paratrooper. He had the most intense blue eyes I've ever seen. Even when he was in a good mood—which honestly seemed to be most of the time—those eyes penetrated like laser beams. That night, however, General Wickham was decidedly *not* in a good mood. In battle, whether it is a massive confrontation such as the Normandy Invasion or a simple meeting engagement between two squads in the jungle, the one thing that every commander at every level yearns for is information. "What in the hell is going on out there?" is probably the most frequently used infantry expression in all the world's languages since the beginning of military time. The corollary of this burning requirement is that the higher one climbs up the military food chain the more one becomes accustomed to being well informed by staff, subordinate commanders, and the like. So that the absolute worst thing for a man of the command level and seniority of General Wickham to endure is to be a mushroom: kept in the dark and fed B.S. That was precisely the situation in which he found himself during that cold, dark night in Seoul as events swirled around him. There he sat in the middle of the command bunker that had been designed for him to fight the next war from and he could not influence events happening right outside the compound gate.

In the months that would follow, John Wickham described the events as a "rolling coup." It was clear that on the night of 12/12, as the Koreans referred to the incident, Chun Doo-hwan and his cohorts were simply beginning what would ultimately result in a takeover of the legitimate civilian government of Park's successor Choi Kyu-ha. Chun later offered apologies to Wickham and sent emissaries in explanation but Wickham had none of it. He was furious because he felt Chun had insulted him at several levels—professional, military honor, and as a representative of the United States. In his excellent account of the events of that night and the months that followed, *Korea on the Brink,* Wickham captured the anger, disappointment, and frustration of the senior American leaders in South Korea. "The lawless seizure of power has interrupted the political progress of recent weeks [following Park's assassination] and displays utter disregard for certain objectives we have been pursuing, to include development of a professional military which would abide by law, remain apolitical, and support the constitutional process." As a measure of his utter contempt for Chun and his colleagues Wickham referred to them in a report to Washington as "politicians in uniform." That's about as nasty as it can get from a professional soldier.

All the way up the ranks to President Jimmy Carter the anger and frustration over Chun's actions had severe repercussions. One of the first actions was cancellation of the annual Security Consultative Meeting, a defense minister to Secretary of Defense level meeting that took place in alternating venues, usually Honolulu and Seoul. The decision to cancel the meeting was made to show that things were not to be "business as usual." Everyone was reduced to walking a fine line of increasing frustration. No one wanted to seem to give approval to the rolling coup but neither did they want to convey too strong a message of non-support that might be misinterpreted by North Korea. It was an exceedingly difficult time for the ambassador, William Glysteen, for the generals in the field, and for those of us at the lower levels who were trying to maintain cordial, professional relationships with our South Korean counterparts. The anxiety and tension lasted for several months. The getaway bags were still packed and stacked by the door.

Much of the frustration expressed by John Wickham was shared by Ambassador Glysteen and others of us who continued to hope that South Korea could break out of the pattern of change of power by military coup. As the weeks and months passed and Chun slowly accreted power, each time sending a representative to General Wickham and the ambassador with typically weasel-worded letters of excuse and apology, the situation seemed to get further and further from a positive solution.

Chun was using as a justification for his actions on the night of 12/12 and following that the army chief of staff, General Chung Seung-hwa, who had been dining alone at one of the Blue House "safe houses" on the night in October when Park was assassinated, was complicit in the assassination. He cited his position as head of the Defense Security Command, saying that it was necessary that a "proper investigation" be carried out. One of his actions on that night of 12/12—in addition to seizing control of Army Headquarters and the Ministry of National Defense—was to arrest General Chung. As then Colonel Hwang Won-tak, who was senior aide to General Chung, tells the story, "a group of soldiers approached General Chung's quarters late at night. We had been alerted earlier that units were moving about the city in an odd manner. We were attempting to determine what was happening when this group of what appeared to be Special Forces approached. The officer in charge said that they were here to arrest General Chung. The junior aide, a major, who stood beside me, reached for his pistol and was shot several times but survived. It was a miracle that I was not struck." Fortunately for Colonel Hwang, his presence at a retirement ceremony for a sergeant major the night that Park was killed was sufficient to exonerate him from any of the conspiracy theories that were being bandied about and the subsequent investigations that ultimately found General Chung guilty.

Hwang Won-tak and I first met and became friends when he was told by the Chun faction that he had to leave the country or risk arrest. I was assigned to the military assistance group. We tried to have him accepted as a military student at the U.S. Army War College in Carlisle, Pennsylvania, but were unable to make

that happen. In desperation we cast about and constructed a typically Korean solution. If Hwang enrolled in a graduate MBA studies program that the University of Southern California conducted
on the Yongsan Compound, the Korean army would consider him
"enrolled in a foreign country's school" and therefore "no longer
physically present in Korea." Form was more important that substance. For the next two years Hwang and I were classmates, and
he bought the time needed for the Chun faction to cool off. After
graduation Chun Doo-hwan parked him far away from troops in
Taegu for a year until he decided to utilize Hwang's incredible in-
tellect and exceptional language skills. Hwang served as the first
Korean representative to the armistice commission and later as
national security advisor to President Kim Dae-jung and as South
Korean ambassador to Germany.

## Visitor from the Pentagon

At one point while all this was going on, early in 1980, the command was to be visited by Nicholas Platt, then deputy assistant
secretary of defense for East Asian affairs. A career foreign service officer, Platt worked for Michael Armacost at the Pentagon. I
had recently been reassigned to the Joint Military Assistance
Group in the capacity of plans and programs officer. Because of my
experience at the Korean Army College and as special operations
officer at the Combined Forces Command I was asked to assist
Colonel Thomas "Reb" Sims in his capacity as liaison officer at the
Ministry of National Defense. His was a highly sensitive job and
he was setting new competency standards in it. Reb had been putting together a dossier on Chun and his associates—the rest of the
living, active-duty Taegu Seven Stars and their supporters—for
our commanding general and to pass on to General Wickham and
Ambassador Glysteen. Our other friend and colleague, Colonel

Jim Young, was then the assistant army attaché at the embassy. Through our contacts, knowledge of Korea, and circles of friends we were able to collectively provide a stream of extraordinarily good information to General Wickham. He appreciated this since he was feeling increasingly isolated because of his deliberate but paradoxical policy of distancing himself from Chun. That, coupled with personal antipathy toward the man, had severely limited information flow from the Korean side. This was something, as noted previously, that commanders cannot tolerate. We were trying to make up for that.

Unfortunately, just before the Platt briefing was to take place, Reb's mother was taken ill. He immediately flew back to Texas to be at her side. I prepared to present my briefing and his also. As is the norm in any military organization we had a rehearsal. Our chief of staff, a navy captain, had me present the briefing to him prior to Platt's arrival. It was an involved briefing detailing Chun Doo-hwan's activities and those of his group, along with sensitivities that we had picked up from secret contacts in the Korean army. At this time it is critical to note, Chun still maintained that he had no political interests. John Wickham did not believe him for a moment, nor probably did William Glysteen. The ambassador, however, was a product of the cautious State Department system that was temperate in all things and reluctant to make a call, so he continually temporized in his messages back to Washington. I had my own analysis of the situation, which I included in the briefing. It focused on a single key point: if Chun in his capacity as Defense Security Commander retains this position and adds the position of head of the Korean Central Intelligence Agency that would be a firm indicator that he intended to finish the rolling coup by taking over the government entirely. "First he will lock up both the military and civilian intelligence functions," I said, "then he will make a move on the government because no one will be in a position to hinder him." By owning all of the internal intelligence, his people would be able to sniff out and suppress any opposition. To me it was plain: first the KCIA then the presidency. When I presented this to the navy captain he commented, "That is exactly the kind of briefing that we ought to give to a deputy assistant secretary of defense."

When Deputy Assistant Secretary Platt arrived for his briefing that winter morning, he must have already been having a bad day. Whatever the reason, he seemed very impatient and waspish. I was less than three minutes into a fifteen-minute presentation, still a long way from the key point, when he interrupted, harrumphing, "this sort of thing is my daily fare." Platt then asked one or two perfunctory questions, terminated the briefing, and left. As bad as I felt for myself—I was mortified—and for the embarrassment my failure caused for the army general who ran the military assistance group, a fine, supportive officer Major General Orlando Gonzales, I was incredibly frustrated that we were unable to make what I thought was a critical point with the one man in Washington who was focused exclusively on Korea. Later Platt's escort officer, a lieutenant colonel friend of mine, reported back that as they drove away Platt murmured, "I shouldn't have cut off that major." But he did and there was no way to make up for the omission.

Within six weeks after the Platt debacle Chun Doo-hwan announced that he was taking over the post of director of the KCIA in addition to his Defense Security Command responsibilities. Long before summer he had consolidated power, declared martial law, and taken up occupancy in the Blue House as the new South Korean president. Word back from the Pentagon was that the move took them by surprise.

## Revolt in the Southwest

The Cholla provinces in southwestern Korea were part of the old Paekjae kingdom of ancient times. Long ago the rivalry with the state to the east, Shilla, had been intense, often peaking in warfare. The Shilla kingdom was just about contiguous with the present-day Kyongsang provinces. Even though the names of the places have changed in modern times, the ancient animosities persist. Park Chung-hee and Chun Doo-hwan, along with his cohorts, were all from Kyongsang. One of the major opposition party leaders during the Park era was a man named Kim Dae-jung. He was from Cholla. He had been arrested, beaten, imprisoned, kidnapped from Japan, and saved from summary execution at sea only by firm intervention of the U.S. authorities. The animosity and rivalry between them reflected both the ancient feuds and modern suspicions. Immediately after the assassination of Park, his vice president, Choi, who assumed leadership, in a gesture of magnanimity and reform, nevertheless released many political prisoners, including Kim Dae-jung.

Because it had been Chun who initiated the 12/12 incident and the rolling coup, dissatisfaction among the South Korean people grew increasingly intense, led by the most visible opposition leaders, especially in the Cholla area by Kim Dae-jung. Chun, along with others who supported Park, looked at many in the opposition, particularly Kim Dae-jung, as having pro-communist, pro-North Korean leanings and distrusted and disliked them for it. Kim had been in exile in western Japan among the disaffected Korean elements there whose loyalties to Kim Il Sung and North Korea were well known. Military leaders are typically very conservative; they prefer to err on the side of caution, not risk. Consequently they will automatically oppose anyone who threatens what they see as good order. Professional dissidents such as

Kim Dae-jung have a deep-seated antipathy for the military that they see as an institution dedicated to the suppression of freedom and human rights. The Park assassination of October 1979 set these two factions on a collision course.

Protests in the streets of the nation grew increasingly vocal and violent, especially in the Cholla provinces and its provincial capital of Kwangju, in particular. The almost nonstop sequence of street demonstrations, protests, strikes, and open slugfests made the American command extremely jittery. Every eye turned to North Korea. Would it intervene under the ruse of "restoring order to our oppressed southern brethren?" It was the usual Kim Il Sung rhetoric but it could not be lightly dismissed. Equally worrisome was the increasingly intense reaction of Chun and his people to the disturbances. In the city of Kwangju, in May 1980, the situation finally boiled over. Local protestors outside a major university reported that regular army Special Forces soldiers "speaking in Kyongsang accents" had confronted them. The gasoline of the ancient rivalry met the spark of present-day agitation. Within minutes the situation got out of hand as the soldiers sent to defuse the demonstration lost control and attacked civilians on the street. It had been problematic just how long soldiers like the Special Forces—independent-minded, action-oriented, and tough—would put up with the barrage of punches, rock-throwing, Molotov cocktails, name-calling, and attacks from the crowd. Retrospectively neither side had clean hands in the affair, although each, predictably, protested its innocence.

Within days the situation had turned into a full-blown revolt. Armed citizens had seized military weapons and vehicles. Firing was common in the streets. Everywhere in the city bodies lay strewn about as if blown there by an ill wind. Chun declared martial law and threw a cordon around Kwangju. The American authorities were totally in the dark, hearing only snippets from the American Peace Corps volunteers who had been trapped there, many of whom had performed with remarkable selflessness and bravery. As the situation grew hotter Chun had military units brought in to control the situation. One unit was a South Korean army division that was posted in the Demilitarized Zone. It had belonged to Chun and was personally loyal to him. When the division was alerted the duty officer called the command bunker in Yongsan and told the duty officer there—an American field-grade officer—that the unit was being repositioned. The American said "approved" and noted the movement in his official log along with his comment.[15]

From this seemingly innocuous event a huge misunderstanding has sprung up about American involvement in what came to be known as the "Kwangju Incident." Some of the confusion is legitimate, and involves people who have not been exposed to what may seem like arcane command and control structures but are in fact serious procedural matters that must be observed scrupulously. Most South Koreans think that the U.S. commanding general in Seoul has operational control over South Korean forces. If that is the case, they reason, then the Americans could have withheld approval and forbidden the division to move to Kwangju. By not exercising that

---

[15] Years later when I spoke with General Bill Livesey about the incident he commented on the unfortunate choice of words that the duty officer entered in the log that night. "We didn't have approval or disapproval authority," Livesey noted in his tight Georgia twang. "But the duty officer was rattled. No one was expecting to receive that kind of call. He knew he couldn't deny the South Koreans the right to move their own units, so he wrote 'approved' because he didn't know what else to write. He would have been much better off—and so would we over the years—if he had simply written 'noted' in the log. That would have shown that the Korean unit movement was appropriately notified to the Combined Forces Command but removes any notion of collusion or cooperation from the act. Ain't hindsight always great?"

control the American then gave overt or, at a minimum, tacit approval to Chun's brutal repression of the uprising.

Other observers fully understand the issues but feign ignorance for political reasons. There are those on the Chun side who pretend that the Americans *did* grant them permission to move the division hoping to dilute the blame for the excesses of Kwangju. On the disloyal opposition side, career politicians such as Kim Dae-jung listen to the explanation, ask questions, and then go out and tell the press what serves them best.

Most Korean people would be absolutely shocked if they knew just how little control General John Wickham—or any American commander—has over South Korean military units in peacetime. He had no control during the Kwangju Incident. They would be even more stunned if they found out how little Wickham and the Americans knew about what was actually taking place in Kwangju during this time. When the Chun forces threw up a cordon around the city it blocked all normal lines of communications. Telephones were down, amateur radios were nonexistent, and travelers were carefully screened before they were permitted to pass through the military cordon. Obviously, journalists were forbidden to enter the area under threat of arrest. The time had long past when American officers accompanied South Korean tactical units, so even that avenue was closed. I was asked to come to the defense attaché's office at the embassy one morning right after the revolt started in Kwangju. There, Colonel Don Blottie, the defense attaché, met and briefed me on what we knew about Kwangju. It was precious little. Blottie was a fine officer with a keen mind and although he was highly competent, he was not a Korea specialist. As a consequence he did not have the personal relationship contacts that take years to develop. Jim Young on his staff had those contacts. Blottie had Jim out fishing for information. Blottie got in touch with me directly, although he knew that I worked for the advisory group. Blottie was aware that the chief of staff had expressly forbidden members of the advisory group to speak to anyone outside of the organization about information that we picked up from the Koreans. He had the infantile idea that the Koreans would actually tell us something in confidence that they would not tell other Americans or even other Koreans simply because we were in the advisory group.

I had tried in vain to explain that what we were hearing from our Korean friends and counterparts were not confidences but messages that they brought to us with the express purpose of having us relay them to proper American officials. The chief of staff, a navy captain, may have had some skill steering a ship but he was totally at sea when it came to working with the South Korean military. I was being approached on almost a daily basis since 12/12 by former classmates from the Army College and others who knew me with messages that they had been instructed to bring from their superiors. On several occasions the officer actually sat across from me and read from a script! When I pleaded with the chief of staff that it was vital that I be authorized to communicate this information up the chain of command—some of the messages were from general officers at the Ministry of National Defense at the two- or three-star level—he warned that he would place me under disciplinary action if I did.

Colonel Don Blottie was aware of these restrictions. He was also under intense pressure from the ambassador and the commanding general to open every line of communication possible. As a consequence we began to have regular tennis matches at Blottie's invitation at the embassy tennis courts located at Compound Two near the embassy. It became my cover to pass information to him without arousing navy suspicions. Later, when the situation got too urgent to wait on phony tennis matches I would call Blottie. If he signaled that the coast was clear—the navy captain lived near to his quarters—I would drive after dark to a spot several blocks away, hide the car, and walk to Blottie's quarters to report.

At one point I'm convinced there were only two or three solid lines of communication coming up from Kwangju to the Americans. My most reliable source was a former student of mine at the Korean Military Academy, a very brave and dedicated individual, much more characteristic of the current and future crop of South Korean officers than of his predecessors who came up in time of political intrigue. He was a newly minted second lieutenant of infantry undergoing branch specialty training at the combat arms training center near Kwangju when the insurrection broke out. He and I were periodically in touch. He phoned and said that he needed to speak with me. That began a gutsy sequence that he maintained for several weeks. The officer students were fully aware of what was happening in Kwangju because the troops were using their training facilities as a base. They spoke with other officers and the troops. On occasion they ventured into Kwangju with a few of the patrols. For a while it was a real combat zone.

My former student would use Sunday, his one day a week off, and depart from Kwangju area on the earliest express bus on Sunday morning. He would come to Seoul, brief me, rush back to the bus terminal and return in time for evening curfew. It had to be an exhausting, boring trip but he thought it was his duty to let the outside world know what was happening. Years later we discussed the possibility of the military becoming involved with politics. "Those days are over!" he said emphatically. "No one in my class or younger would ever support such activities again. We are committed to democracy."

It was in this tenuous, back-door manner that General Wickham was receiving only bits and pieces of information from the running firefight that was Kwangju. Far from being the puppet masters in the Kwangju Incident, the U.S. forces from the top general and ambassador on down were almost completely in the dark about affairs there. Why did the United States not take a more aggressive role to depose Chun or to punish him? As Ambassador Glysteen said, "we are not colonial masters." It was not the business of the United States to interfere to that degree in South Korea. We saw the security issue—the North Korean threat—as the overwhelming area of our responsibility. It is always a tempting tightrope to walk to meddle in other's internal affairs. As we saw happen in South Vietnam that can and usually does lead to tragic consequences. Guide, advise, assist, and set an example, all those are good tactics for the United States to follow with our friends. But it is wrong to interfere strongly. Those South Koreans who blame the Americans for allowing Chun to continue in power would be more justified in criticizing the Unites States if it had come in and forcibly removed him. Kwangju at last was restored to peace but the bitterness and confusion over the incident remains.

## Defense Industry Growth

During the period of the early 1980s South Korea—at U.S. urging—devoted at least 6 percent of its gross national product to defense. At this time the defense industries that the late President Park had set in place were beginning to crank out products that were moved directly into the South Korean army inventory. As this process continued and expanded another of the "law of unintended consequences" gremlins struck. As long as the South Korean military had been largely cooperating with and dependent on the United States as a primary supplier for defense products, such things as interoperability were not a major concern. Now that South Korea was going further in the direction of equipment of its own design and manufacture, planners began to have serious concerns about common logistics stores, supplies in time of war, and the ability to communicate successfully between different systems. As higher and higher technology was incorporated into increasingly sophisticated defense systems these issues became critical.

Another consequence of pushing the South Koreans onto an independent path was that they no longer felt obligated to take U.S. advice. Heretofore one of the most influential American military officers in South Korea had been the chief of the military assistance group. By the mid-1980s that organization bordered on the anachronistic. The position of chief was downgraded from a major general's position to a full colonel's and the organization focused increasingly on arranging training in the United States for Korean officers and NCOs who were participants in the American international military education and training program. One of the major levers and persuasive tools with the South Korean military had been casually cast off by forcing them to go their own way in the defense industry.

A healthy byproduct of increased defense spending and awareness by South Korea was a slow improvement in capabilities so that some time in this period South Korea crossed the point where it no longer could have been defeated on the battlefield by North Korea. It would still be years before this was realized by all concerned but from hindsight it is now clear to see that the curves crossed about 1985. From that time forward South Korea was a leader in the region in every area. Hand in glove with the improved defense capabilities was a sharp economic upswing that made South Korea a role model for developing countries. But that was yet to happen. We had to get there first.

In spring 1981 a Security Consultative Meeting was held in San Francisco—the first called by the Reagan administration and the "make-up" date for the 1980 meeting cancelled in pique by the Carter folks. I was an action officer representing the military assistance group. This was one of those rare bilateral meetings where both sides want to paint the best face on things. Over the weeks prepping for the event and the intense three days of the meeting itself we met frequently with our Korean counterparts to work out many details. One of the quirks of a Confucian-based culture such as South Korea's is that their ideal meeting—business or government—is a meeting in which all the details are worked out well prior to the actual moment that the principals come together. At that final, glorious meeting of the bosses everything is supposed to go smoothly, in a nonconfrontational, harmonious manner. Unusual for Americans, Secretary of Defense Caspar Weinberger seemed to understand and appreciate this philosophy.

Weinberger was unlike many American heavy hitters who say, "have something substantive for me to do at the meeting. I don't want to just sit there and chat and smile. I want to do something!" They fail to realize that the most productive thing that they *can* do is to chat, smile, and build a relationship. Weinberger grasped this. He was comfortable pushing issues down the food chain for the staff to resolve. This is exactly the way Koreans address potentially confrontational issues in order to keep them from becoming "face-loss" issues. Accordingly, things worked smoothly. At the eleventh hour of the last day we were down to the short strokes in what had been a very positive meeting.

The venue at the Presidio of San Francisco was awe-inspiring with its views of the glorious, ever-changing San Francisco Bay, the Golden Gate, and that triumph of American civil engineering, the bridge across the mouth of the bay. I could not help looking out into that space and recalling that day when Dad, Mom, and I sailed under the awesome bridge returning from Asia. Dad, if you could only see it now, I thought, the Korea that you helped preserve and defend. How proud you would be of those people! Every morning I drove a rented Chrysler K-car through the back gate of the Presidio with a couple of fellow officers. The scent of the eucalyptus trees was so invigorating and uplifting that everyone just knew that we were going to make the day a success.

By the last evening of the last day the only remaining sticking point was some language on the ever-important joint communiqué. Now drafts of the joint communiqué had been worked for weeks prior. But that final night we were caught in a good news-bad news situation. The good news was that the atmospherics had been so positive at the meeting that the principals wanted stronger language than was present in the original draft. The bad news was that we had no time to pull off the final coordination. We were pleased at the success but daunted by coordinating language not only among each country's representatives but then also across Korean-English language lines. By about ten o'clock that evening everything was cleared except for a particular supportive phrase. The Americans had balked at something presented by the Koreans. We seemed at an impasse. Mid-level staffers were growing restless. The Secretary was flying back to Washington later that night. This language had to be fully cleared before then or the success we enjoyed would be dampened. For reasons I still do not understand the paper ended up in my hands—and I was probably the junior staffer there (perhaps that is exactly why). It occurred to me through the fog of a long three days and a desire to have dinner and a glass of fine California wine—we had worked straight through—that I was the only one in the group who spoke Korean. We had been depending on a translation of the Korean language into English by the South Korean staffers, our counterparts. Some of them were facile but not fluent English speakers. "Let me see the original document in Korean," I said. Someone ran across the street to the Fairmont Hotel to get a copy. After examining both documents side by side, I was able to tweak the respective languages to get what I thought were the results each side hoped for. Then we ran the side-by-side translation past my Korean counterpart for approval. Within an hour the paper was vetted by respective bosses and we were released. My chief, Major General Gonzales, read the final communiqué, put his hand on my shoulder and said, "Bless you, Gordon." I was a bit shocked to discover the depth and intensity of his concern for his mission: support and improve the defense capability of South Korea.

Back in Seoul, General Wickham was as happy with the outcome of the Security Consultative Meeting as General Gonzales had been. Wickham insisted on pinning a staff medal on me and several others who had made the meeting successful. While in San Francisco I had been asked if I would like to come to Washington to work in the Office of the Secretary of Defense. At the ceremony I asked General Wickham about choices. An infantry division assignment or Washington? He thought for a moment, intense eyes never leaving mine. "Go to the Pentagon," he ordered. A day later his assistant, Colonel David Lynch, sent me a copy of the backchannel message the general had sent to my future boss, Eric von Marbod. It was a strong enough recommendation to get a middle of the night phone call from the capital. My pal from Washington Chuck Jameson was elated. "Von Marbod is shaking the army assignment system to have you here," he reported. Within a week or two it was all settled. We packed to move from Seoul. This would be our nineteenth household move in sixteen years. It had undeniably been four exciting years in South Korea: first American to graduate from the Korean Army College, charter member of the Combined Forces Command, special operations officer, military assistance officer, and a job offer from the Pentagon. Present for the assassination of Park Chung-hee, the rolling coup, the Kwangju Incident, running my first marathon, the Security Consultative Meeting, and a full plate of North Korean terror threats. What ex-Green Beret could ask for more than that? It was a time of crisis and uncertainty for South Korea but had been a valuable learning experience for me. I left with mixed regret and anticipation: I hated to miss the excitement and would miss my friends, but the new adventure of a Pentagon assignment lay ahead.

# CHAPTER 9

# Democracy Blossoms in the South

For the next six years I followed Korean events from Washington, D.C., first from the Pentagon where I worked security assistance programs in the Defense Security Assistance Agency, part of the cluster surrounding the Secretary of Defense. Later, I had been recommended for the Marshall State-Defense Exchange, a program whereby eighteen uniformed officers of all services go to the State Department for a tour of duty and eighteen foreign service officers come to Defense. We would be working at the policy level, and I was excited in the spring of 1984 when I reported in to be the political-military advisor to the assistant secretary for East Asia Pacific affairs. It was a time of increasing global stress and Asia was no exception. Ambassador to South Korea Richard "Dixie" Walker was followed by James Lilley. Both men were in Seoul accomplishing the delicate work of dealing with the military regime, constantly keeping a balance of promoting U.S. interests in moving toward democracy while making certain that the security situation was given adequate attention. The

parallel American military leadership that supported the ambassadors was uniformly excellent. Nevertheless, Chun Doo-
hwan, now president, continued to present problems. He was
tough on internal dissent and had a general's reluctance to release authority. Despite these faults, the government of South
Korea was able to win award of the 1988 Summer Olympic
Games to Seoul. It was a marvelous catch and would lead to
changes within Korea and with Korea's relationship to the
world. But those changes were yet to come—as with any triumph, first there must be a trial. North Korea issued hysterical
threats to sabotage the Olympic Games unless ridiculous concessions were made. And South Korea was heating internally to
the boiling point.

Chun Doo-hwan led the country with a sterner hand than
even Park had used, but with poorer results. By summer of 1987
the shine was definitely off the penny. Any affection, loyalty, or
trust the people may have had in Chun was gone. Student
demonstrations against Chun had been a regular event since the
early 1980s. One of the professors at the prestigious Seoul
National University stood on a balcony on campus one April and
drew a deep breath. "Ah," he said, "the smell of tear gas. It's a
sign that spring is truly here." As long as the demonstrations
stayed on campus they were tolerated. It was almost like a
Japanese kabuki theater where the same play runs for hundreds of years and everyone knows the plot, the outcome, and
even individual lines. Demonstrations would usually be scheduled to start no earlier than midday. (No need for the college students who may have been out late the previous night to rise
early.) Bored police waited nearby in large, olive-green diesel
buses with metal mesh screens to protect windows from a stray
rock. The policemen would be alerted to suit up. When they put

on their gear the riot police looked like major league catchers gone *Star Wars.* "Darth Vader outfits," the expatriates called them. But when the special riot control policemen removed their black helmets they looked just like the kids who would appear with white headbands throwing rocks and Molotov cocktails. Indeed, many of these men had been students the year before and may have demonstrated themselves. But now roles were reversed because they were performing their national service duties. Every young South Korean man has to make the choice of military branch or risk being conscripted. As a sweetener, if a young man volunteered for the Korean Marine Corps or the national police he got six months chopped off his three-year enlistment. But the Marine Corps doesn't give those six months because it is easy duty; sooner or later the kids have to pay for it. That time can come when a campus begins to erupt and the police stand shoulder to shoulder behind transparent visors and body shields. With little warning, student demonstrators race toward police ranks and pummel them with everything that can be thrown—rocks, bricks, paving stones, and Molotov cocktails. Police restrain themselves and take the punishment. Occasionally, if demonstrators are trying to move somewhere off campus, the police will form a blocking line. At those times hand-to-hand combat becomes common. Demonstrators kick, punch, and club the police. The police reciprocate. A heavy shower of tear gas is the typical signal that police patience is at an end. Usually certain unspoken rules are enforced, however. People get beat up but the idea is that no one gets really hurt. Yet sadly, the rules were not always followed. In 1987 demonstrators in Pusan intentionally lured police into the upper floors of a house that they had soaked in gasoline. As the demonstrators escaped out the back they set fire to the building. Several policemen were horribly burned to death. The nation was shocked. Public reproach against the demonstrators was strong and for many months demonstrations stopped. Murder was a line the Korean people thought ought not to have been crossed.

Korean people were not the only ones exasperated with students. Foreign expatriates, especially military or businesspeople, had a short fuse with the demonstrators. For the military it probably brought back memories of the anti-war demonstrations of the Vietnam era. For the businesspeople, demonstrations block traffic and are filmed in a particular way by cable news so that it gives the wrong impression. To viewers who see only the news film, it looks as if the entire country is rioting and in flames. This overemphasis on civil disturbances makes businesses reluctant to invest in South Korea because they fear the stability of the government and the financial systems. On the other hand, in that hot summer of 1987, students, laborers, and the general public had a legitimate cause. They wanted to bring about the end of authoritarian military rule and transition to full democracy. This time the students left their campuses and took most of the country with them. Each day demonstrations, frequently turning to mini-riots, took place in the center of Seoul. The country was getting hot enough for the lid to blow.

I could tell how tense it was because I was back in Korea, on the streets, gagging on the tear gas. It was a different feeling. For the first time in twenty years I did not have a uniform hanging in my closet. With mixed emotions I had left the military, accepting an offer from GE Aerospace to open an office for them in Seoul. I took temporary lodging at the Westin Chosun Hotel, a modern structure that was built on the site of the original Chosun Hotel, a national landmark with a fascinating history. My office was on the other side of City Hall, now dominated by a giant Olympic countdown clock, within easy walking distance from the hotel. Every afternoon I dodged through ranks of riot police who would look up with frank curiosity at the odd foreigner passing by with suit and briefcase while they licked their wounds, repaired their equipment, and prepared to face the crowds yet again. Demonstrators, either cheerful citizens on a lark, or more threatening wild-eyed students on crusade, could appear at any turn in the road or from any alley or subway station. They were not threatening but they tended to be magnets for tear gas, pepper spray, and fire trucks. I lost at least a couple of pairs of shoes to soakings in the ubiquitous puddles of water from fire hoses or terminal scuffings on debris fields of broken paving stones, rocks, bottles, glass, and assorted crockery that marked every demonstration site like the high-water mark of an obnoxious flood. Throughout the transit I learned to hold a handkerchief—preferably damp—to my face to ameliorate the effects of the tear gas. Yet, it was strangely exciting and a lot of fun. Legions of reporters and photographers covered Seoul. The Westin was an important hangout for them since it was close to everything happening and had good communications facilities and an excellent bar. These men and women of the press were better prepared than I—each one had acquired a personal gas mask. But the stuff got into everything, including hair and clothes. After running the daily gauntlet I couldn't wait to get upstairs to shower and change, but the newsies reveled in the stink and stench of battle. The lobby so reeked of gas from their clothes that the hotel staff ran around bleary-eyed.

But despite the obvious civil unrest, the summer of 1987 was somehow different than previous years and other demonstrations. It seemed to me that the South Korean people had made an attitudinal transition. They had passed a significant milestone in their bumpy road to democracy. It was as if they were for the first time so confident in their physical security vis-à-vis North Korea that they were no longer willing to trade open, participatory government for security under an authoritarian ruler. The public sophistication level had risen dramatically. South Koreans were a bit embarrassed at the succession of coups d'état and authoritarian rulers that marked their postwar history. They were tired of the endless belt-tightening campaign, a controlled economy, and what they perceived as too great a gap between the ultra rich and the emerging middle class. It was a fairly common sight at demonstrations, especially as they turned into the public riot scene, to see many young men who looked more like thugs and criminals than like students. This was because they *were* thugs and criminals and looked at the demonstrations as excellent opportunities to hurt the hated police and get some positive credit for it. But in summer of 1987 many of the people on the streets were salary men, workingmen and women, clerks, laborers, and professionals. It was a popular uprising, a widespread demand for a change of systems that transcended class, profession, and region.

Chun Doo-hwan faced a dilemma. The constant demonstrations and public unrest were staining South Korea's world image. Each demonstration-turned-riot gave North Korea an opening to protest the location of the Olympics and try to muster world opinion against Seoul. Already there were some quiet rumblings about including North Korea in the Games or relocating. A loss of the Games would be an unacceptable set back for South Korea. Chun was stymied. If he got tough and really cracked down on the demonstrations he risked further world approbation and the real possibility of losing the Olympics. If he stepped down voluntarily the demonstrations would stop. But did he want to give up power?

Could he risk it? After extensive consultation with many advisors, including his military academy classmate and confidant Roh Tae-woo, Chun chose to step down and turn affairs over to Roh. Contrary to what political opponents predicted would simply be a reprise of authoritarian military rule, Roh almost immediately called for free elections to be held just weeks away in the fall of 1987. Suddenly democracy began to bloom in South Korea. The country rejoiced; the Olympic Games were secure. Almost immediately investigations of Chun's activities were initiated. Several presidential candidates were announced, including previously jailed dissidents. Vocal opposition leaders raised their voices in harsh criticism of past policies and demanded a chance to participate in the political process. It was an amazing but incredibly rewarding sight for those of us who had followed Korean affairs for so many years to see men like Kim Young-sam, who had been imprisoned for his opposition, and his political opponent, rival opposition leader Kim Dae-jung, who at one time had been kidnapped from Japan by Park Chung-hee's KCIA and marked for death, now rise up to participate in an increasingly open political process. The campaign and election brought observers from around the world to South Korea including political satirist P. J. O'Rourke, whose essay "Seoul Brothers," contained in *Holidays in Hell,* captured the flavor of the times—heavily seasoned with ubiquitous pepper gas—with outrageous humor and surprising empathy for the Korean people.

At the October election South Korean voters conservatively chose stability over radical rhetoric. They overwhelmingly brought Roh Tae-woo—legitimately this time—into power for a constitutionally limited, single five-year term. He was the last of the general-presidents and the first elected in a relatively free, open election. It marked the first of several peaceful transitions of power, and the first in modern times in which the people had a major voice and had serious choices. Oddly, over the next two elections his opponents, Kim Young-sam and Kim Dae-jung would follow him in that order. It was a triumph for democracy. A delayed triumph, but a triumph nevertheless.

Very few of us old Korea hands would ever have thought that Seoul would host an Olympic games. We might not have laughed outright at the suggestion—most are far too polite to do that—but we would have chuckled to ourselves. Despite odds against it and some of the worst conditions for athletic events in August, the award was granted and Seoul came out the winner. As an old Korea hand myself I was too discreet to inquire too loudly about the possibility of money changing hands with the selection committee members. But however it came about, it was a big deal—maybe the biggest deal ever for Seoul. No one could ever have predicted a Seoul Olympics, but happen it did.

Eight years earlier Leonid Brezhnev, then premier of the Soviet Union, decided to add Afghanistan to his hit list and sent scores of his troops to take it over. The Soviets discovered a real military quagmire, not a *New York Times* military quagmire that occurs within the first forty-eight hours of a Republican administration, but a quicksand battleground that ate up Russian troops and equipment with an enthusiasm not seen since Hans Guderian raced his Panzers eastward across the steppes. In response to this naked act of international aggression, President Jimmy Carter imposed a boycott on the 1980 Moscow Olympic Games. In response to war, he cancelled the one peaceful thing the world did together. In 1980, South Korea was planning to attend the Moscow Olympics, an opportunity that they viewed as bringing them one step closer to normalizing diplomatic relations with the Soviet Union, the primary sponsor of North Korea. President Carter instructed his Secretary of State to order all U.S. diplomatic missions to put maximum pressure on its friends, allies, and acquaintances to join the United States in the boycott. South Korea, being the stand-up country it is, joined the boycott—through clenched teeth, but joined it nonetheless—even though they viewed it as a tragically missed opportunity. South Korea still supported the administration that had done little for it other than threaten it with the withdrawal of military support and harass it for human-rights abuses.

It didn't require a fortuneteller to realize that the Soviet Union and Eastern Bloc states would not be coming to Los Angeles in the summer of 1984 for the Olympic Games. It was a great Games for the United States, but as enjoyable as it may have been to binge on medals something seemed missing in certain sports. So when the name of Seoul popped out of the hat for the 1988 Games the world was ready to gear up for the largest Olympic Games ever and one that everyone would attend. Everywhere you looked in Seoul in those days of preparation you saw the sign: SEOUL TO THE WORLD; THE WORLD TO SEOUL. Countdown clocks dominated City Hall and other large buildings. Olympic fever was rising. Construction on the south side of the Han River—just about the only area where room for expansion still remained—boomed. Inside the city proper renovation projects dominated any venue that might be used. A massive apartment complex rose near Chamshil, the primary Olympic venue. Interested Koreans were able to apply in a lottery-like fashion for the right to purchase an apartment in the new complex after the athletes departed. It was as close to a sure thing on an investment as one could have.

## The Northern Fly in the Olympic Ointment

Selection of Seoul as host city for the 1988 Olympics may have driven a stake into the heart of North Korea. The North tried everything it could do from diplomacy to threat of boycott to request for participation to actual terrorism to either get invited to play as a co-host city or to destroy the Games and force them to be relocated. It started out nasty and got worse. By this time, South Korea had far outstripped North Korea economically, socially, and even diplomatically. Having started the competition with most of the marbles in 1945, North Korea had by 1988 squandered so much of its birthright as to be economically as well as morally bankrupt. The South Koreans publicly made polite responses to the North's increasingly shrill pronouncements and threats. The Olympic Committee patiently ruled on one ridiculous request after another and at one point probably would have conceded to a North Korean request to have a few of the activities in Pyongyang but the North pulled out when its bluff was called. The last thing North Korea can stand is an uncontrolled visitor flow. Still the tensions grew as the big clock over City Hall counted down the days, hours, minutes, and seconds to the opening of the Games. To South Koreans, this was much more than a mere sporting event—as proud as they would be over that. This was an international affirmation—by enemies as well as by friends—that South Korea had reached a level of development and maturity in the world that made it capable of hosting the quadrennial world sporting event, the Olympic Games. Adding Seoul to the list of Los Angeles, Rome, Moscow, Paris, Berlin, Tokyo, Melbourne, Munich, and other famous cities was an honor few Koreans could have predicted and none could resist. They were determined that arriving athletes, visitors, and staff would find the best, most wonderful venue ever. They wisely postponed the Games one month until

September, when as if a switch is thrown, the nasty, polluted, hot, humid inversion layer of air that dominates in late July and August magically lifts and cool dry days with a sky as high as the hopes of the people of South Korea dominate the city.

But Kim Il Sung and his erratic son had different ideas. South Korean authorities were ever alert for terrorist acts. They had a long memory of assassins dispatched from western Japan, infiltrators coming across the beach from midget submarines at night or racing down from the Demilitarized Zone with blood in their eyes. They remembered how North Korean agents in 1984 exploded a pagoda in Burma that decimated their cabinet and almost killed their president. Would the next move be even more egregious, some wondered. Would the North Koreans attempt to fabricate a major incident in order to frighten the world away from Seoul? It was possible.

The reality struck on November 29, 1987, when Korean Air Lines Flight 858 coming from Abu Dhabi to Seoul was blown up over the Andaman Ocean off Myanmar killing 115 innocents. Two passengers, posing as father and daughter, boarded the flight in Baghdad and got off in Abu Dhabi leaving behind a radio filled with explosives. When apprehended two days later at the international airport in Bahrain as they waited vainly for a flight to Rome, where they were to meet North Korean handlers, the pair bit into cyanide-filled filter cigarettes.

The man succeeded, dying quickly. The woman, twenty-five-year old Kim Hyun Hee, bit on her cyanide but had the cigarette slapped away by a policewoman, who thus saved her life. Kim was evacuated under guard to Seoul where for several days she was neither tortured nor subjected to intense interrogation but simply chauffeured around and given tours of the bustling city. At first she kept her cover story of being a Chinese tourist on a Japanese passport (which the Japanese authorities said was forged). Her cover as a Chinese national enraged the People's Republic, as North Korea tried to shift blame for the bombing onto them. It was not until weeks of witnessing the highly visible lie to all of the years of North Korean propaganda that Kim Hyun Hee turned to her guard, a Seoul policewoman, and said, speaking in Korean for the first time, *"Mianhamnida, ohni"* (I'm sorry, elder sister) and acknowledged being an agent of North Korea. She was tried, sentenced to death, and then received a presidential pardon on the grounds that she had been brainwashed.[16]

One of the primary benefits of capturing Kim Hyun Hee alive is that she gave a complete, voluntary confession about her involvement in the terrorist act. She had been recruited by the North Korean security agency at an early age for training as an agent. In a James Bond–like scenario she achieved remarkable physical fitness, learned to kill with her hands or with a variety of weapons, and became adept at posing as both Japanese and Chinese. According to Kim this was her first mission, and when selected she was told that her mission to down the aircraft was personally ordered by Kim Jong Il in an attempt to disrupt the 1988 Seoul Olympics. Like many North Korean agents she had been

---

[16] Given the Korean predilection to forgive anything from someone with youth and beauty (something they share with Americans), one wonders if the seventy-year-old man would have been given a pass had he survived. On the night that she made a public appearance on Korean television to give her confession I was at our GE country manager's apartment for an office party. Just about everyone from the office—managers, secretaries, and support staff—gathered around the TV and watched as Kim Hyun Hee appeared. Spontaneously all the Koreans drew in a breath and whispered, *"ipoyo"* or "pretty." One suspects that had their roles been reversed and her chomp on the cyanide had been harder than her operational partner's that the sour-faced old man would have swung from a rope. Instead, she became a media star, received many offers of marriage, and is living well in Seoul today.

told of the brutality of the Seoul regime and the harsh conditions under which South Koreans lived. During her chauffeur-driven tours of Seoul where she observed the people cheerfully going about their day-to-day business, she realized how the North Koreans had lied to her and tricked her. Conscience pangs set in for the 115 people she had killed.

After her confession, an American official who spoke Korean interviewed Kim Hyun Hee. He assured himself that Kim and her agent partner had indeed been dispatched from North Korea and reported it to higher headquarters. Authorities at the State Department added North Korea to its list of terrorist countries. President Reagan made a personal request to the Soviets that they not boycott the Olympics as the North Koreans were urging. Both the president and Secretary of State George Schultz were assured by the Soviet foreign minister that they would attend. It would have been twelve years since the world participated in an Olympics and most nations thought that this was a must-attend event. Thanks to the two previous boycotts and new South Korean President Roh Tae-woo's policy it appeared as if the world truly was coming to Seoul.

## Five Rings over Seoul

Suddenly, after a ghastly August in 1988, a period in which lung-scalding pollution, oppressive heat, and strength-sapping humidity reached new highs—it was as if the Creator had flipped a switch. The sky lifted, pollution disappeared, the Han River flowed blue, the air lightened, and the city sparkled. Massive green spaces, land-reclamation projects along the Han River, were opened to the public. They had been landscaped into vast parklands and opened up the riverbank to access by picnickers, joggers, and strollers. Boats plied the Han, offering sightseeing and food. The new Olympic Expressway from Kimpo Airport to the Olympic cluster was a joy to drive, especially on a Sunday morning before anyone woke and you could zip up to speedometer-burying rates without another vehicle on the road.

Despite an aura of confidence South Korea was on pins and needles for the event. Nothing was left to chance, for although the threats from North Korea had not abated, most of the athletes, staff, and international visitors paid little attention to them. Visitors saw South Korean soldiers in camouflage uniforms patrolling the airports in pairs and standing on raised platforms in the ticketing, arrival, and baggage claim areas with loaded submachine guns (now all of South Korean design and manufacture, thanks to the threatened Carter pullout).

One of the more spectacular segments of the highly advertised opening ceremonies was going to be a collection of thirty skydivers who would form the five Olympic rings. Each group of five jumpers wore a distinctively colored jumpsuit to match his ring mates. They would assemble in the air duplicating the rings, free-fall a bit, then separate and land inside the stadium and re-form the rings. As someone with a measly 150-plus parachute jumps under his belt, I thought that seemed like an incredibly complex maneuver, and one so highly visible that it was fraught with potential disaster. One jumper failing to hook up would spoil the show. Quite by chance, in the Itaewon shopping area I stumbled on an old friend and boss from my Special Forces days, Bruce Wicks. Bruce was now a full colonel leading the U.S. Army parachute team, the famous Golden Knights. He was now in Seoul with the Knights who had already begun jumping into the stadium. "The Koreans don't want to take any chances," he confided. "We'll have some of their guys with us but mostly it will be the Knights making the jump." On opening day it went beautifully as the hookup of thirty jumpers fell in perfect rings through the crystal blue Seoul skies. But after they landed, formed the rings, gathered their chutes, and left the field to thunderous applause from the Opening Ceremonies audience they all kept their goggles on. They didn't want to advertise all those blue, green, and hazel eyes.

Tickets for the Games were scarce. Fully a year before they began the GE Aerospace country manager circulated to business managers an order form for them. The plan was to distribute Olympics tickets to strategic customers. I ordered tons of tickets: opening ceremony, closing ceremony, preliminary events, finals, major sports, stadium sports, venue sports—everything. After review, the country manager called me into his office and gave me a puzzled look. "You ordered more tickets than the rest of the managers combined," he said. "Why?" I explained that these would become coveted items but didn't convince him. He called his boss in Hong Kong who chided me to be more "realistic" in my needs. Reluctantly I cut back, but each cut seemed to draw blood. The month before the Games were scheduled to begin I drew up a distribution plan: Who gets invited to use what tickets? Originally it seemed like a good idea to escort a prized customer to a big event such as the opening ceremonies, but with my ticket stack cut so heavily I decided to host something pregame at my house and let the customers use the tickets without me.

Suddenly Olympic fever swept the country and the demand for tickets—any kind of tickets, to any event—soared. At least both the country manager and his boss grudgingly admitted that they had "underestimated" the demand. Suddenly mine was the most popular office on the floor, with other managers there to beg tickets. Even the country manager urged me to "share" my tickets. Sadly it was too late. I gave away an archery set or two but the rest were spoken for. It gave me an enormous amount of pleasure to give the only two Opening Ceremony tickets I had (I originally ordered six pair) to Hwang Won-tak. My old friend from the "rolling coup" days was now a major general and senior South Korean official. He and his wife enjoyed the experience immensely. At a dinner later, Jim Young offered a toast to General Hwang: "Eight years ago Chun Doo-hwan tried to have you killed. Now he's under arrest facing criminal prosecution and you're attending the Olympic Games!"

It would have been nice to have the North Koreans at the Games too, although realistically none could have been allowed back home after they had seen Seoul. The North Korean propaganda machine cannot stand up to truth, which is why they continue to keep themselves sealed so tightly. Shades of the Hermit Kingdom of old.

## The Present-day Demilitarized Zone

It is certainly possible to be a military man and not like the outdoors. But you can't be Special Forces and want to drive a desk all day. One of my great pleasures has always been the wild country— the mountains, oceans, forests, and jungles in which the wild critters live. A totally unexpected pleasure is what is happening on the Korean Peninsula. Cheerfully unhampered by man, nature works steadily to reclaim the Demilitarized Zone for itself. Reports abound of the return of rare and endangered species that were indigenous to Korea and have been extirpated elsewhere. Bear are seen now on a regular basis and there are whispered rumors of tiger sign being spotted. The DMZ has become a wildlife and bird refuge. Nesting areas for rare birds have made certain spots magnets for birders who excitedly watch their quarry through binoculars while patient, bemused South Korean infantrymen watch over them. Several years ago, North Korean soldiers wantonly fired into a flock of the amazingly large, incredibly rare, and stunningly beautiful Siberian cranes—virtually the national bird of Korea—killing several. The resultant outcry was more harsh and angry than if humans had been killed. Korean people by the millions yearn for the day when the DMZ can be officially converted into a huge national park. I hope I'm around to enjoy it with them.

# CHAPTER 10

# Tyranny Destroys the North

The two decades of the 1970s and 1980s were a roller coaster ride for North Korea, first up then sharply down. By the latter part of the 1970s Kim Il Sung and Kim Jong Il, who began to be increasingly involved with substantive issues, watched what appeared to them as an American defeat in Vietnam followed by a sharp U.S. pullback from Asia. It looked to them like someone who had played too close to the fire jerking back after a bad burn. For a bit it even appeared as if the United States was going all the way back. The indications of the second half of the 1970s, when the Carter administration gave the world the impression that the United States was pulling inside its shell, once again spurred the North Koreans to reach farther and more aggressively than they might have otherwise. Despite the hermetically sealed nature of their regime the Kims were savvy enough to see what was going on around the world. It appeared that communism under the Soviets and the Chinese was just about to make the big breakthrough. Soviet influence was expanding while America's shrank. Peace and anti-nuclear movements swept Europe and North America. The United States seemed to dash from one foreign policy crisis to the next, giving the appearance of having lost control of the situation. There was every reason for Kim Il Sung to ramp up his military capability in all sectors, including the nuclear. And that is precisely what he did.

Virtually from the inception of his rule as dictator of North Korea Kim Il Sung had it in his mind that one day he too would possess nuclear weapons. Early on he pestered Stalin and later Mao for support for a North Korean atomic bomb program. North Korea—mineral rich compared to the fertile but otherwise resource-poor South—has large amounts of uranium ore and other key minerals required for a program. They just needed the know-how to develop it and top cover to keep activities clandestine. These they hoped to get from either communist partner. Kim had tried the Soviets first but Stalin, having only recently acquired atomic weapons himself, was not eager to share his knowledge with North Korea. Kim Il Sung received the same answer a few years later from Mao after the Chinese communists went nuclear. Neither was interested in seeing a nuclear-capable North Korea. In modern international circles a nuclear device filled the same niche that a Colt revolver did in the old American West: it was the ultimate equalizer. No country—particularly an authoritarian one—appreciates the idea of what it considers a subordinate state moving up to a level of parity. Thus neither encouraged a nuclear North Korea.

Perhaps it was in their minds—with ample justification—that the appearance of nuclear weapons in North Korea would accelerate nuclear development in both Japan and South Korea. World War II was far too recent for either the Soviets or the Chinese to cotton to the idea of a nuclear Japan. Nor did the prospect of either North or South Korea—both countries they regarded as small and relatively unimportant—being in a position to upset the delicate balance of Northeast Asia in a manner that disadvantaged either the Soviets or the Chinese. So although Kim Il Sung was temporarily put off by his partners, he continued to explore options.

In the 1970s and 1980s U.S. satellite photography, imaging, and other overhead intelligence gathering was extremely secret. The program itself was classified a notch higher than Top Secret. Even the code name for the satellite program—Talent Keyhole—was classified confidential. For that reason the entire overhead information acquisition process was spoken of as "codeword." One person might ask, "Is he codeword cleared?" or another might say, "I think this intell might have come from codeword sources." The first time a warrant officer at the embassy told me that the name itself was classified I chuckled. He didn't. Even in those days with the relatively primitive systems compared to what flies now, the products were startling. You couldn't quite zoom down on a man smoking and read his nametag, but a good analyst could read volumes from photos taken at various times of the day, month, and year. He would build up a file over time to compare and contrast. Certain structures, for example, always have a signature construction pattern. We learned some of this in Special Forces training when we were training on target assessment techniques. What did a steel mill, electrical power plant, cement factory, munitions plant, chemical refinery look like? Number and quantity of smokestacks, input of raw material, cooling waters, smoke output, size of electrical input, and many other indicators disclosed much to a trained eye.

To a highly skilled image interpreter what we did was kid stuff compared to the sophistication they displayed. For example, they were able to tell with certainty in 1982 when the North Koreans began to construct a reactor at the Yongbyong facility. A few years later they were able to watch a building designed to produce weapons-grade plutonium be erected. Most alarmingly, U.S. analysts were able to determine where North Koreans fired off explosives in nearby test pits that matched the kinds of pits produced by explosives that would be configured in a specific manner to detonate a fission bomb. That is the same kind of nuclear weapon that destroyed Hiroshima and Nagasaki.

For the year I spent as a student in the South Korean Army College at Chinhae, 1977–1978, we focused much more intently on the Korean military situation than I would have done had I attended our U.S. equivalent program at Fort Leavenworth, Kansas. As a result we fought and re-fought the Korean War many times, and, naturally, explored the defense scenario of a possible North Korean attack on South Korea in great detail. It was startling for me to learn that my South Korean counterparts fully accepted the fact that Kim Il Sung possessed certain types of poison gas agents—specifically a blister agent similar to mustard and a nerve agent like VX—and would use them in conflict. In those days weapons of mass destruction (WMD) training in U.S. schools was perfunctory at best. The Koreans took it much more seriously. Our Korean instructors typically began the North Korean attack scenario with use of these chemical agents to assist the North Koreans in breaking through South Korean-American defenses. They also anticipated use of poison gas on Seoul to disrupt supply lines, inflict maximum casualties on the South Korean civilian population, and cause general chaos. I had no doubt that poison gas raining out of the sky over a city of fourteen million would have done exactly that. Frankly, it was a chilling scenario and one that none of my counterparts took lightly. We studied various prevailing wind directions to learn anticipated points of use and notional downwind patterns. Even though we regularly planned for enemy poison gas use we did not, at first, plan for use of nuclear weapons by the North Koreans.

But later in the course, a special section was introduced. It involved a scenario in which the invading North Koreans blew their way through the defending South Korean lines by use of tactical-yield nuclear weapons. While we were setting up the situation on our maps and overlays, in a manner reminiscent of every officer training school in the world, I pointed to the map. "The North Koreans have got nuclear weapons?" I asked my student sponsor, Lieutenant Colonel Lee Chong-ok. After so many months of hand-holding me he was accustomed to my behavior, considered too inquisitive by the conservative South Korean officer corps. He raised an eyebrow and shrugged. "Just do the problem," he grumbled, jabbing a finger at the map. "You ask too many questions!" he added, returning to his work.

Despite contrary guidance from the Chinese and Soviets, Kim Il Sung was determined to have his own nuclear capability. We'll probably never know why he felt so strongly about having a bomb. From a practical standpoint, his motivation is less germane to solving the issue than the existence of the weapon in the first place. Looking around the world at other dictators it seems to be a trend that having the "ultimate" weapon at their disposal gives them a sense of invulnerability. The confrontational relationship that existed between North and South Korea (despite the fact that high tension levels were his own doing) and continued presence of the U.S. forces in South Korea unsettled Kim Il Sung. The North Korean dictator probably thought he would buy some insurance making his own nuclear weapons.

How comfortable could Kim really feel relying on the Soviets or Chinese if crunch time came? With his megalomaniacal personality he could easily be called a "control freak." He would bitterly resent any dependency, real or imagined, on either Moscow or Beijing. Kim Il Sung would only be secure if he controlled his own fate. He could be expected to take all necessary steps to hedge his bets and protect himself—and damn the consequences. Kim was also aware that U.S. forces stationed in South Korea had at one time possessed nuclear weapons, although under the prevailing U.S. "neither confirm nor deny" policy it was unclear whether these weapons remained on the peninsula. From a practical standpoint, why would he ever trust what was told to him by the United States? He issued lies and propaganda on a regular basis; he had to assume that everyone else did, too.

As far as destabilizing the neighborhood—particularly in regards to Japan going nuclear—Kim probably thought that Japan was capable of assembling components already produced and ready at hand to make a nuclear device if it felt its national interest required it. From the elder Kim's perspective that would not be an altogether unpleasant state of affairs because it might raise the old specter of a regional threat from Japan, distract attention from him, and drive a big wedge between relations with Japan, South Korea, and the United States. It was always his intent and policy to break up the coalition opposing him. He was a master at exploiting every crack in the façade, every possible point of leverage, in order to separate allies. He even did it with the Soviets and Chinese. Correctly reading the emotion of the world community regarding nuclear weapons, Kim Il Sung realized that he could best distract from his own program by focusing world attention on real or potential programs elsewhere. North Korea sent trained scientists and specialists to Pakistan, Iran, Iraq, and other countries to assist them with their nuclear-development programs. This policy of exporting nuclear technology—against all treaty conventions—proved effective. It has remained the policy of the younger Kim Jong Il and the North Koreans to the present day.

By 1990 pressure was on North Korea to accept weapons inspectors. It had signed the Nuclear Non-Proliferation Treaty in 1985 but had restricted the occasional inspector to a small Soviet-supplied facility that was quite out of date. U.S. Central Intelligence Agency photography—courtesy of the Talent Keyhole overhead program—indicated a major expansion that CIA Director Robert Gates feared had the North Koreans at the verge of a functional nuclear weapons program. Meanwhile, a team of UN weapons inspectors, led by the director of the International Atomic Energy Agency inspection team, Hans Blix, of Sweden, were briefed by American CIA analysts on what they thought was happening at the North Korean's Yongbyong nuclear facility. When the team arrived they found the facilities larger than anticipated but not as far developed as Gates feared. To their shock, the North Koreans proudly presented them with a vial of refined plutonium, the element that in eight- to twelve-pound quantities is sufficient for bomb manufacture. Many worried that the North Koreans were too far down the road to stop. As North Korea careened into the 1990s like a runaway truck on a winding road, it was clear to many of us that the wheels were coming off. The nuclear contingency was there and had to be addressed, but the balance of power had shifted when no one was watching. The engine was breaking down, but if you get hit by a broken-down runaway truck you can be just as dead as if you are run over by a late model. It was too soon to count North Korea out. Sometimes an enemy is most dangerous when he feels most desperate. But the indications that the country was deteriorating out of control were unmistakable.

## A Darkened Image

From satellite photography we had seen something remarkable. A strikingly graphic NASA photo taken from a Shuttle flight over the Korean Peninsula at night revealed the awful truth. Looking down from space, when the earth is dark, an astronaut can pick out South Korea and Seoul easily. They are glowing jewels of sparkling lights. Seoul itself is almost a solid splash of light, beaming prosperity into the night sky. But the contrast with North Korea is stark, so extreme that you can almost trace the precise boundaries of the Demilitarized Zone just from the photograph. The North is a black, desolate wasteland. Only a few feeble, weak lights shine in Pyongyang. The effect is staggering in its implications. One of the defining moments of the modern industrial age was the invention of inexpensive, ubiquitous lighting. Prior to the invention of the electric light and the technology that brought it to the world, people feared the night. Their lives were regulated by available natural light supplemented poorly with sputtering oil lamps, candles, fires, and torches. Electric light civilized the world and changed it forever.

Now, in the dawning of the twenty-first century, at the start of a new millennium, most of the world basks in electric light and enjoys the many health, lifestyle, and economic benefits that accrue from electricity. But in North Korea, a mere thirty-five miles from a thriving megalopolis, a nation of twenty million souls hunkers down at night in medieval darkness, fearing the evils in the dark and fearing even more the tyranny of their own autocratic leaders. It is an anachronism of staggering proportions and heart-wrenching sadness. How awful to live a brief, harsh life unable to benefit even a little from products that most of the world takes for granted.

The stark economic difference between the two countries mirrors the contrast in light. None of the highly visible wealth of

Seoul is apparent in Pyongyang. Seoul, the capital of South Korea, is brightly alive—vibrant, growing, thriving. People clog the sidewalks and subways, traffic is jammed, and stores burst with a range of products of every description. Pyongyang, the capital of North Korea, is dark and lonely, a grim façade of a city, a decaying corpse with rouged cheeks and painted lips. Pyongyang is a huge Potemkin village of tall buildings, modern subways, and omnipresent monuments to Kim Il Sung, but with no people in sight. Stores have no goods to sell, no customers to purchase them, and no money in circulation for a transaction even if they had products available. It is in a downward spiral into an economic black hole. Extraordinarily wide boulevards crisscross the city, yet a blindfolded man could cross safely for nothing but the occasional Party limousine or military vehicle ever uses them. The privileged few among the citizenry who are permitted to live in the capital are gray, faceless people who scurry about with expressionless faces. Their Kim Il Sung buttons are firmly attached to their lapels, prominently displayed. Their eyes are downcast and their minds are as closed as their lips.

Everywhere in North Korea it is the same. The people are uniformly repressed. Virtually nothing is spent on infrastructure improvements or on standard of living upgrades. The leadership makes only a few limited kinds of national investment: it maintains the million-man-plus armed force that sits poised and ready to attack South Korea, and it spends lavishly on the communist party and its leaders. No cost is too high if it promotes the personality cult of the dysfunctional father-son team of Kim Il Sung and Kim Jong Il. The Party leaders live in secret luxury while their people eke out an existence just above the starvation level— if they are among the fortunate few. The unfortunate simply go hungry. Outside of Pyongyang the countryside reminds observers of a typical poor third-world country. It has mostly dirt and gravel roads, a few narrow two-lane concrete roads, no electric grid, poor bridges, primitive communications, and crude buildings. It is a land caught in a terrible time warp, all due to the twisted dictatorship of men who revel in power at the expense of their own countrymen.

The small number of foreign visitors are monitored constantly. Their minders make certain that they are kept away from the gulags, prisons, and areas of mass hunger. "I didn't see anyone obviously starving," a recent visitor told me, "but then I didn't see anyone who was overweight either." When asked how much of the country he had been allowed to see, he acknowledged, "Very, very little." The countryside reminded him of South Korea forty years ago, but worse. Only visitors such as Ramsey Clark, Jimmy Carter, and Madeline Albright are such self-delusional true believers that they doubt what their own eyes see. Supposedly astute visitors such as they are submit to North Korean restrictions and conditions that would make them justifiably howl in protest if a country like South Korea imposed them. They will allow their visits to be completely controlled, access severely limited, and they will never challenge their hosts on human rights violations. They will absorb all the propaganda the North Koreans can shove down their gullets and then regurgitate it to the world on their return. People like Carter, Albright, and Clark will complain of the mite in someone else's eye while ignoring the boulder in their own. So while Kim Il Sung and Kim Jong Il receive a pass from the foreign sycophants who visit them, the people continue to starve.

European doctors, such as German physician Norbert Vollertsen, return with wrenching photos of children who are so undernourished that their growth patterns have been stunted. Vollertsen displays photos of children in confinement centers wearing striped pajama uniforms. He was so shaken by the Nazi death camp–appearance of the children that he was spurred to action. "How could a German like myself see something like that and not act?" he asked. Vollertsen is now banned from North Korea and spends his time trying to organize and inform world opinion against it. Food aid people speak movingly of the dire need for increased food assistance. But how could this be the case since North Korea was the largest recipient of U.S. and other countries' foreign aid in food, fuel oil, and other essentials, more than any other country? All this aid and yet it still fails to meet minimum standards for its people. Why is this?

One reason is that clearly the military and the communist party have first claim on all resources in the country. First priority of available mass rations always goes to the army. Even if the actual food intended for relief is not siphoned off for the military (and indications are that most of it is given to the army) then it becomes fungible. In other words, food aid frees up other food to go to the military. Either way the military gets first call on the food so that even with a population flirting with mass deprivation and starvation, it is kept fit. Recent indications are that food excess to Party and military needs is shipped out of country for sale to bring in hard currency. Party members, particularly the top leaders, do not lead a life of austerity and want. How otherwise to explain the fact that a country that intentionally starves its citizens into submission is also the world's number one importer of expensive French cognac and brandy? Party leaders, especially the Dear Leader himself, and military leaders live lives of sybaritic luxury far removed from the underclass of workers and peasants they profess to adore.

A recent escapee from the "peasants and workers paradise" is living in hiding in Japan. He is a Japanese national who was recruited more than a decade ago to be sushi and gourmet food chef to the Kims. He is hiding in Japan because he ran from the Dear Leader and fears that a North Korean hit squad would casually take him out—or worse, kidnap him back into the belly of the beast. The man, who goes under the pseudonym of Kenji Fujimoto has a hot-selling book in Japan that details the bacchanalian lifestyle of Korean leaders, especially Kim Jong Il. The stories are particularly repugnant when juxtaposed against agonizing scenes of starvation, mass imprisonment, death camps, and torture. Kim Jong Il imports delicacies from around the world and North Korean people try to survive hard labor on two cups of gruel daily.

Typically, a betraying symptom of a decaying nation-state is refugee flow. This should not surprise us. When people are hungry, sick, threatened, or repressed their first instinct is to get far away from what is causing their pain. In this case, the cause of their pain is North Korea itself. But in North Korea even opportunities to flee are limited. Heading south is out of the question. A concentration of military personnel in manned defensive positions and the dense mining of the Demilitarized Zone make escape to the South infeasible. Nor is it possible for someone to escape by small boat the way that tens of thousands of Vietnamese refugees did after Saigon fell in 1975. The Soviets and their puppets brought with them a system of secret policing, informants, and punishments when they came into North Korea in 1945 and imposed it upon the society. The Kims have improved upon the system in the following decades. Every now and again a fisherman will defect, but the opportunity for a citizen to construct a boat and head south without someone informing on him is virtually impossible.

With oceans on two sides and an impenetrable border to the south, that leaves the border with the People's Republic of China to the north as the best possibility for escape. North Koreans fleeing in that direction would find familiar faces. Even prior to World War II there were rather large numbers of ethnic Koreans living north of the Yalu River (the Amno Kang in Korean). South Korean visitor, S. J. Kang, GE's country manager in Seoul, made the pilgrimage through China to the North Korean border. He returned with an album of snapshots of villages, stores, and shops that could have been villages thirty years ago or earlier in South Korea. Signage is in hangul, the distinctive alphabet of the Korean language. He said that the food in restaurants was familiar, with the traditional fiery kimchee a standard side dish. The primary difference was the wide noodles in the soup, a distinct preference in northern cuisine. It was nostalgic in a way, Kang said, because it reminded him of his boyhood. At one point several years ago, the ethnic Korean residents in China told him, it was commonplace for North Korean citizens to cross the river back and forth into villages in China. They would come across to find work and to purchase a few things to take back. In those days most would return to North Korea. The flow was a then mere trickle and was not of concern to either country.

But then life in North Korea deteriorated at a more rapid rate. Recent visitors from the region say that the border is tightly sealed. Occasional shooting is heard at night as North Koreans try to escape under the gimlet eyes of the guards. Refugees are routinely shot. From what we have learned from the few who have made it to China and hidden themselves, conditions are far worse that what we are allowed to see in Pyongyang. Reports from the refugees crossing the border are appalling. Some of these brave souls have been rescued by efforts of the Defense Forum Foundation under the leadership of Suzanne Scholte. She has arranged for them to testify at Congressional hearings, especially before engaged Members such as Kansas Senator Sam Brownback.

As conditions deteriorated in North Korea, the refugee flow increased. Although refugees are often difficult to interview, some stories emerged. At first they spoke of deteriorating economic conditions that lowered living standards and made life harsh. Then they spoke of widespread hunger, of starvation, death, and unchecked disease. Then the chilling tales of cannibalism emerged. Reports of families consuming the bodies of their starved children or eating corpses were common. At that point, North Korea and China separately clamped down on border traffic. The North realizes that an unrestricted exodus will bleed the impoverished country of the only resource it now possesses—cheap labor. Without people there will be nothing to support the artificiality of the Party or the army, and the entire sordid affair will collapse in a manner similar to East Germany and the communist Balkan states. That is an unacceptable outcome for North Korea, of course, and for the moment, also unacceptable to China, primarily because of these same refugee implications.

It has become a preferable course of action for North Korea to restrict the refugee exodus as brutally as possible. Stringent security measures are imposed upon the border. It is a scene so painfully familiar in failing communist countries: guards face inward to keep citizens from fleeing. It is reminiscent of Hungary after the 1956 revolt or East Germany before the Berlin Wall was torn down. We see it everywhere communism has taken hold and then deteriorated—Cuba, Cambodia, Vietnam, and the Soviet Union. The Chinese are loath to receive any more Korean refugees for economic, political, and diplomatic reasons. They fear that unrestricted immigration could turn into an unstoppable tidal wave of millions of refugees if North Korea goes down quickly, as many observers anticipate it will do. The Chinese doubt their ability to deal effectively with the hunger, health, crime, and population-control issues of such a flow, much less the expense. This is more of a challenge than the Chinese wish to accept. China has therefore made forcible repatriation of refugees a national policy. Even those few North Koreans who are permitted to travel and who try to defect in places such as Beijing are sent back to North Korea where they face imprisonment, torture, and death. Chinese patrols routinely pick up refugees trying to hide along the border villages and send them southward. Word has trickled back that these forcible returnees and their family members are routinely rounded up by North Korean secret police and sent to forced labor camps. But life is so horrid in North Korea that even facing terrible risk people still flee. Life inside is a dark, unspeakable nightmare that is so overwhelmingly oppressive that the West cannot even imagine what it must be like.

## All in the Family—North Korean Succession

Kim Il Sung was the odd combination of an hereditary Yi Dynasty ruler infected with a particularly virulent form of Stalinism. As noted previously, he outlived both of his mentors—Stalin and Mao—and made them envious of his degree of absolute control over his country and the pervasive personality cult that he instituted. He remained in power through ten U.S. presidencies. At just what moment it occurred to Kim Il Sung to install his son Kim Jong Il as successor is something we are likely never to learn. It was a process that Kim eased into. If nothing else, the man held his cards close to his chest. For years there existed a barely penetrable veil of secrecy around the son, a situation that only served to fuel speculation and rumors. Everyone wondered: Who is he? What is his purported role? Many of the rumors revolved around Kim Jong Il's eccentricities: he was a bizarre filmmaker, almost a self-styled de Mille in a mad totalitarian world. Other rumors had him as somehow not fully functional either in brainpower or in mental health. Kim Jong Il for years never met foreign dignitaries, was seen only rarely in public, and was mentioned only tangentially on the few occasions that his name was given in the North Korean press. Perhaps this was all part of an intricate design on Kim Il Sung's part, a way that he had of first convincing himself that the son was worth grooming for the position and would be able to rise to the challenge. It was a tantalizing portrait. Figuring out Kim Jong Il was like trying to describe a crowded room yet being able to look at it only through a keyhole. Regardless it was Kim's intention—long before he let the rest of the world know—to make his son his successor. What better place to learn the job of totalitarian ruler than in the intelligence service?

It was apparent fairly early on that Kim Jong Il had been positioned to play a leading role in North Korean external terrorist activities. Certainly by the early 1980s it was clear from confessed North Korean agents that he was personally involved in operations. This operational supervision role may have been one of the combinations of testing and training that his father had in mind when making the appointment. The younger Kim was responsible for such terrorist operations as the Rangoon bombing, the sabotage of Korean Air Lines flight 858, the kidnapping of film professionals from Hong Kong, and the abduction and murder of Japanese citizens over a period of several years. He was a bad actor from the start but was considered by many—including me and several of my contemporaries—as being far too junior to be a serious contender for North Korean leadership. A colleague, a former Marine and a senior Foreign Service officer, spoke derisively of Kim Jong Il as "too weak to take leadership from men who fought Japanese and Americans while he was squatting in the gutter in diapers sailing wooden twigs and chips in the sewage." Among many of us who thought we were in the know that was a fair consensus. We blew that call.

Another error on many of our parts was the assessment of the famous Kim Il Sung tumor, a huge, strange growth on the back of his neck. "He can't live much longer with that thing," I recall saying optimistically. That was in 1978 when he had sixteen years left to live. But Kim Il Sung was smarter than we were when it came to preparing the ground for hereditary succession. He was exceedingly patient about bringing Kim Jong Il into prominent leadership positions. Kim Il Sung nonetheless continued to chug along in apparent good health despite our most sanguine predictions about his possible forthcoming demise.

In retrospect, it may have been for the best that he did live so long. During his lifetime, North Korea was stronger than it is now. It was capable, according to most intelligence estimates, of fighting at least a thirty- to ninety-day war, which would give it ample time to win it—by overrunning Seoul and suing for a ceasefire. Its greatest risk would be to have the status quo restored antebellum—the line of the Demilitarized Zone. It was widely speculated among Korea watchers that one technique Kim Jong Il might use in event of an unplanned succession would be to initiate a war. He would thereby pressure most of his rivals within North Korea to side with him. Everyone is thankful that that option was not exercised.

The odd aspect of the North Korean succession process—assuming that anything about North Korea is usual—was that it *was* hereditary. For a quintessential authoritarian regime such as Kim Il Sung's to be inherited successfully, political safety nets had to be put in place to protect the successor even after the old man died. It would be one thing to announce a successor and receive agreement from all concerned while Kim Il Sung was alive. It would be quite another to make that agreement stick after he was unable to influence events. If the history of succession among European monarchies and the Soviet Union is considered as a model, the chosen successor is just as often beheaded, imprisoned, or exiled as he is revered. But of all the labels that might apply to Kim Il Sung, "fool" is not one of them. He was bright enough and sufficiently ruthless himself to realize that mere diktat would not guarantee that Kim Jong Il would survive another sunrise, much less fill his shoes if left to his own devices.

We will never know the actual mechanics of Kim Il Sung's process of succession. It is likely that even victims of the old man's tyranny and intimidation only saw the small role that they occupied in the larger scheme. Nevertheless, we do know one unassailable fact: Kim Jong Il is now in charge of North Korea—and he had to get there through the machinations of the elder Kim. If we build on the premise that in most communist states succession is given either to a single strongman or to a temporary alliance of several strongmen who compete until one emerges, then it is highly unlikely that a fifty-something Kim Jong Il could have been sufficiently old enough, experienced enough, or have a strong enough internal political organization on his own to make the grade. We must assume that the elder Kim put a failsafe mechanism in place.

First, the younger Kim could not have been simply sprung on the competitive leaders or on the country cold. There had to be some preparatory work. This began when his name or the oblique title, the "party center" appeared more frequently in the North Korean press. While there was little point in putting him in front of the populace, who had no say in government, it did make sense to work him into the communist party apparatus so that he could begin to build his own dependency networks and tight relationships. In order to ensure his succession there needed to be a sufficiently strong base of support for Kim Jong Il within the Party leadership or at least the rising Party leadership. He would need those people whose ambition and venality were sufficiently for sale that they would pledge fealty to the younger Kim in turn for rewards of power and position.

Simultaneously, the elder Kim needed to exercise caution. This movement to build up his son could, if unmanaged, morph into an unplanned internal coup to dispose of the younger Kim. And such a move was not farfetched given the unscrupulous nature of North Korean communist party members. So as Kim Jong Il was pushed higher and higher up the Party ladder he had to increasingly assume some operational function. It was decided at an early stage that his quirky personality made him an unlikely diplomatic representative of the regime. Perhaps the father decided that the son may have been a bit too unstable to permit him unfettered travel for extended periods of time in cities of the West. Therefore, Kim Jong Il worked the operational side of the house in the terrorist and anti-South Korea effort. Apparently his performance was satisfactory in these endeavors; at least he worked his way up to the standards of his father.

It is quite likely, although at this point impossible to prove or document, that the elder Kim put in place a terror situation that would sufficiently influence potential rivals to his son as to render them impotent. Throughout history, hostage taking has been common practice. For example, in feudal Europe wives, children, and relatives were exchanged with an enemy to guarantee future compliance. Throughout the Shogun days of old Japan, it was customary for the Japanese feudal lords, the *daimyo,* to leave loved ones at Edo Castle in Tokyo while they journeyed out to their fiefdoms. When their turn came to rotate back through a stint at the castle the *daimyos* they replaced left their relatives. It was a largely effective system that dampened enthusiasm for collusion and revolt against the Shogun. And some modern version of that system of intimidation and fear was probably put in place by Kim Il Sung in order to solidify and protect his son. One can imagine any number of working scenarios: a large villa somewhere where the hostages live in quiet, secluded luxury under the constant guns of Kim Jong Il's security goons who will murder the lot on command. Or the security guards could be placed one-on-one with some key family members, awaiting the word to kill on a private radio. Other blackmail or intimidation methods may be in place—these people can be very imaginative when it comes to horrific activities—but however it worked, safeguards were put into place to protect the son. In all likelihood the original system or a modified version remains in place today.

Kim Il Sung's process, from concept to announcement to place Kim Jong Il officially into line of succession, took about ten years, from the early 1970s until 1980. That October, the big announcement was made at the Sixth Workers Party Congress in Pyongyang. The younger Kim, who had been a Party Central Committee member, was then kicked upstairs to the Politburo, the Military Commission, and the Party Secretariat, the three essential elements of the government that control North Korea. The reality of control in communist North Korea is that the will or desire of the people is not something to be garnered or earned. The leader simply dictates to them. After the 1980 announcement, Kim Jong Il began to be officially called the "Dear Leader." It was required that he be referred to only in that manner. Meanwhile, the personality cult machine was cranked into high gear. Printing presses ran uncountable copies of his photo to be hung in every office, store, factory, and home in North Korea. Songs were written about him. It became customary for him to be referred to officially as the source of all good things that were happening. For example, if a government official dealt with a citizen he would tell the citizen that the goodness of the Dear Leader was responsible for the service he was receiving. It was all designed as part of a conscious movement to in effect deify Kim Jong Il in the same manner as his father had been. Although Don Oberdorfer reports that "affection for Kim Jong Il in North Korea is much more limited than it was for his father," how does one measure genuine affection in a repressive society? It is obvious that the intent of the policy is to create among the citizens a dependency upon the so-called Dear Leader, not an affection for him.[17]

## The Old Man Dies

In July 1994, shortly after his triumph against Jimmy Carter, Kim Il Sung died, apparently of a heart attack. He was eighty-two years old and had ruled North Korea since 1945. Kim Il Sung was at a mountain villa when he was stricken. Weather was inclement, restricting travel to land vehicles—helicopters that tried to fly were grounded. But even land vehicles could not negotiate the unpaved road from the main highway to the villa, so they were not able to evacuate Kim to a medical facility. Fifty years of absolute rule and he was brought down partially because of lousy infrastructure. There is a message there somewhere.

Around the region, nations braced for chaos. Would the designation of Kim Jong Il as successor hold, or would there be a power

---

17 *The Two Koreas,* 350.

struggle? Inside North Korea the elder Kim's plan unfolded in secret. For the next several months it was somewhat murkier than usual in North Korea. There appeared to be behind-the-scenes drama unfolding as Kim Jong Il fought for control. First he appeared to be on top, then sliding downward. Yet, by the end of a year he was clearly in charge. Kim the elder's nefarious succession plan, to continue indefinitely the repression of his people in the person of his son, was complete. From outside we watched tensely and wondered what would the next North Korean move against the South be?

# CHAPTER 11

# The Growing Nuclear Threat

As much as I think I know about Korea I am always discovering something new. In a conversation with Korean scholars I learned as an adult the concept of "Han and Chong," which is known to every Korean child. Understanding these ideas made me appreciate the closeness of the relationship Korean people share with one another, regardless of where they live. Han and Chong are the psychic glue that binds Korean people together in the face of all outside forces despite geography or politics. Han is deeper than the intellectual level of consciousness. It burrows deep and lives down inside a person's heart where the most intense emotions lie, waiting to rise. Han evokes a memory of shared bitterness and common adversity. Han means having to endure and subsist together under the worst adversity in order to make the eventual triumph that much sweeter. Merely saying the word "Han," a Korean person will typically point to his chest or gut with an open hand and bow his head slightly. Calling on Han is not a thing to be taken lightly because it invokes ethnic ties woven through thousands of years of history. It calls on the listener to transcend the superficial and focus on the real, the immediate. It is a call to a racial unity that automatically excludes the foreigner. When Han is invoked, a Korean wrong is supported by fellow Koreans even in the face of a foreign right. Han is serious business.

In keeping with the Taoist sense of balance and harmony—the yin and the yang—most everything in Asia has two sides. The counterfoil to Han is Chong, a similar binding sense, although less developed. Chong focuses more on the positive aspects of life, of love and goodness, and therefore receives less attention than Han. After all, people are drawn to tragedy. (If you see Koreans leaving a movie theater sobbing uncontrollably, you know that they have just had the time of their lives.) Still Chong is an important aspect of Korean culture. Chong serves as an appropriate counterweight for Han. It is the philosophy that explains the traits of kindness and friendship that most Koreans display as a matter of course and for which they are justifiably proud as characteristic of their culture. Taken together Han and Chong have enabled the Koreans to endure what many consider a brutal history.

Donald Gregg, former U.S. ambassador to South Korea, captured the Han philosophy when he described the Korean attitude toward foreigners by saying that "it seems to some that nothing good has ever come to Korea from overseas. As a consequence they look with suspicion at any foreigner, especially those claiming to be acting in the Koreans' best interests." Certainly the classic Korean proverb in which they see themselves as a shrimp among the whales of Japan, China, Russia, and America has some historical validity. "When the whales collide," the Koreans say, "the shrimp gets hurt." That has been the case in the past. Life is tough, the Korean people will acknowledge, on a national level no less than on the personal level.

But Korean people operate at many levels. At an ethnic level it could be said that xenophobia and exclusion of foreigners are desirable. But at an individual level Koreans can be the most friendly, hospitable people in the world. Paradoxical, contradictory? In Korea, you never know which one you're going to encounter. Once when I lived in Seoul I was driving home in the evening, probably around eight o'clock or so, and had stopped in traffic for a light near the City Hall. Suddenly from out of the nearby subway station, hundreds and hundreds of students poured out into the streets and began to run down the lanes made by the idling automobiles. They wore headbands and carried signs reading "Americans Go Home!" and "Yankee Out!" The students looked intense and focused as they flowed. Alone in the car and totally blocked in by other traffic I was without recourse. I decided to just sit back and let things happen. As the students raced past several glanced into the car and began to slow. I could hear the dreaded words "*mi-guk saram*," or "American" murmured. Then suddenly I began to hear "Hello" and "How are you?" and all of the phrases that they learned during their six or seven years of English lessons. They were practicing their language skills on me! The kids stood around grinning, waiting for a response. Tentatively at first, I began to respond with greetings—a smile and a wave. They responded enthusiastically. By then several had gathered hoping for a chat. But voices called to them. They smiled apologetically, waving farewell as they ran off to rejoin their friends in the anti-American demonstration. In a few minutes the kids were gone, the light turned green, and I drove home shaking my head in wonder. Such is the classic South Korean dichotomy.

The concepts of Han and Chong come with built-in inner conflict. They bind Korean people together against foreign influence, and yet Koreans like and admire foreign things and people. And

Koreans are especially proud of their hospitality. Koreans shared the hardships and scarcity of colonization and war. This deprivation contributed to a deep work ethic and drive to success. But the act of enjoying that eventual success brought with it a guilty feeling that they are being too materialistic and losing the spiritual, moral core that makes Koreans special. This moral conflict confuses many modern Koreans. Elevate the concern one level and the South Koreans are bitter about national division but are simultaneously fearful that too-rapid unification could cause the entire economic fabric—that they previously had thought was so strong—to rip apart. A burning desire for racial and national reunification—a manifestation of Han—is therefore tempered by an unwillingness to lose the good things in life that cost so much time and effort to begin with. When the culture becomes burdened with the guilty feelings that result from this conflict the easiest course is to transfer blame to outside forces—Americans, Soviets, or others—and by assuming the mantle of the victim, relieve the guilt that weighs heavily upon them. This phenomenon is also a constant undercurrent in Korean society.

All of these forces came to play in 1988 as the Olympic Games kicked off. The Olympic slogan was "Seoul to the World; the World to Seoul." What could be a more classic Han versus Chong dilemma? As it turned out, Koreans were a bit shaky when the World arrived with all of its brashness, informality, and cultural eccentricities. But, wow, did they ever win the Seoul to the World part. Newly elected South Korean President Roh Tae-woo used the Olympic Games success as a springboard to diplomacy. He quickly embarked on his visionary northern policy—an outreach to the Soviet bloc and China. In so doing he adroitly demonstrated the value of a free-market South Korea while successfully minimizing the threatening image that North Korea tried vainly to perpetuate. We're willing to co-exist with North Korea, Roh's emissaries said. By contrast, North Korea's protestations seemed pointless and shrill. Roh extended an olive branch to the Eastern Bloc countries as well. He led his diplomatic charge with capital investment and lots of it. South Korean money poured into the southern China coast, the Eastern Bloc from Poland through the Balkans, and into the remote Soviet border republics such as Azerbaijan and Turkmenistan. Roh successfully positioned South Korean businessmen and diplomats inside Eastern Bloc countries for business purposes. Countries such as Hungary and Czechoslovakia, which saw a chance to break from the Soviets with the advent of glasnost and perestroika, began to look to South Korea as an economic and political role model, an interesting twist from the superior European colonial attitude of the nineteenth century. Roh's strategic gambit yielded unexpected but positive results. When the Soviet system and its satellites collapsed a year or two later the South Koreans were already on the spot ready to work with the newly emerging governments. Watching the process of painful transition from communist to democratic country, South Korean officials gained an appreciation for the magnitude and rapidity of internal disintegration. Could this happen to North Korea? was the question on everyone's mind. When East and West Germany were reunited it was widely viewed as a model of how things might eventually develop between North and South Korea.

In a departure from previous policy, Roh invited nations that recognized South Korea diplomatically to extend that recognition to North Korea also. We would even agree to let both states be admitted to the United Nations concurrently, South Korean diplomats told their counterparts. It marked a huge surge in South Korean confidence. Previously each country strove to gain international recognition at the expense of the other. Predictably, the North Koreans felt the pinch. They had been excluded by the Olympic Committee because of their own boorish, threatening behavior and then excoriated by the international community because of the terrorist act of blowing up an airliner. Pyongyang grew increasingly isolated and economically depressed while South Korea's economy and status in the world soared. By using the Olympics as a carrot along with encouragement from loans, investments, and business opportunities, the South Koreans made significant headway into diplomatic territory previously uncharted and forbidden. Diplomatic missions opened around the world for the South Koreans.

The 1988 Seoul Olympics brought with them many exciting things, ranging from the athletes themselves to the visitors, and to the political, economic, and diplomatic initiatives they sparked. Remarkably the most significant outcome happened without conscious plan or intent. The period of the Games—preparation, execution, and aftermath—marked a major developmental crossing point for the two Koreas. The trend had probably been underway for years but like any major paradigm shift, it required time for observers to become aware of it. From the period of the Games onward South Korea was on an unstoppable developmental rise while North Korea slid evermore rapidly into ignominy and irrelevance. Imagine the progress of each country almost like a classic supply-demand curve: one rises while the other falls. From hindsight it is perfectly clear.

Free-market democratic institutions were booming in South Korea. A peaceful transition of power—the first of several—had taken place. The economy grew, suffered some setbacks, shrugged them off, and continued to expand. To the practical-minded citizens of South Korea this meant an increasingly longer lifespan, lower infant mortality, higher standards of living, greater productivity, and a far freer life than Korean people had ever known. The belt-tightening, the sacrifice, the air-raid drills, and national conscription, all the difficult times had finally begun to pay off. In contrast, North Korea had started high, with a distinct advantage in available natural resources, population base, and outside support. North Korea walked a radically different course, under total control by a maniacal regime that only wished absolute power regardless of how many innocent lives were destroyed. There was no way that a highly controlled society and economy could grow and prosper. It was and continues to be based neither on the consent of the governed nor on the welfare of the populace, but on maintenance of a destructive, corrosive, hateful ideology that corrupts all it touches. Such a regime is a cancer spreading inside itself, and while it spreads, it inflicts so much hurt. This is the very process that is taking place on the Korean peninsula: one a case of prosperity and freedom, the other a spiral into brutality, totalitarianism, and darkness. Korea is a classic, timeless object lesson in the stark contrasts between democracy and communism. And the point of crossing, where the inexorable march of democracy triumphed was the Olympic Games. How appropriate.

So the glories of the 1988 Seoul Olympics in the long run were not measured by number of gold medals won, although South Korea won a good share, not in number of athletes, and how many nations attended. The Games marked a moment when free people no longer had to fear total oppression or conquest from a hostile neighbor. North Korea can cause problems and do a lot of damage but from that point forward its perverse dream of conquest was forever stifled: North Korea can never again successfully conquer South Korea. The roots of freedom are too pervasive and too deep.

## Sticker Shock

In the late 1980s the Berlin Wall fell and East and West Germany were reunited. While we had all known or suspected for decades how badly the East Zone was suffering under the Soviet boot, it was not until the Iron Curtain was pulled open wide that the true extent of the economic, political, and human stagnation was displayed for the world to see. This revelation brought shock and horror to the West Germans who knew that they would be receiving the repair bills and signing the checks. It was a classic case—on a mega scale—of entering into an irrevocable contract, then "discovering" a hidden cache of exorbitant costs. The initial cost estimates of East-West unification—which were already high—skyrocketed dramatically. Clusters of zeroes accrued faster than in a Pentagon budget proposal. Bitter statements by German politicians and citizens in the more prosperous West reflected their intense dissatisfaction with the unwanted new responsibility for their Eastern brothers and sisters. They were expected to pick up the tab on what had been the equivalent of a forty-year long, unsupervised frat party held by the Soviets in a neighbor's house. The irresponsible Soviets had metaphorically broken all the windows, knocked down the doors, and peed on the carpets before passing out in a pool of their own vomit. But grousing and complaining did nothing to halt the growing tide of Easterners moving into the West seeking lost relatives and better everything: better jobs and pay, better medical care, housing, food, and an infinitely better ambience.

When the South Korean leaders saw what was happening in Germany it took them a nanosecond to run estimates of what their own numbers would be in event of a North-South reunification. When they totaled the estimates the bottom line gave them extreme sticker shock. The reverberations went right to the top. Not

long after the Berlin Wall fell I had a private dinner with an economic advisor to President Roh Tae-woo's Blue House. He confided
that even though the stated public policy of South Korea would remain "Unification now!" the real policy post-Germany had quickly
become "reunification later—much, much later," preferably on
someone else's watch. The consequences of what they would find
when the Bamboo Curtain was pulled aside was almost unimagin-
able. Considering that on a worst day, communications and interaction between East and West Germany had been better than on
the best day between North and South Korea, they were scared.
"What we are going to find is going to be awful," the economic advisor said softly. "We simply had never looked closely enough at potential costs of reunification. We assumed that the greater social
benefits would overcome any financial burdens. And we were willing to endure those burdens for the greater good of the Korean people. Now, we fear that abrupt reunification could collapse the
economy of the South." For the first time among South Korean people a widespread desire to maintain a prosperous, comfortable
standard of living trumped the ethnic demands of Han, to reunite
the separated Korean tribe. A few days later at a luncheon with a
Hyundai Heavy Industries president I raised the unification question. He confided to me that his chairman had decided that immediate reunification would be extremely detrimental to the economy
and to business in general. "We were very naïve in our approach,"
he said. "What we have seen take place in Germany frightens us.
It might ruin even so large a company as Hyundai." So what could
be done? "We must proceed cautiously and try to build up enough
of an economic base in North Korea so that they will not collapse."
Won't that prolong the regime, I asked? "Perhaps," the Hyundai
president shrugged. "But to do otherwise risks a disaster that
would wreck us all." At a later luncheon with Daewoo Heavy

Industries, President K. H. Lee spoke of quiet initiatives that Daewoo Chairman Kim was making to open manufacturing zones in North Korea. "It would assist us in maintaining worldwide cost competitiveness," he said, "while allowing a steady flow of hard currency into North Korea. It is a solution that will benefit both sides." It was abundantly clear from both executives that these initiatives to North Korea, although ostensibly private, were done with the approval of a fully informed South Korean government.

### Spies and Inspectors

By 1992 I had moved to New York City to take charge of an old organization, the Korea Society. In order to grow the organization we expanded programs to include a greater number of public policy activities, current affairs discussions and seminars that involved key persons such as UN representatives, ambassadors, and the like. Optimism was in the air regarding the North Korea-South Korea relationship. Seoul had established inroads into the formerly communist countries in Eastern Europe and Russia and the People's Republic seemed pleased with a more harmonious Korea. While continuing to mutter, North Korea seemed significantly less bellicose than it had proven in the past. Both countries were preparing for admittance into the United Nations as regular members in September of 1992. At a luncheon in New York the respective ambassadors spoke a few words and North Korean ambassador Ho Jong sounded a note that sounded remarkably friendly, inclusive, and peaceful. The South Korean ambassador was cautiously optimistic and stressed the need for vigilance and mutual trust. On the way out, one of my friends, a long-time Korea hand mused. "Who would have ever thought that we would be listening to a North Korean representative who sounded more reasonable than a South Korean representative?"

Within weeks the idyll was shattered. Reality, not always pretty, but always demanding recognition, had punched through the clouds. In Seoul there was a massive roundup of North Korean secret agents. A ring of more than sixty people was arrested, including a woman who was a ranking member of the North Korean Workers' Party hierarchy who had lived clandestinely in South Korea on several occasions. These were agents that North Korea had insisted for months were not there. But South Korean authorities had monitored their activities and had them dead to rights. Don Oberdorfer wondered if the spy bust was politically motivated. He noted that "timing [of the arrests] raised eyebrows . . . especially because managers for ruling party candidate Kim Young-sam were unhappy with rapid improvement of relations with the North." Why were they unhappy with a development that seems so desirable? Oberdorfer speculates that the Kim Young-sam people thought that cordial North-South relations favored opposition party candidate Kim Dae-jung, at the time the strongest rival to Kim Young-sam. Kim Dae-jung was significantly more leftist than the opposition and was a vocal proponent of greater engagement with North Korea. Supporters of rival Kim Young-sam accused their opponent of promoting an appeasement-based policy. The implication drawn by Oberdorfer and other Kim Dae-jung supporters was that by arresting the spies and overstating the seriousness, if not the existence of the espionage ring, the ruling party intentionally jeopardized what was really a solid relationship between the two Koreas. If only that had been the case.

Despite all of this warm and fuzzy relationship building that the spy arrest supposedly ruined, the North Koreans were discovered to be proceeding apace with their clandestine nuclear development program. North Korea was in the process of excluding international inspectors from key installations and accusing them of being "agents for the American CIA." In point of fact, if North Korea genuinely wanted to improve relations with South Korea it would have pulled the spies out on its own accord, before they were discovered. The incumbent party simply pointed out the dangers inherent in trusting North Korea too blindly. No one in South Korea did anything to upset the harmonious applecart: the North Koreans had already knocked it over by their demonstrably hostile and duplicitous actions.

In 1992 the United States and South Korea each held a presidential election, and in both elections a spoiler candidate played a major role. In Korea the candidacy of Hyundai's chairman Chung diluted the vote for the conservative candidate and brought in Kim Young-sam. In the United States EDS's Ross Perot took enough votes away from the Republican incumbent George H. W. Bush to give a victory to Democrat Bill Clinton. As party changes will do in Washington, the new administration recycled in many foreign policy stalwarts including Warren Christopher, Strobe Talbot, and Madeline Albright. The Clinton administration nevertheless favored a domestic focus over foreign policy. But then abruptly the smoke screen that North Korea had placed between observers and its nuclear development program was pulled away. To the shock of the new administration, it was apparent that the North Koreans were considerably further ahead than anyone had thought. There was an immediate scramble to develop a policy and course of action, a process in which all major cabinet posts, especially Defense, State, and CIA had a voice. There was talk of military options, even the possibility of a war.

Meanwhile, South Korean voters selected the candidate that they considered the most conservative, at least from a security and economic perspective. Kim Young-sam had merged his opposition party with the mainstream party—a move that some of the more radical observers called a "sellout." Despite the presence of the usual diverse crowd of splinter interest parties, it came down to a contest between Kim Young-sam and the indefatigable campaigner Kim Dae-jung. For many voters the latter was still a bit too radical and left-leaning for their tastes. They were concerned that he would be too soft on North Korea at a time when it was aggressively continuing its nuclear arms program and flooding South Korea with spies. On that point Oberdorfer was correct: whether the timing was propitious or opportunistic, the mainstream party took full advantage of it.

Kim Young-sam was the first president since the dysfunctional succession of Choi Kyu-ha following Park's assassination who was a pure civilian. He had no military ties but was viewed more positively by the military than was Kim Dae-jung, who was more vocal in his distain and mistrust of the military. It is likely that the transition from Roh to Kim was smoother as a result. Certainly the electorate felt more comfortable with a man at the helm who was at least willing to face the North Koreans squarely and not bend too far to accommodate them, which they feared Kim Dae-jung would do.

## North Korea Raises the Temperature

The South Korean and U.S. forces had reinstituted the annual Team Spirit training exercise for 1993. This exercise, designed expressly for reintroduction of American forces to Korea in event of a general war, always unsettled Kim Il Sung. Such exercises were held all over the world, not just in Korea, but that fact did not pacify the North Korean dictator. Although it was not conducted with an aggressive intent, North Korea found Team Spirit extremely intimidating. In 1992 the exercise had been voluntarily cancelled in an effort to give a "confidence-building measure" to

North Korea. It was revived in 1993, however, specifically as a protest of the lack of good faith bargaining on the part of the North Koreans in regard to the nuclear inspections. The North Koreans used the resumption of the Team Spirit exercise to excuse their previous deceptive actions and to raise their accusations to a higher pitch. In March 1993 North Korea pulled out of the Non-Proliferation Treaty, claiming that the United States was planning a nuclear attack against it. With both Seoul and Washington in the process of bringing aboard new executive branch leaders, the timing was, to say the least, uncomfortable. It is quite probable that Kim Il Sung, who had been securely in power during the tenure of quite a few American and South Korean leaders, was testing both of these new, untried presidents on his terms.

Despite mounting rhetoric about the "paradise living conditions" in North Korea that its propaganda machine unceasingly cranked out, by December 1993, it was clear that North Korea was tanking economically. It had registered yet another disastrous year on all fronts. Food supplies were reaching scandalously low levels and the world began to hear the first reports of hunger in North Korea. It was no longer possible to hide the desperate conditions there. Sympathetic governments and nongovernmental organizations began to send food aid and medical assistance but any donation was tightly controlled and, it was strongly suspected, funneled off to the Party and the army first. How had the situation become so desperate so quickly? Simple, the entire *juche*, or independence of North Korea, was exposed as pure fiction. For decades the North Koreans had depended on major clandestine support, primarily from the Soviet Union. The final fall of the Soviet Union removed the main prop that was keeping Kim Il Sung's regime upright. As its longtime supporter toppled, Kim no doubt recognized that he was facing a disaster of his own. The system he had so brutally nailed together was failing to provide even a modicum of the "peasants and workers paradise" it was touted to be. Economic desperation may have been yet another stimulant for him to proceed apace with his nuclear program. Perhaps Kim Il Sung realized that it was the only bargaining chip he had left in his stack. When even a mouthpiece organization such as his own Party Central Committee described the situation as "grave," it alarmed Korea watchers.

During the following year—until summer of 1994—the crisis in Korea reached the boiling point. Yet, the Clinton administration's Korean policy can only be described as incredibly confusing and totally uncoordinated. Korea was not where it wanted to spend time and effort. Even reporters favorable to the administration describe the disjointed bilateral meetings with North Korea and the shotgun approach of separate official and semiofficial initiatives. Too often one agency did not bother to tell other agencies or principals what they were doing. It was foreign policy chaos.

Within Seoul, Ambassador James Laney and General Gary Luck were trying desperately to improve America's deterrence posture on the peninsula. Laney had even made a special coordination trip back to the United States to try his best to get the various agencies and individuals involved in the process coordinated with each other. He met with only limited success. In the Pentagon the chairman of the Joint Chiefs of Staff and Secretary of Defense were dusting off War Plan 50-27, the often-revised plan for general war in Korea, and were updating it. Military leaders had assured the president that it was possible to eliminate the Yongbyong nuclear research and processing facility by air strike. But the caveat? Such a strike would likely start a general war. Word of this planning had reached Seoul and had startled Laney and Luck with the apparent pace of planned execution and lack of coordination with the U.S. forces stationed in Korea, and with the South Koreans themselves.

On the UN side Thomas Hubbard and North Korean ambassador to the United Nations, Ho Jong, continued to meet in New
York in a Dickensian scenario where progress was measured in
micro-inches. Hubbard appeared to be getting nowhere with the
North Koreans. Meanwhile, reports from UN weapons inspection
teams, led by Hans Blix, were increasingly strident in their concerns about the possibility of North Korea diverting civil-use nuclear power generation materials into materials for weapons
purposes. Intelligence information from various U.S. agencies
often conflicted but in general seemed to support Blix's assess-
ments. There were calls based on these reports to raise the North
Korean issue at the UN Security Council level, although at that
point none of the major players—especially Russia and China—
supported the idea of sanctions. Robert Gallucci was elevated to
an ambassadorial level and told to get all of this confusion sorted
out. He tried, although there seems to be little evidence of success.

Meanwhile on the North Korean side, the rhetoric was heating up with the usual talk of turning various cities in South Korea
and Japan into "seas of fire," and of threats that "UN sanctions
mean war." About the only thing that North Korea always has
plenty of is bullying, blustering noise. This time it found an audience that believed its threats and gave credence to them—always
a dangerous situation. On the U.S.-South Korean side, the Team
Spirit exercise for 1994 was announced and plans proceeded apace
to reinforce the existing 37,000 American troops in South Korea.
President Clinton, alarmed at the speed of developments and ap-
praised of the possible costs of war in human and financial resources, attempted to dispatch two U.S. Senators to meet
personally with Kim Il Sung but was rebuffed by the North
Koreans. Across the board the consensus in the United States and
South Korea appeared to be that war was inevitable.

What is the core issue here that caused so much heat? The technological issues incumbent with nuclear power use, nuclear fuel reprocessing, and nuclear weapons production are complex and confusing to the layperson. But the bottom line is that the North Koreans *had* nuclear power plants. They had agreed under terms of the Non-Proliferation Treaty to let outside inspectors look at the plants to make certain that nothing was being misdirected into a weapons research program. They were nonetheless denying the inspectors access and they were conducting highly suspicious research and development programs that led UN and other nuclear technical analysts to believe that they were violating their word.

In reaction to increasingly tough requests that they honor the agreement, the North Korean leadership was threatening war, obfuscating issues, bullying its neighbors, and stalling progress in meetings. In an attempt to deflect blame the North Koreans pointed fingers at everyone from the United Nations to the United States to South Korea for challenging their sovereignty or violating their independence. At this juncture, the United States and South Korea thought that they had little recourse but to fall back on extreme measures if the North Korean intransigence continued.

Adding to the tragicomedy was the fairly steady parade of visitors to Pyongyang, ranging from the conservative Reverend Billy Graham to the liberal reporter Selig Harrison. Each either delivered messages to Kim Il Sung or returned with ones from him. Graham's message to Kim from Clinton, although the minister tired to soften it, was a blunt demand for Kim to back away from his nuclear development program. As expected, it drew an outraged response. Harrison conversely brought back rosy belief in all of Kim's promises. One useful nugget that appeared in Harrison's comments was an indication that North Korea might be willing to resume negotiations if it received assistance from the United States.

Meanwhile, perennially failed peacemaker Jimmy Carter decided to intervene. Despite multiple requests from the Carter people, Clinton had refused him permission over the past several months to go to North Korea. But this time Carter announced that he would go there as a "private citizen." On hearing that, Clinton relented and had the Carter team accompanied by Dick Christenson, a career foreign service officer who spoke excellent Korean. Carter landed in Seoul on June 15, 1994, and motored to Panmunjom where he and his crew walked across the Bridge of No Return into North Korea amidst appropriate drama and suitable press coverage from both sides.

What did Kim Il Sung think of all this? Here comes to Kim's capital a former president of the United States—the most senior American ever to visit Kim—accompanied by a serving senior diplomat and a squad of former government officials. Yet, he professes to be a mere private citizen. Kim had to look at this gambit with a wink and a nod. In the tightly ground cultural lens through which Kim Il Sung viewed the world, it was absolutely impossible for Carter to be anything less than a special, personal emissary from President Clinton. Kim would have assumed that the "private citizen" label was Carter's face-saving device in the event that he was unable to cut a deal with North Korea. That alone was sufficient to signal Kim that he was desperate to make a deal. The not-so-subtle signals, such as his hyperbolic public pronouncements about peace being the most important part of his mission, and that war was to be averted at any cost, were more than enough to telegraph Carter's—and by logical inference, Clinton's and America's—complete anxiety. The setup was such that Kim thought that he was being legitimately approached by the Americans.

So as he watched television film of Carter waving from Panmunjom, Kim Il Sung must have enjoyed a moment of quiet triumph.

The scenario that he worked so hard to put together was happening at last. Faced with the most dismal economic news he had ever received and a prospect of a worsening economy, devoid of his long-term sponsor, and desperate for outside assistance, Kim had, by adroitly using the threat of nuclear weapons and general war, brought a novice American government to his desk bearing gifts.

Thus began a series of meetings that if held in Italy would have been a viewed as comic opera. The cameras recorded Carter stopping his entourage on the wide, deserted Pyongyang Boulevard in mid-thought. Next, he jumped out of his limousine and conducted policy discussions with his team on its hood. Frantic messengers were dispatched like ancient couriers racing to the DMZ with messages to be sent to Washington on a contingency basis. The process became so bizarre that for a while Carter was in Pyongyang on CNN while Wolf Blitzer stood on the White House lawn asking him questions. A stunned Clinton foreign policy team, including Al Gore and Sandy Berger, meanwhile watched television monitors in the West Wing in puzzled bemusement as the former president ad-libbed policy for the current president who had been upstaged out of the picture.

In the end all Jimmy Carter accomplished was to adroitly maneuver, cajole, and pressure Kim Il Sung into accepting everything that the North Korean leader had hoped to receive in a plan that was known as the "Agreed Framework." Terms included the construction in North Korea of two light water reactors that would accommodate its power needs but not be used for weapons purposes. North Korea agreed to remain in the Nuclear Non-Proliferation Treaty and have a summit meeting with South Korean President Kim Young-sam. In addition, North Korea would receive hundreds of thousands of tons of fuel oil to "make up" for the loss of power due to their "voluntarily" shutting down the

Yongbyong reactor facility. Also, the assistance program would be accompanied by tons of food aid and other in-kind material. As Oberdorfer notes, "Pyongyang played its card brilliantly, forcing one of the world's richest and most powerful nations to undertake direct negotiations and to make concessions to one of the world's least successful nations. *The nuclear threat proved,* up to a point, *to be Pyongyang's great equalizer.*" [Emphasis added.] We shall see how this identical strategy is being used by North Korea today with the hope that it will yield similar results.

Carter, on return to Seoul, modestly called his trip "a miracle." Some say that Carter's mission averted war. They credit him with defusing a tense confrontation and possibly saving millions of lives. It was to be one of the many acts for which the former president was awarded the Nobel Peace Prize. Yet was it really so, or was this merely a case of *post hoc ergo proper hoc* logic? (The cock crows and the sun rises; therefore the cock crowing makes the sun rise.) Even though there are analysts who think that North Korea really was on the verge of initiating a war, it is very difficult to say with certainty. Obviously in such a hermetically closed nation, little trickles out that the dictator does not want made public. There is a certain sense of gamesmanship with Kim Il Sung, who may have been pressing as hard as he could press banking on the United States and South Korea to cave. If that was the case, he read his adversaries perfectly.

Events subsequent to the Carter visit and the Agreed Framework have disclosed that the North Koreans cheated on the agreement from the onset. They switched the emphasis of their nuclear weapons program from plutonium-based to uranium-based and relocated the facility. They gladly accepted the foreign assistance, funneled most of it into keeping their military capability alive, and let the foreigners stay dumb and happy. While it is possible, even easy, to take shots at Carter and Clinton, that is not profitable. We need to learn from our mistakes. The entire Carter trip and the Agreed Framework, which looked so promising at the time, turned out to be a duplicitous fiasco. It is important that we recognize North Korea negotiating tactics and strategy for what they are, and act accordingly in the future.

## Democracy Wins Again in South Korea

Despite endless internal corruption trials involving yet more scandals, this time associated with the Kim Yong-sam administration, South Korea entered a vigorous year of presidential campaigning in 1996. By election time it had been touched by the onset of what would come to be known as the "Asian financial crisis." Despite all this bad news, October 1997 marked another giant step forward for South Korean democracy. Perennial opposition leader Kim Dae-jung was elected president. For the third time executive power had transferred peacefully in South Korea, despite the fact that Kim Dae-jung was intensely disliked and distrusted by the military. It was a scenario that even the most optimistic observer years earlier would have thought incomprehensible. It had to have been a bit of a personal sense of triumph for the former American ambassador Don Gregg as he saw the man whose life he had been instrumental in saving years earlier elevated to the highest office in his land by an involved electorate.

Kim Dae-jung, more than any other major South Korean president, was convinced that accommodation with North Korea was possible. He proposed to seek this accommodation through what he called the "Sunshine Policy"—supposedly a meeting of equals. But in reality it could be more appropriately called a "policy of appeasement." Although it was not known at the time, his much-lauded Sunshine Policy involved bribing the North Korean players. Kim Dae-jung was determined to leave a legacy, and that legacy would be a landmark North-South drawing together. He wanted to be recognized by a Nobel Peace Prize, and he was. Everything seemed good and harmonious on the peninsula. For those of us who had watched through suspicious eyes for decades it seemed far too harmonious to believe.

And then the money ran out—and so did the subterfuge. The list of Kim Dae-jung's accomplishments loses their luster when we know that hundreds of millions of dollars in South Korean chaebol money bought and paid for them. While lionized abroad and praised initially at home for bringing an accommodation of peace to the troubled Korean peninsula, his real legacy is considerably harsher: he bought a fabricated, phony peace while turning a blind eye toward North Korean duplicity. Covered by the playacting, the North Koreans worked feverishly for five unhampered years on clandestine nuclear arms research and manufacture and missile production. And far more heinous, Kim's Sunshine Policy created a bogus atmosphere of harmony and goodwill on the peninsula while hundreds of thousands of his fellow Koreans were starved, tortured, or slapped into concentration camps by a brutal regime with which he was playing games. Kim Dae-jung is still under investigation for his part in the bribery scandal. One can only hope that he is made to pay for some of the harm he has done to the North and South Korean people.

## The Nuclear Boil

By September 2002 when Roh Moo-hyun was elected the new South Korean president, the fat was truly in the fire with North Korea and its nuclear program. Although North Korea continued to deny it, there was increased speculation that it was violating the Non-Proliferation protocols. Two years earlier, in the United

States, George W. Bush had been elected president. The transition between administrations was time-consuming after eight years of opposition party White House occupancy. As the staffs were put together it became evident that the principals would be an interesting mix. Some had had experience in George H. W. Bush's administration. Others, such as Paul Wolfowitz, Richard Armitage, and John Negroponte, were key figures from the Reagan days. It was clear from the outset that this administration would be substantively engaged with foreign affairs. Nevertheless, Bush was tardy devising a Korea policy. By June 2001, some five months after he assumed office, a policy was at last in place but it was never implemented. In response to terrorist attacks against the United States in September 2001, policies around the world were urgently reassessed. Countries were evaluated by how they opposed or supported international terrorism. Given a solid history of supplying and participating in terrorist operations and an increasing sense that North Korea continued to aspire to be a nuclear power, Bush correctly labeled North Korea as a member, along with Iraq and Iran, of an infamous "axis of evil." His remarks were met with predictable shock and horror by the appeasement-minded in this country and abroad, including in South Korea. The North Koreans replied with the usual barrage of hostile, repetitive accusations and denials.

By the beginning of the new century—indeed the new millennium—faces and places around the world were undergoing change. In North Korea the anachronistic heritage of a repressive regime continued unchecked. But they were about to be called to task to answer to the free world for their transgressions.

# CHAPTER 12

# What Next for Korea? Observations, Opinions, and Options

In 1993–1994 I transitioned from executive director of the Korea Society in New York City to a writer and commentator. I moved to an alpaca and llama farm in the Catskill Mountains of New York, began raising these fascinating animals and using the ultra-soft fiber they produce annually (they are not killed for fiber, we just give them a spring haircut) to make elegant garments such as scarves and shawls. After more than eighteen years in big cities with high-stress jobs, I was coming apart around the edges. I needed a change: some clean air, quiet countryside, contemplative solitude, and stress-reducing animals. I needed time to think and sort things out. Most of all I needed to begin writing. To pay bills and keep my hand in the game I booked myself out as a consultant, trainer, and coach, preparing clients to work effectively in Korea and East Asia. This period afforded me the opportunity to do more public speaking, especially to veteran, civic, and student audiences. I began to show up on various talk radio shows across the country and became a regular commentator for national and local television outlets. Although I am carrying a laptop instead of an M-16 these days, and jumping out of pickup trucks rather than C-130s, I continue to focus on Korean affairs and stay connected to Asia.

Since I've been working independently, the world has continued to turn. America has been attacked and infiltrated by terror groups. We've successfully fought two major wars that were geographically oriented, in Iraq and Afghanistan, and are combating the ephemeral specter of global terrorism in its organizational form. Our country is pledged to hunt down and eliminate terrorists and the countries that support international terrorism. Quite naturally, when assembling such a list of rogue nations, North Korea floated to the top. That is not surprising. For decades they have conducted widespread terrorist operations on their own and are active supporters of other rogue nations that wish to possess weapons of mass destruction. It would be entirely in keeping with the North Koreans to sell WMD to terror organizations as well. Hard cash, not morality or legality, carries the day in Pyongyang. The crisis in North Korea, although it is boiling hot, is therefore not new. We've been dealing with it in one form or another, first with the elder Kim, now with his son, for more than fifty-five years. We fought a war to thwart their aggressiveness and many people have devoted major portions of their lives—sometimes even sacrificing them—in order to keep South Korea free. Through these difficult times, America, together with its South Korean ally, has exercised patience and restraint in dealing with the often-hysterical threats emanating from North Korea. Deterrence has worked; war has been averted on the Korean peninsula. Moreover, by its rapid internal decay, North Korea is reduced to a blustering, threatening bully, incapable of winning a conventional war. But it is capable of launching terrorist attacks using nuclear weapons or other forms of weapons of mass destruction aimed at helpless civilians.

Wherever I travel, people ask me the same important questions. How bad is this crisis? Will there be a war? Can the United States strike North Korea militarily? Should it? And whatever it does, will it have to go it alone or with allies?

One of the major world concerns in recent years is that North Korea claims to possess nuclear weapons and is threatening to use them. Many voices, including mine, have called for a resolution of this issue. We've been dealing with the totalitarian regime of North Korea for a long time—too long in fact. Why focus on just another stopgap measure? Suppose we raise sights higher. What if we look at a picture bigger than the nuclear program alone? What if we initiate an action directed at regime change? Let the United States join with South Korea and its regional partners and get rid of the atrocious dictator and his WMD threat once and for all, liberate the oppressed North Korean people, reunite the Korean peninsula under one democratic, free-market government, and give every Korean a chance to enjoy a better life. Certainly this is a worthy goal. But is it realistic?

First, we must look hard at North Korean military capabilities. Frankly, North Korea has grown relatively weak. While it still fields a large army, its systems are old, its tactics outmoded, and the motivation of the troops suspect. Twenty years ago we estimated that North Korea could fight a ninety-day war without outside support. Considering the present stage of internal decay, two weeks of war would probably just about deplete all of its reserves. The North Korean military, although still possessing the gross numbers of old, has stagnated and grown less effective. They are not a paper tiger, however, and we ought to expect that the troops in the better units will fight well, but they are hardly as formidable as when they were well supplied and backed up by two giant neighbors—the Soviet and Chinese armies. There is considerable speculation that in conventional weaponry the primary North Korean improvement has been in the field of short- and medium-range missiles. The accuracy of these missiles is questionable, as is the payload capability. Given the accuracy limitations observed in testing, a North Korean missile may be more a terror weapon to be directed against a helpless civilian population than a serious military tool capable of destroying a selected target with any precision. The only impressive trick left in North Korea's bag is the nuclear threat. But that is a terrorist move, not a legitimate military strategy.

In the other systems—artillery, armor, air, infantry weapons, communications, logistical, transportation, and support capabilities—the North Koreans have lagged far behind the South Koreans. Even though the North Koreans spend a large percentage of their GNP on defense and the South Koreans spend 6 percent or less, the difference in available funding is staggering. In other words, relative to the South Korean military, the North Korean military is in decay. Again, that is not to say that it cannot inflict pain. You can be just as dead when shot from an obsolete weapon as you can when shot from a modern one. Could North Korea pour human wave assaults into a meat grinder of South Korean and U.S. firepower? Unfortunately, it could. It would incur huge casualties with no gain. Then the system would collapse.

No matter how one analyzes the particulars, it is clear that North Korea could not prevail over South Korea even if the latter stood alone. With the United States shoulder to shoulder, adding not only force of arms but also strength of will to the sometimes-vacillating South Korean political leadership a North Korean win is out of the question. If it were not for what former National Security Advisor Richard Allen calls "the unfortunate geostrategic location of Seoul," defending against North Korean aggression would not even be a major issue. To acknowledge the point that CATO Institute's Doug Bandow and other observers have made, it is unquestioningly true that the North Koreans could perpetrate an unacceptable level of damage on South Korea and the American and foreign community residing in Seoul. Conventional weapons alone would wreak havoc with the citizenry, causing untold casualties. If weapons of mass destruction were to be employed, the catastrophe would be horrific and unacceptable. But such a scenario implies a North Korea willing to do a thing that not even Imperial Japan was willing to do at the end of World War II: commit national ritual suicide.

South Korea is another story. On the military side the South Korean army of approximately 600,000 is well trained, intelligent, and capable. The South Korean military fields trained, motivated, healthy soldiers with excellent weapons systems and a solid logistical support capability. The South Korean Air Force is equipped with modern U.S. jet aircraft and has the tools, manpower, and know-how to fly, fix, and fight them. The navy and marine components are the smallest of the services but are quite capable. South Korea also has a reserve service requirement (it has an active duty universal military service requirement for all young men) that allows them to field reinforcement units in an emergency. Militarily, the South Koreans are tough, ready, and capable. They are professionals, who have come a long way since the days when I was a student at the South Korean Army College. While the South Korean educational system still retains too much rote memorization, South Korean military leaders are far more imaginative and capable than they were in those stratified years. Even without the presence of the U.S. forces, the South Korean units are fully capable of defeating an attack by North Korea. Yet, they still face the critical issue of anticipated civilian loss of life with Seoul located so inconveniently close to the Demilitarized Zone, a place that President Bill Clinton on a visit called "the scariest place in the world."

Nor is the military any longer the dark eminence lurking in the political shadows waiting for its opportunity to seize power. Those days are gone forever in South Korea. Several of my student officers, from my English language classes at the Korean Military Academy, have reached senior levels. "It could not happen with us," they said emphatically when I asked about possible military interference with the political system. "We are committed to democracy." The present chief executive, Roh Moo-hyun, and his immediate predecessor, Kim Dae-jung, are not friends of the military. Nor are they especially respected by the military—but they were supported fully by them. The South Korean military recognizes the sanctity of the presidential office. They have proved by their behavior that they are committed to democracy—just as they say they are.

It was an article of faith for us during the Vietnam War that the toughest national soldiers were always the South Koreans. Later, having them as my classmates at the Army College in Chinhae, I came to know these officers on a close personal basis. One of our classmates in Class 23 was a winner of the Hwarang Medal, the South Korean equivalent of the American Congressional Medal of Honor, the highest valor award given. Almost every other one had cycled as I had through the Southeast Asian wars. Some were also Special Forces, others were combat arms, aviators, or support branch officers. There was absolutely never a question in my mind of their professionalism or their bravery. Later I watched the young men I taught at the Korean Military

Academy take charge of their units and exhibit the utmost bravery
when required. The courage and dedication of the South Korean
military is beyond question. The strength of will and the courage of
the South Korean politicians and public in general are of greater
concern.

The weakness in South Korea is not military but political and
moral. On the political side things are rather wishy-washy in Seoul.
Problems started with Kim Dae-jung's Sunshine Policy movement:
it was all hogwash. Investigation disclosed Hyundai and other
major South Korean conglomerates had paid massive bribes to the
North Koreans. Kim Dae-jung was completely aware of what was
happening, consequently becoming a compromised leader and a
covert partner of North Korea. As former National Security Advisor
Richard Allen notes, "Kim's Sunshine Policy . . . depended in large
measure on North Korean goodwill. During the final months of his
presidency, Kim, who was awarded the Nobel Peace Prize for his
breakthrough with the North, was confronted with the chilling fact
that, during his five-year term, North Korea was hard at work developing a secret uranium enrichment program." After the scandal
was revealed and the entire mess exposed as a fraud, Kim, "eager
to preserve his legacy, pressured Washington to be 'reasonable' with
North Korea," Allen further notes.

As a consequence of Kim's desire to protect his reputation, despite the cost to his country, his opponent to the north, Kim Jong
Il, was under little pressure either to reform or to abide by the
Nuclear Non-Proliferation Treaty that he had accepted. When
caught red-handed violating the nuclear agreements and challenged by Assistant Secretary of State for East Asia Pacific Affairs
James Kelly and other American officials, North Koreans admitted their transgressions but refused to apologize for them.
Instead, North Korea reverted to type and adopted threatening,

bullying tactics. These actions, and the huge national loss of face incurred because of Kim Dae-jung's reprehensible behavior, upset South Koreans, who are both embarrassed and confused.

As a result, we observed in both the Kim Dae-jung and now the Roh Moo-hyun governments, a rather bizarre movement by the South Koreans toward a neutral stance. I use the term "bizarre" because the South Koreans, as Allen observes have "stepped into the neutral zone and now pretend to be a role of mediator between Pyongyang and Washington, declaring that both sides must make 'concessions.' The cynicism of this act constitutes a serious breach of faith." It has also, as Allen correctly notes, reinforced the ever-present North Korean objective of splitting apart the coalition poised against it, most especially the bilateral relationships between South Korea and the United States. The North Koreans have blatantly appealed to Han, the ancient ethnic glue binding the Korean people, and, to their shame, many South Koreans have responded positively. So at this juncture of affairs the North Koreans are quite likely to be rating the political will of the South Korean government and people as rather low if it came down to a confrontation—certainly so in the face of a physical confrontation. In some manner, this attitude from South Korean leadership seems to be reflected in what can only be described as a combination of wishful thinking and denial by much of the South Korean public who are frantic in their desire to pretend that a North Korean threat does not exist.

It is a difficult attitude to fathom. It manifests itself by a willful disregard for North Korean aggression. Or as a vague sense that all this has somehow come about because of a latent American-North Korean animosity. They need to be made aware of the consequences of their indifference, and the need for their active involvement and support. After all, it is the fate of their families and countrymen that is at stake here. But South Korea has earned its independence and worked exceedingly hard and long for democracy. Ultimately the choice of options must lie with the South Korean people. We can only hope for the sake of all that they make the best choice.

## China Leads

The People's Republic of China is the key player in the region. "China," former ambassador to both China and South Korea James Lilley says, "is absolutely an essential participant in resolving a crisis situation in North Korea." And with his penetrating, analytical mind, there are few outsiders with a deeper understanding of the Northeast Asia region than Jim Lilley.

China has been called North Korea's only remaining friend. Yet, given the stresses of leadership succession, SARS, and an attention-demanding economy, China may not want to be its friend any longer. North Korea has become an embarrassment. China is increasingly inclined to cut off the flow of the ceaseless welfare demanded by a blustering, whining North Korea that contributes nothing but irritants to China's international development goals. If conflict flared, China would likely stand neutral in a war, no doubt positioning troops along its border with North Korea to keep refugees out and to be in position to hop in any direction it deemed necessary to protect its interests. China would hope to salvage enough political clout from a conflict to come out a winner. But it would never encourage or support war.

China is itself in a period of transition. It is far less interested in ideological expansion than it was in the early days of aggressive communism. Decades of economic growth and relative prosperity are bringing slow political reform. China has become a nation that values this economic growth and seeks a harmonious and stable relationship with its neighbors and in the region. China's president, Hu Jintao, on a visit to Washington made it clear that he is firmly committed to a peaceful resolution of the lingering acrimony between the two Koreas. There can be no question that Hu views a recalcitrant, aggressive North Korea as a major hindrance to China's policy of unchecked economic growth. This is one of his major concerns because the economy is the engine of modern China. Hu has even expressed comfort with Japan's role in the region, going so far as to give the nod to a modest Japanese military buildup. But Hu would be horrified if Japan were so pressured by the situation in Korea that it elected to develop nuclear weapons itself. This is an unexpressed, but lingering fear that Hu shares with others in the Chinese ruling clique. Equally troubling to the Chinese leadership is the prospect of an unchecked refugee flow from North Korea into China. Refugees are already a serious problem, and they only number in the low thousands. Imagine if that number skyrocketed into the millions? The thought of it keeps the Chinese awake at night.

The North Korean situation also carries dire economic consequences for China. No matter how you try to portray it, economically, North Korea is a black hole for Chinese money, fuel oil, food, and supplies. North Korean belligerence constantly focuses international attention on friction in the region rather than highlighting the atmosphere of harmony. Not only does North Korea absorb far more than it contributes but it also chases away potential regional investment by its aggressive stance. None of this pleases Chinese leadership.

China, on the other hand, is entirely comfortable these days with South Korea—a major departure from past days of open hostility. Ever since the successful Northern Policy, which was initiated by previous South Korean president Roh Tae-woo, ties between South Korea and China have grown close. Today they have never been tighter. Politically, the two countries get along well. Economically, the level of South Korean investment in China is high and rising. China has enjoyed being a trading partner with South Korea and has learned that the two countries are no longer implacable enemies. A reunited Korea under the kind of leadership that South Korea has exhibited would not worry China about exposing its flank to an enemy. A Korea that walked a bit of an independent path would continue to be a strong buffer between the ancient enemies China and Japan. Korean unification would have positive collateral consequences, such as accelerated industrial development of the now dirt-poor region of China that borders North Korea. If that area from the mouth of the Tuman River across to the Yellow Sea could begin to look more like the highly prosperous China South Coast and less like Dogpatch it would be to the benefit of all concerned. Economic prosperity lends a great deal of social stability to an area. Development of the now-depressed border territory would contribute positively to the net economy of China and would also benefit China by reducing resources required to police and regulate this volatile area. Purely from an economic standpoint there are zero benefits to China to keep propping up the Kim Jong Il regime.

While economic reasons may be persuasive to convince the Chinese to dump North Korea into the ashcan of history—a place it has earned and so richly deserves—none are sufficiently compelling by themselves. What may convince China that it is in everyone's interest to move toward positive resolution of the Korean question once and for all is the issue of a nuclear Japan. There is a vast difference in regional stability and the manner in which diplomacy is conducted between a Japan that might have a nuclear weapon *one day* and a Japan that formally announces that it *has* nuclear weapons. Gene Hanratty, former U.S. Army China specialist, says "Japan's pacifism could well be tested if North Korea continues to test missiles by firing them over Japan and to build up some sort of nuclear arsenal." Should it be confirmed that the North Koreans have embarked aggressively on building nuclear weapons, Hanratty continues, "the only alternative in that circumstance would be Japanese development of nuclear weapons. That is an alternative no one in Northeast Asia wants to see—especially China."

An added, not-insignificant benefit to China of a peaceful Korea is that the presence of U.S. troops—37,000 in South Korea and 40,000 in Japan—could be reduced significantly. The number in a reunified Korea would probably be cut to almost zero, mostly a symbolic regional presence, home porting for some U.S. Navy ships, and perhaps an airbase. A majority of the troops in Japan would be drawn down, reflecting tension reduction. For China this could only be good news, for the significant presence of American troops in South Korea has been looked at by them for decades as a threat to the sovereignty of China.

By far the most troubling issue facing the Chinese is the specter of millions—perhaps even double-digit millions—of North Koreans fleeing across their border to escape an imploding, self-destructive Kim Jong Il regime. The Chinese are right to worry. After all, where else can North Korean refugees go other than north? The southern border is loaded with the highest number of soldiers on both sides, plus the deadly minefields of the Demilitarized Zone. With oceans to the east and west and too few boats, the best escape route for disgruntled North Koreans is to head to the Chinese border. It is not the mere numbers of refugees alone that scares the Chinese government but their abject poverty. The poor souls who flee North Korea are teetering on the edge of starvation, wracked by serious illness, and desperate enough to do whatever might be necessary to keep themselves and their families alive. The potential for abuse—prostitution, slavery, and crime—is so high that the social issues alone are terrifying. In fact, humanitarian leaders, such as Suzanne Scholte of the Defense Forum Foundation report continually of "the horrible human rights situation in North Korea." All of these things, Scholte tells us, are happening now along the North Korean border in China. And the refugee flow is a mere trickle compared to what it could become. The prospect of a raging torrent of troubled humanity spilling across the fence virtually forces the Chinese to resort to the expedient policy that they know will work: keep the North Koreans south of the border, and forcibly repatriate those caught crossing illegally. It is a harsh policy but, when viewed through Chinese eyes, somewhat understandable. Chinese leaders will likely be willing to prop North Korea up indefinitely rather than risk being overwhelmed by refugees. Solving the refugee issue is therefore the key to unlocking the North Korean conundrum. Fix it and the door will open to solutions of the remaining issues.

There is already a model we could learn from in Southeast Asia. Thailand was wracked by a similar—albeit smaller in raw numbers—crisis following the fall of Vietnam and the horrific rise to power of the Khmer Rouge in Cambodia. Refugees of all kinds fled west into Thailand to escape the insane violence of the killing fields of the despotic communist rulers. Later, after Vietnamese forces invaded Cambodia and overthrew the Khmer Rouge, even those killers fled into refugee camps. The situation along the border was volatile, sensitive, and desperate—as most refugee problems can quickly become. The solution that worked in Thailand was to establish a string of tightly supervised and controlled camps under the overall jurisdiction of the UN Human Rights

Commission to give the camps an international legitimacy. Many governments and nongovernmental organizations sent contributions in the form of funding, supplies, and volunteers to the camps. Physicians, logisticians, and health specialists and managers were dispatched to the camps to make certain that health, sanitation, food, security, and immigration issues were taken care of properly. But as in any endeavor, there are lessons to be gleaned from the Thai experience, both positive and negative.

A similar model can be constructed in China—tailored specifically to accommodate Chinese sensitivities and to handle the needs of North Korean refugees. Funding for such an operation could be generated from the countries most involved: the United States, Japan, and South Korea. European, Asian, Australian, North American, and South American assistance can come from countries that generally are receptive to supporting humanitarian needs around the world. A buffer zone could be established with a clear understanding on all sides that North Koreans fleeing the camps would be subject to Chinese law as it applies to other illegal aliens.

The purpose of the camps would be to establish a safety zone where abused North Koreans could recover their mental and physical health, participate in educational programs to bring them into line with current affairs, and even receive vocational-skills training prior to ultimate resettlement back in North Korea. There may even be cases of resettlement to South Korea on a case-by-case basis because of family exigencies or other unusual factors. But the ultimate purpose of the camps—other than that basic human decency cries out for us to help the unfortunate North Korean people—would be to allow the dictatorship of Kim Jong Il to collapse without endangering the population either internally or in neighboring countries. When the word begins to spread of the open sanctuary in China, the people of North Korea will vote with their feet. The anticipated huge outflow of people ought to be sufficient, if not to cause Kim himself to relinquish power, then perhaps enough to generate internal action against him. The consortium of regional allies will have to be fully prepared to meet whatever emergency arises in what will become an extremely fast-moving, fluid situation. A comprehensive menu of scenarios and options will need to be prepared and thoroughly vetted through the relevant players prior to embarking on the strategy. It will be much like a war plan in complexity and thoroughness but its purpose is to prevent war.

This isn't your father's China any more. The actions and pronouncements of recent and present leadership have shown that, and here is the opportunity for China to prove it to the world. It must be an active member of a committed coalition to isolate and force regime change in North Korea. China has long been the closest thing North Korea has to a friend, and while that relationship is visibly chilling, the Chinese are ideally positioned to present at least a somewhat sympathetic face. China may well accept a deposed Kim Jong Il and resettle him. If the international coalition decides that regime change is necessary, it is highly probable that Chinese diplomats will have to bring some harsh, unwelcome messages to the Dear Leader himself. Again, the big question: Is China up for this level of responsibility? Is China willing to accept the risks involved to have a more politically stable East Asia? I addressed the problems, especially that of the refugees, with a Chinese-American friend who said emphatically, "No! China will never agree to accept more refugees from North Korea." When I asked whether her opinion would change if the refugee situation was constructed on the Thai model, she reconsidered. "They might agree to that," she said, adding "but only if someone else paid for it." Considering that refugee camps are less expensive than light water reactors and infinitely less expensive and more humane than war, it ought to be possible to find deep-enough pockets internationally to pick up the tab to save millions of human lives.

The burning question is of course, "What makes you think that Kim Jong Il will sit quietly by and let this process happen?" Although it is not always polite to answer a question with a question, my initial response is, "What will he do other than rant, rave, threaten nuclear war, and carry on like crazy?" In other words, a continuation of the very acts upon which he has depended for years, and that he is using at this moment. Kim Jong Il is rapidly reaching the point where he is running out of options. Certainly he holds the nuclear hammer—or we are concerned enough that he does that we do not want to test him on it. But that is strictly a one-time use. And it is akin to holding a huge revolver to his own head and squeezing the trigger. Bill Clinton was correct when he said that if Kim uses nuclear weapons he and his country are dead. Kim Jong Il ought to be told, quietly but officially, preferably by a high-ranking Chinese official speaking on behalf of the international consortium, that such an act will bring instant retaliation of the most personal sort. In other words, he will be killed if he does anything to generate hostilities. The same conversation would be an appropriate occasion to remind him that voluntary departure might be the safest course of action. The beaches in Cuba are always nice this time of year.

Nothing, of course, is as simple as we would like it to be. There are serious issues involved with this strategy. One of the biggest concerns has to be Kim Jong Il's personal lack of international sophistication. He has minimal international exposure and for decades his human information sources have been committed to telling him only what he wants to hear. The tricky thing about

North Korea has always been its impenetrability. Information does not get in or out. Former senior Federal Bureau of Investigation counterintelligence specialist Skip Brandon remembers that the FBI rated its ability to penetrate North Korea as the "most difficult of all intelligence targets." He explains further that "because of the closed, totalitarian nature of their society we were always nervous that their agents might be tailoring reports to what they thought their superiors wanted to hear." Given their culture, that would be a very reasonable characteristic to expect of North Korean intelligence service operatives. Brandon warns, "our fear always is that those same superiors will then make critical policy decisions based on skewed information." There is only one real decision-maker in North Korea, and the intelligence service reports directly to him. So will logic penetrate the delusional mind of Kim Jong Il? We know that he sees the world through a lens of his own manufacture and chances are excellent that lens is warped from reality. He may really believe that he is as strong as he thinks he is, that America is a soft, decadent country, and that South Korea can be bribed or bluffed into any course of action that he desires. Convincing him of the futility of his position is a major challenge. Are there other steps that might help him make up his mind?

Prompt military action is an option. But while military action in Afghanistan and Iraq accomplished its missions, it is not the first choice for resolving the Korean problem. North Korea could not win a war but it could inflict unacceptable damage on South Korea and Japan. It is critical when dealing with Kim Jong Il, however, that he continues to *think* that the military option, while not necessarily at the top of the list, is still definitely on the table. Removing that threat without a verifiable quid pro quo is foolish negotiating technique and seriously weakens the American position. The history of negotiations with dictators whether, Hitler,

Stalin, Saddam Hussein, or Kim Jong Il, has taught that a carrot without a stick is useless. It is worse than useless, actually, because a perceived unwillingness to use force if pressed encourages these lunatics to greater excess and aggression. It is therefore crucial to effective negotiations that the stick be prominently displayed, even if the United States does as Theodore Roosevelt counseled and speaks softly around it. Naturally, no military action ought to be initiated frivolously. There must be adequate justification and a clearly defined, reasonably attainable goal. It is important that all courses of action be thoroughly analyzed and considered in terms of possible cost—to people and treasure—and in terms of desired outcome, prior to military engagement.

But, people ask, why is it necessary to go through all of this? Why bother to keep the military option open even if you know in your heart that it would be a last-resort option under any circumstances? The reply is simple: to remove the military option unilaterally places the United States and its coalition partners in a weakened state for all negotiations. Unless and until a reliable reciprocal agreement can be obtained from the North Korean opponent the military option must be kept alive. Someone like Kim Jong Il would view its withdrawal not as a confidence-building measure but as contemptible weakness.

What does having a military option do for diplomacy? Paradoxically, it strengthens discussions. Using a one-two punch of diplomacy backed by a military option produces focus on both sides. It keeps parties rational and motivated to hammer out a mutually acceptable solution. Yet there are times when a rogue state is so caught up in its own propaganda and inflated glory that even a military threat cannot bring it to rational discussion. The North Koreans will use what has worked in the past as a model for what they think that they can get away with in any ongoing discussions. For a time America's record was harmful to negotiations. Unwillingness to use the military option effectively—in the case of U.S. actions in Somalia and elsewhere—sent a message of appeasement and peace at any price to opponents around the world. It said loud and clear that the United States was unwilling to stand up for what it said or to accept casualties to do what it knew to be the right thing. That kind of a message guaranteed continued North Korean hostility. On the other hand, a successful conclusion through precise application of violence—for example, victory in Iraq and Afghanistan—demonstrates that the United States is indeed willing to use force if pressed to carry out policy that it and its allies interpret as correct. This is a complete paradigm shift from the past. The North Koreans will need to digest it. From this point forward they ought to expect the United States to reject blackmail, bribery, and appeasement. Therefore, an essential element of successful negotiations with North Korea—and, ironically an avoidance of war—has been winning the war in Iraq. The North Koreans would otherwise continue to consider America the paper tiger it has been in the past.

Again, China must play a positive role here. Kim Jong Il needs to feel the strength of the consortium marshaled against him in such a manner that he knows that none of the tactics that he has employed in the past will succeed this time. Additionally, he needs to hear from a Chinese diplomat the key message that China has run its course with North Korea and that the time for personal relocation is at hand. This combined action plan will be effective as long as all concerned have the strength to stay the course. It will at times seem exceedingly dangerous, but it pays to recall that Kim has now seen the results of American military action. Despite his own propaganda, the realization must be forming that he cannot realistically stand up to a determined South

Korean-American military operation. From there the path leads to escape or suicide. Essential to the new paradigm—the one Kim Jong Il must grasp—is a new U.S. policy of resolute determination, vision, and patience—backed with strength. The War in Iraq was watched with "shock and awe" in Pyongyang. Since the North Korean military, just like Iraq, is a clone of the Soviet forces the United States in effect showed Kim Jong Il how he would be defeated in detail. The message of focused strikes aimed at the person of Saddam Hussein was not lost on the Dear Leader. It wouldn't take more than a millisecond to change his title to the "Dead Leader."

Whatever eccentricities Kim Jong Il possesses, a death wish does not seem to be one of them. So unless we think that the Dear Leader is ready to pull the temple down on his head like Samson and commit national suicide, the Iraq lesson has sent an incredibly relevant, strong message to him. First and foremost, Kim Jong Il realizes that it is no longer in his power to win a war. This is not going to be an easy lesson for him to digest. For someone accustomed to making life and death decisions with frivolous carelessness, Kim is unlikely to be able to consume this elephant of a revelation all in one bite. He is going to need to chew on it a while and ingest it in chunks. That will take time but the more time passes the more convinced of his military weakness he is going to become. His minions may figure it out before he does—and that may influence their behavior.

## Multilateral or Unilateral?

Primarily because the North Koreans realized that under the former president of South Korea, Kim Dae-jung, the South Koreans had taken the military option off the table, they were able to manipulate and steer negotiations comfortably. Not only that, but the

North Koreans were well rewarded for their efforts. Bribery scandal investigations in South Korea speak of "hundreds of millions of U.S. dollars" paid to North Korea just to show up at the conference table and look pretty. The North Korean leadership probably still thinks that it can continue to do the same under President Roh Moo-hyun. Continued South Korean government vacillation is one of the primary reasons that the United States insists on multilateral meetings with North Korea and not bilateral ones as the North Koreans request. One of the criticisms of the Bush administration is this idea of bilateral negotiations and meetings between the United States and North Korea. "What does it cost us to talk to them?" Sure, that sounds reasonable. Talk, what can that hurt? After all, Americans are coached from youth that talk is better than precipitate action. What the critics may not understand it that from the North Korean standpoint the goal is not to negotiate with the United States, but to divide it from its friends and allies in the region. This is exactly what the North Koreans were doing by continuing to encourage bilateral talks during the Clinton administration: divide and conquer. In essence, what could be expected after conducting extensive bilateral talks with the North Koreans is a targeted, well thought-out campaign to split the United States from its friends and allies through calculated rumor, disinformation, and bribery. Negotiation with North Korea is hardball, not beanbag. This is sufficient reason to maintain the current policy of multilateral talks only. But there are others.

Another issue with a strictly bilateral approach in this instance is that one-on-one begins in a confrontational, win-lose format. The North Koreans come to the table with a highly defensive posture. They are programmed to mistrust and dispute any U.S. démarche. They will promise to agree to UN supervision on cessation of WMD programs, anything in return for support in kind and in specie, but as we have seen, will lie, cheat, and evade. On the other hand, a group conference with a minimum of China, Japan, South Korea, and perhaps Russia present, would diffuse the confrontational aspects of a bilateral negotiation and allow for some face-saving actions on the part of other participants.

Surprising for many American observers who tend to see these things in binary, black-and-white terms, the South Koreans are likely to be sympathetic to the North Koreans on some issues but for their own reasons. Certainly South Korea fears North Korea's erratic tendencies. But South Korea also craves a relationship that neutralizes the North Korean threat while providing the South Koreans with a source of cheap labor and maybe even a market for some of its low-end consumer products. As we have learned so far, Korean people on both sides of the Demilitarized Zone are highly conflicted by the fifty-year-long love-hate relationship. They are culturally imprinted with values that differ strongly from some in the West. The ultimate reuniting of the two countries into a single people is never too far from any person's mind, especially in the abstract. As a consequence, on many issues the South Koreans would act more as colleagues with the North Koreans than the Americans might expect. This could actually be a positive in a multilateral conference, but only if the South Koreans stay as team players and do not cook private side deals with Pyongyang. There has to be team discipline for the strategy to work.

Japan is a necessary participant in any conference because it is such an historically strong player in the region. Japan wields enormous economic power backed by solid military capability that many overlook. Due primarily to the bipolarity of the Cold War and the mutual threat that was for decades perceived in the region from the Soviet Union and China, it was increasingly in U.S. interest to see Japan expand its military capabilities. While this was happening, both sides downplayed the nature of the improvements by focusing on mutually agreed and self-enforced limitations. Japan is a formidable military power from a self-defense and short strike perspective. It is seriously considering a sophisticated missile defense system. Every North Korean missile test pushes Japan harder in the direction of upgrading not only their defensive capabilities but also the offensive improvements that even a decade ago would have seemed to exceed Japan's stated needs. It is helpful to note that the frequently cited proscriptions in Japan's Constitution regarding war (Article IX outlaws war as a national policy) were written and imposed by a conquering, albeit highly admired, foreigner, General Douglas MacArthur. Constitutions can be amended should the gravity of the threat seem to warrant it.

So also could the Japanese exercise a nuclear development option. No one involved in the region wishes to see this happen. China particularly would fear an openly nuclear Japan. Nonetheless, in coalition negotiations those are the unstated, off-the-table items that everyone knows exists but no one talks about. What Japan really brings to the table in this case is a strong economy and an ability to deal with North Korea on a relatively unemotional, business-like plane. The North Koreans certainly have jeopardized that relationship in the past with some of their erratic acts such as kidnapping innocent civilians, running drugs, laundering money, staging terrorist operations, and firing missiles close to Japan. These actions were not taken to win friends but rather to intimidate, especially firing the missiles. As a potential source of huge capital investment for North Korea, Japan nonetheless ranks right up there with the United States.

It is a positive sign indeed to see the alacrity with which Japan is moving to action as the crisis builds in Northeast Asia. It also speaks well of Japan that the moves it has taken to begin to squeeze North Korea are being done without undue fanfare and with absolutely no provocative rhetoric. Given a series of fairly high-level meetings that have taken place, it would appear that Japan's moves are part of a coordinated strategy involving, at a minimum, the United States and South Korea. It is this kind of pressure that will have more influence on Kim Jong Il than would public, dramatic pronouncements that would force him to stand fast rather than lose face. Japan has been an entrepot serving North Korea for a long time. It has also been a rich source of hard currency, primarily from the Korean yakuza. The open two-way access Pyongyang enjoyed in Japan is denied. Currency shipments are being curtailed and in the busy port cities North Korean ships—many used to carry contraband of illegal drugs (heroin and methamphetamines), counterfeit currency, and weapons—are being thoroughly searched. Cleverly avoiding use of the "B word"—blockade—the Japanese are indulging in an undeclared one. They use subterfuges such as "port inspections," "safety inspections," and the like to hold North Korean ships in port for weeks. Even if the ships are not carrying contraband the action shows that North Korean authorities must still be extremely cautious about transiting Japan or risk seizure of the cargos and increased world condemnation.

Other countries committed to freedom, such as Australia and Singapore, are joining in quiet but unmistakable moves to intercept and thwart continued criminal or terrorist activity by North Korea. North Korea has too long been permitted to engage in mobster-like activities in order to acquire foreign currency. Once it realizes that it will no longer be able to do so without penalty, it will have to change. A good name for this might be the "anaconda strategy." The anaconda, a huge snake that inhabits tropical South America, has a reputation for squeezing its prey to death. But that is not, strictly speaking, the case. What the anaconda does is wrap its prey in huge coils. It tightens down to the extent that the prey cannot move or expand its chest cavity. When the prey exhales the anaconda in a flash tightens down just enough to accommodate that difference. And repeats the process. Soon the prey suffocates. That is the effect of the undeclared blockade of North Korean shipping. Just keep tightening down until they can't continue present illegal activities. The essential requirements for success in the multilateral area are unity of effort and clarity of message. It is imperative that the North Koreans hear the real message.

The best option is to keep the carrot of some support as well as the stick of military action in full view. Meanwhile, all players must agree in secret that the ultimate goal is not continuation of the status quo, but regime change as soon as possible with minimum damage. The only way I can foresee accomplishing this admittedly challenging mission is for the United States to enlist the full cooperation of the regional powers, most particularly China, Japan, and South Korea. The quietest, most efficient way to bring down Kim Jong Il is not by direct confrontation but by bleeding North Korea to death. At the moment Kim holds two groups of people hostage: the citizens of Greater Seoul and the unfortunates who live in North Korea under his heel. He uses both groups to guarantee his longevity and individual prosperity. Certainly, some of his minions are quite willing to stand with him and enjoy the authority they wield and the luxurious crumbs that fall from the Dear Leader's table. It has been shown historically, however, that given sufficiently deteriorating conditions these trusted allies will turn on the leader who has lost the magic. The way to accomplish this is through implosion.

When a rancher has a sick animal that poses a danger to itself and others either through spreading disease or aberrant behavior, the animal is "put down" or destroyed. It is restrained so that it cannot cause damage and then is killed in as humane and gentle a manner as possible consistent with safety. This is in essence what must happen to the regime of Kim Jong Il. He ought to be required by the international community to answer for his many crimes against humanity, especially those atrocities committed on his own people. In the short run it may be efficacious to give him the escape route that the ancient Chinese strategist Sun Tzu counsels ought to be offered to enemies. He may accept the opportunity to flee in splendor. But whether his reign of terror is terminated by exile, imprisonment, or execution is less important than that it end and end as soon as possible. Like a berserk animal, Kim Jong Il must be restrained from further damage to his country and to others.

In some ways he has made this task easier by his abominably awful reign. Following the train wreck that characterized his father's economic policies, Kim Jong Il has adroitly managed to bring North Korea so close to the precipice that he is "hanging ten" over the black pit of economic disaster. That is the good news. The bad news is that the helpless people of North Korea continue to endure the pain of his policies because he always reserves sufficient funds to pay for the luxurious lifestyle that he and his cronies enjoy. In that he typifies his class: corrupt communist dictator. These people are brought down by their excesses and, in time, so shall he.

The danger arises in what desperate terrors Kim Jong Il may unleash in a last-ditch effort to retain control and blackmail neighbors into keeping him afloat. This is justifiable cause for worry. His potential actions are difficult to assess. Miscalculation potentially risks the lives of millions of innocents. Our sense of concern and responsibility is, of course, a point that Kim Jong Il imagines strengthens his position. Yet his conscienceless behavior weakens himself terminally in the long term, although for a brief moment he may think himself in control of the situation. He is not; others are. And the time is ripe for those others to act in concert and remove him.

In order to push Kim Jong Il into the oblivion of history, into a place he has so richly earned, combined action will be required to achieve the final implosion of his regime. The key players in this drama are of course China, Japan, South Korea, and the United States. The United Kingdom will be a partner. Russia can be helpful. In order to execute a proper squeeze on Kim Jong Il it is necessary that all players be in synchronization. Pressure must be real, fixed, increasing slowly in intensity, and unwavering. It must be made abundantly clear to Kim that continuation of present policies is unacceptable, and will, if continued, be addressed with force. Whether or not the consortium intends to exercise the military option, it must be taken seriously. It must be there as an implacable stick: not overtly threatening, but something that may not be overlooked

Meanwhile, a quiet exit ought to be arranged for Kim Jong Il. Until the very last minute in these cases there are always the questions of who wants him, who would accept him, or even if he will accept an offer to flee. Power of an absolute nature must be extremely heady as well as corrupting. It appears to have an addictive nature. Relinquishing such power voluntarily must be a wrenching experience. But having the offer on the table—visible as much for him to see as for those in close proximity to him to know it exists—is critically important as the endgame plays out. For at the last minute it is certainly possible that one of his cronies will take independent, summary action in order to save his own hide. Such things are not a certainty by any stretch, but are far from unknown historically. If the corps surrounding him thinks that its only options are to remain in power or to die, it would be inclined to fight on. If on the other hand its members see that there might be a way that they could escape with some of their miserable hides intact, they might also opt to select that option, even if it means stepping over the body of Kim Jong Il to get to it.

Northeast Asia is vital to the security of the United States and represents the present and future in our mutual economic growth. China, Japan, and the United States are three of the world's largest economies. It is reasonable to think that South Korea—now also a major economic power—would, given time, lead a reunified Korea to new economic heights. Wouldn't it all be much better if the region could focus on economic development with only the minimum necessary for adequate national security being diverted to that sector? It is yet another reason to insist on radical reform—regime change—in North Korea and to press for eventual reunification.

The United States is going to be one of the principals in funding, and will take the lead in planning the military option. After Afghanistan and Iraq, the twenty-first century version of Teddy Roosevelt's "Big Stick" policy is now a consideration that America's enemies overlook only to their peril. It is hardly necessary—in fact would be counterproductive—if the United States were to answer North Korea's inflamed, hyperbolic threats and blustering in like manner. That kind of ranting is a recourse of the desperate and the weak. North Korea is now both. Quiet, firm leadership with focus on ultimate objectives and a willingness to be strong in the face of a dictator is required at the moment. Fortunately America has the leadership in place to handle such a crisis. The major U.S. role will be to establish firm presence in the region and reiterate the U.S. commitment to defend South Korea against aggression. It may be necessary to take dramatic but non-provocative steps to establish in Kim's mind that America is not a paper tiger but is fully capable of destroying him in the event he oversteps his bounds.

If America is impatient it is going to miss some opportunities. Patience applied properly in this case avoids war. Undue haste risks it dramatically. The challenge of the century is before us. It is up to all right thinking people to respond. The people of North Korea are waiting for their moment of liberation!

*De oppresso liber.*

# Index

295

DEMCO

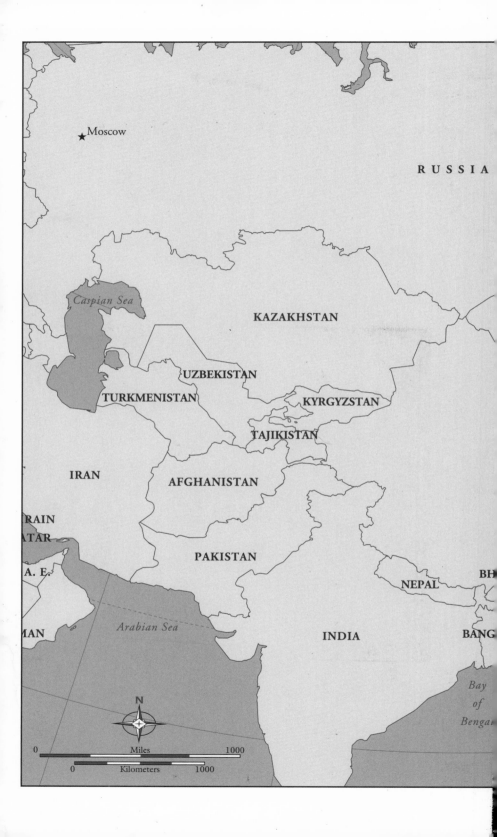